FANTASY OF SALVATION

FANTASY OF SALVATION

LAW EMEKA MODEME

© 2020 LE Modeme

All rights reserved. This book or any portion thereof may not be reproduced or used in any manner whatsoever without the express written permission of the publisher except for the use of brief quotations in articles and reviews.

Printed in the United States of America

Second Revised Edition, 2020

First Edition, 2019

ISBN 13: 9781999884741

Ameze Resources Limited

18 Torcross Road
Manchester

M9 0GP

England, United Kingdom

www.amezeresources.com

Email: Law@amezeresources.com

DEDICATION

To Godwin Okafor Modeme, my late father and a gentleman

CONTENTS

PREFACE 13
INTRODUCTION 19
1 25
ATONEMENT 25
    ATONEMENT IN ISLAM 28
    ATONEMENT IN JUDAISM 28
    ATONEMENT IN CHRISTIANITY 30
    ORIGINAL SIN 33
2 37
SALVATION 37
    SALVATION IN JUDAISM 37
    SALVATION IN ISLAM 40
    SALVATION IN CHRISTIANITY 41
3 45
SALVATION AND THE ABRAHAMIC COVENANT 45
    A MYTHICAL TALE 47
    A COVENANT OF DOUBTFUL VALIDITY 52
    A PURELY JEWISH COVENANT 55
4 57
SALVATION AND THE LAW OF MOSES 57
    ARE JEWS GOD'S CHOSEN PEOPLE? 58
    DID GOD GIVE MOSES THE LAW? 61
5 65
IS THE MOSAIC LAW DIVINE? 65
    THE LAW AND HUMAN SACRIFICE 65
    CULTURAL, AGRICULTURAL AND DIETARY LAW ... 70

- LAW ON ADULTERY, VIRGINITY AND SEX 71
- LAW ON DIVORCE 75
- LAW ON HOMOSEXUALITY 77
- LAW ON APOSTASY AND BLASPHEMY 78
- LAW AGAINST SPIRITUALITY 81
- LAW ON REBELLIOUS CHILDREN 85
- THE LAW AND SLAVERY 86
- LAW OF WAR 87
- OTHER LAWS 90
- IS THERE SALVATION IN THE LAW? 91

6 93

SALVATION THROUGH JESUS CHRIST 93
- DID ADAM AND EVE COMMIT ORIGINAL SIN? 94
- HAVE HUMAN BEINGS INHERITED ORIGINAL SIN? 95
- DOES BLOODLETTING ATONE FOR SIN? 102
- IS THE SACRIFICE OF JESUS REAL? 104
- EXCLUSIVELY JEWISH SAVIOUR 106

7 110

THE PRICE OF CHRIST'S SALVATION 110
- NO CAREER, FAMILY OR LIFE 110
- NO SEX 112
- NO DIVORCE EXCEPT FOR INFIDELITY 115
- NO WEALTH 119

8 123

IS JUSTIFICATION BY LAW OR CHRIST? 123
- JESUS AND THE ABRAHAMIC COVENANT 124
  - SALVATION THROUGH ABRAHAM OR JESUS? 125
- JESUS AND THE LAW 127

DID JESUS DISPLACE THE LAW?	131
DISCIPLES OF JESUS AND THE GOSPEL	136

9

ISLAM, PATRIARCHS AND CHRIST 139

10

PAUL AND THE SALVATION OF CHRIST 142

THE STORY OF PAUL	142
DID JESUS CONVERT AND COMMISSION PAUL?	143

11

END TIME AND DAY OF JUDGMENT 148

DAY OF JUDGMENT IN JUDAISM	149
DAY OF JUDGMENT IN CHRISTIANITY	150
DAY OF JUDGMENT IN ISLAM	155
WILL THERE BE A DAY OF JUDGMENT?	157

12

RIGHTEOUSNESS OR GRACE? 163

RIGHTEOUSNESS	164
GRACE	166
EXCLUSIVE CRITERIA	168
SIN AGAINST GOD	169

13

DEVIL AND DEMONS AS REASON FOR SALVATION 173

MEANING OF DEVIL, SATAN AND DEMONS	174
MISSION AGAINST DEVIL AND DEMONS	176
CREATIONS OF RELIGION	179
GOOD AND EVIL	187

14

HELL AS PLACE FOR THE UNSAVED 191

- A PLACE OF ETERNAL TORMENT? 192
- WHO GOES TO HELL? 195
- GOING TO HELL IN ANGER 200
- MEANING OF HELL 205
- DIVINE PUNISHMENT FOR EVIL 208
- THE LAW OF CAUSE AND EFFECT 210

15 215
HEAVEN AS HOME OF THE SAVED 215
- HEAVEN IN JUDAISM 216
- HEAVEN IN CHRISTIANITY 220
- HEAVEN IN ISLAM 222
- WHO GOES TO HEAVEN? 223
- A POPULAR MISAPPREHENSION 229

16 233
LOVE AND PEACE 233
- LOVE 234
- PEACE 237
- RELIGIOUS LOVE AND PEACE 239
  - JESUS AND NON-BELIEVERS 239
  - JUDAISM, ISLAM, AND NON-BELIEVERS 243
  - RELIGIOUS EXCLUSIVISM 245

17 248
UNITY 248
CONCLUSION 252
BIBLIOGRAPHY 255
INDEX 1

ACKNOWLEDGEMENT

I am grateful for the inspiration, guidance and strength that enabled me to begin and complete the task of writing this book. I am thankful to Peter Mogbo and Paul Okojie for pre-viewing the book, and Dr. Francis Tansinda, for his invaluable editorial work. I am also indebted to the special persons in my life whose love, support and encouragement enabled me to accomplish this project.

PREFACE TO THE SECOND EDITION

As a person born into a strong Christian home, and who grew up as a Christian, I fully believed in the Bible and Jesus Christ. I had no doubt that the gospels were true. I not only believed that Jesus Christ is the saviour of humanity, I also believed that he was the only way to God and the only means by which people would obtain salvation. Along with other Christians, I believed that non-Christians, unless they repented and accepted Jesus as their Lord and saviour, would be doomed to everlasting suffering in Hell Fire.

For almost four decades of my life, I held these beliefs. Although I was born into an Anglican family, I was later to join the growing Pentecostal movement, and for many years, attended different Pentecostal denominations. About twenty years ago, with a strong Christian zeal, I joined the Bible school of my local church, as a first step to realising what I believed was a call to be an evangelist. It was then, for the first time, that I attempted to study the Bible from the beginning to the end.

However, my study of the Bible raised many troubling questions for which the answers were not forthcoming. As a man trained in law and logic, I could not reconcile many of the events and stories in it with reason, common sense, the universality of God, and the oneness of all people. I could not reconcile many with known historical and scientific facts. I found it troubling that God would choose one people ahead of all others and then instruct them to kill some other peoples and take over their land. I could not understand why only Christians would go to heaven when most of the people in the world are not Christians. I found it difficult to understand why only the Bible could be the Word of God when other religions have their own Holy Scriptures that adherents sincerely believe came from God.

Since as a Christian I had not read the scriptures of other religions and had never attended their worships or meetings, I wondered why I should expect people of other faiths to accept Christian teachings. Given that I was a Christian by birth, I wondered why I should condemn people born into other religions or expect them to leave the religion of their parents in favour of mine. I could not come to terms with the notion that otherwise good people would be condemned to eternity of suffering in Hell Fire because they did not accept Jesus, while notoriously bad people would receive salvation because they accepted Jesus as lord and saviour, even if this was at the point of death. This seemed very unjust and unfair to people who were born into non-Christian homes, as I could easily have been a Muslim, Hindu, Sikh, or Jew, or an adherent of any other religion, an atheist or 'pagan' if I had been born into a different family, part of the world or set of circumstances.

It seemed to me that I had no right to judge or convert anyone since I did not really understand what I believed neither did I have any basis for vouching for its validity since I had done nothing to verify it. I also realised that just as Christians believe that salvation is exclusively theirs through Jesus Christ, people of other religions also believe they are the true worshippers of God and inheritors of salvation and paradise. This means in effect that every believer is also an unbeliever. Effectively, the human family has been divided and disunited by religions the basis and origins of which the ordinary believer does not know.

In addition to all these, I had become very disillusioned with the corruption, deception and exploitation in churches and other religious centres and appalled by the evil people have done and continue to do in the name of God or in defence of their religions. I was acutely aware that despite spending a lot of time in the church, I was spiritually undeveloped. Although there was much talk about personal relationships with Jesus, I could not say I knew this person or had any personal encounters with him despite being 'born again' and speaking in tongues. In spite of pretensions to the contrary, I knew many believers were in the same boat with me. It was clear to me that if I stripped emotions and doctrines from them, my faith and belief would appear to rest on no tangible or concrete foundation.

Convinced that religion cannot bring love and unity to the world or enhance people's spirituality and innate abilities, I had a strong urge to do something positive that would bring people together in love, unity and peace without religious indoctrination and in spite of their race, colour and nationality. However, I was reluctant to abandon my faith in Jesus entirely. I felt that at the core, there must be substance in the gospel, even if it has been the subject of abuse and negative manipulation. The problem, I thought, was not with Jesus but with his followers. I believed that in the teachings of Jesus would be the essential ingredients for a message of universal love, unity and peace. I was determined to bring these out by a scrupulous study of the Bible, especially the New Testament.

It soon became obvious however, that my initial misgivings were well founded. The more I delved into it, the more it appears that the Bible, including the New Testament, is a quintessential religious and dogmatic book. Jesus, it appears was a religious character similar to those that had featured in earlier religions; and his story seems as mythical as the others were. I realised that the Christian veneration of Jesus Christ is not much different from the veneration of the Gods and heroes of many other religions.

The three-fold aims of this book are simple. The first is to use the scriptures to disabuse people of the belief not only that anyone is their saviour, but also that, they need any form of eschatological salvation under the aegis of any religion. Second, to enlighten people about their innate connection with the Divine, and empower them to reach their potentials without any of the handbrakes and obstacles imposed by religious dogma. Third, to propagate a message of love and peace that would transcend religious, racial, national, ethnic and other divisive affiliations. In the end, I hope that people will come to the realisation that humanity is one and that there is neither need nor basis for the divisions and hatred – much of them inspired by religion – that currently cause serious problems for us.

INTRODUCTION

For what profit is it to a man if he gains the whole world, and loses his own soul? Or what will a man give in exchange for his soul? - Matthew 16:26

The three Abrahamic religions – Judaism, Christianity and Islam – of all major world religions, espouse the theology of salvation. For adherents of these religions, the notion of salvation is not only the essence of their faith; it is also the main purpose and culmination of their life on earth. To this end, they invest time, energy and resources in sundry religious activities and observances in the putative race for heaven. Judaism and Christianity share a common foundation and belief in salvation through a divine saviour, although their understanding of the saviour's identity is quite different. In Christian theology, the saviour is Jesus Christ who came down from heaven to die in order to atone for the inherent sins of human beings, release them from satanic control, and reconcile them with God. This sacrifice ensures that believers would enter the kingdom of heaven at the end of time. In Judaism, salvation for the people and nation of Israel comes from Yahweh, although there is no concept of inherited sin nor vicarious liability for the transgressions of others.

The doctrine of salvation for the purpose of admittance into heaven also exists in Islam. However, this is dependent on the observance of Quranic edicts, martyrdom and the mercy of Allah. There is no belief in Original Sin or a messiah, as such. Another religion that upholds the notion of salvation through a divine saviour is Zoroastrianism. It pre-dated Judaism, Christianity and Islam, and apparently influenced their theology. However, Zoroastrianism is today a minor religion with an estimated worldwide population of two hundred thousand. Adherents now largely exist among the Parsis (descendants of Persian who escaped persecution in Iran) of India, in the more remote parts of Iran, and in the Kurdish regions of Northern Iraq.

Contrary to the Abrahamic faiths, in most traditional societies, and in religions such as Buddhism, Hinduism, Sikhism, Jainism, and Shintoism, the belief in innate human depravity or unworthiness, or in the need for salvation, does not exist as such. Generally, these religious-cum-cultural systems deem the human soul to be immortal and involved in an evolutionary cycle of birth and rebirth until the need for further re-incarnation ceases to exist. At this point, the soul re-unites with the creator or remains in the spiritual realms.

Because of their great influence in world politics, religion and culture in the last two millennia, this book focuses on and contrasts the soteriology of Judaism, Christianity and Islam. Not only do these sister religions have different prescriptions on salvation; they each tend to see them as the only valid ones. Believers pass these beliefs on to their offspring who follow them without much inquiry or

INTRODUCTION

objective assessment. Those who do not accept or believe in the theology of particular faiths are labelled pagans, gentiles, infidels or unbelievers. This mind-set has been the main reason for proselytisation and the main cause of religious conflicts, persecutions, violence and exploitation in human history.

Even though many believers would not go out of their way to persecute, destroy, or exploit people of other faiths, those that control the powers of state have often hidden under the cloak of religious superiority to ill-treat 'pagans', take over their lands and expropriate their resources. Moreover, there are always the so-called fundamentalists or extremists who are willing to kill or harm unbelievers in the pursuit of religious supremacy or piety. Incidentally, these people see themselves as the true believers who uphold the undiluted 'truths' of their faith. Furthermore, many believers are often indifferent to the sufferings of people of other faiths, especially when inflicted by fellow believers, there being no instinctive feeling of oneness or solidarity with these victims. There is thus the anomaly that religions that claim to be the route to salvation and God have often been the cause of death and harm to people.

The belief in a divine incarnated saviour, or in the superiority or exclusivity of particular faiths, has seriously damaged human development, relationships and unity, as well as our relationship with God. It undermines the essence and universality of God and engenders profound divisions and separation within humanity. The belief in a saviour also leads to the creation of a separation between human beings and God, and consequently the denial to people of their natural connection with the Divine. Incidentally, while belief in a saviour and religious doctrines empowers religious institutions and their leaders, it undermines and dis-empowers individual believers by filling them with fear and making them vulnerable to manipulation and exploitation. The desire to be with 'the Lord' has led many to not only material and spiritual hardship, but also death under the influence of charismatic and deceptive or ignorant religious leaders. On the other hand, many have committed terrible acts of murder and terrorism in the mistaken belief that this would guarantee them salvation.

This book dissects the salvation offered by Christianity and contrasts it with the Jewish and Islamic schemes of salvation. In so doing, it critically examines the apocalyptic eschatology that underlines the expectation of salvation, the fear of eternal punishment in Hell Fire, and the hope of eternal bliss in heaven. Ultimately, and with deep scriptural, scholarly and philosophical insight, the book explores the question whether the salvation offered by religion is meaningful and realisable; or whether it is fanciful, puerile and counterproductive.

1

ATONEMENT

For all have sinned, and come short of the glory of God; being justified freely by his grace through the redemption that is in Christ Jesus. – Romans 3:23-24

The theology of salvation assumes the inherent depravity of human beings and their need for atonement. The word 'atone' is a derivative of the phrase 'at one'. Atonement is the notion that sinful human beings need to be reconciled with God before they could benefit from divine favour and protection. Atonement, many believe, is achievable through the sacrifice to deity of plant produce, animals or human beings, or the performance of prescribed rituals. However, people have traditionally prized the blood of animals and human beings for the best atoning sacrifice. The idea behind animal and human sacrifice is that the shedding of the blood washes away the sins or wrongdoings of the sacrificer and restores harmony between him and God. Historically, untold numbers of animals and human beings have lost their lives for this purpose in different parts of the world.[1]

Acts of atonement may be an individual or communal undertaking, with the latter usually requiring the sacrifice of larger or multiple animals or human beings. For extremely serious or universal sins, the belief often is that only the sacrifice of a god would suffice for atonement. For this reason, the belief in the expiatory dying of gods prevailed in many ancient religions.[2] Sacrifices are supposed to appease the gods and win back their favour and protection. Animal or human sacrifice typically involves the slaughter or strangulation of the animal on an altar, the collection of its blood, and the sprinkling of it on the sacrificer, alter and surrounding areas. Often, the sacrifice would be burnt, although it might also be buried especially where it concerns the gods or goddesses of the earth or fertility, or the burial of kings.[3]

The animals or human beings chosen for sacrifice would usually be those considered to be without blemish – a factor responsible for the frequent use of children, infants and virgins. The understanding

---

[1] See generally, *The Encyclopaedia Britannica*, http://www.britannica.com/topic/sacrifice-religion; JN Bremmer (ed), *The Strange World of Human Sacrifice* (Peeters Publishers 2007); MA Green, *Dying for the Gods: Human Sacrifice in Iron Age & Roman Europe* (Stroud, Gloucestershire, Charleston, SC: Tempus 2001).
[2] See *Encyclopaedia Britannica*, http://www.britannica.com/topic/sacrifice-religion/Divine-offerings). See also R Girard, *Violence and the Sacred* (Baltimore: The John Hopkins University Press 1993).
[3] Ibid.

behind the use of unblemished animals or humans is that the innocent sacrifice would be a substitute for the sinner whose sins and due punishment would now be borne by the sacrifice. The condemnation or death of the sacrifice means freedom from sin, death or punishment for the actual wrongdoer. The shedding of the blood of the sacrifice is significant because it is believed that, 'the life of the flesh is in the blood, and [...] it is the blood that makes atonement by the life.'[4] In many traditional religions of the ancient world, the sacrifice of animals, human beings or gods for the purpose of atonement was common. As the Encyclopaedia Britannica observes, 'rituals of expiation and satisfaction appear in most religions, whether primitive or developed, as the means by which the religious person re-establishes or strengthens his relation to the holy or divine.'[5]

---

[4] See Leviticus 17:11.
[5] http://www.britannica.com/EBchecked/topic/41872/atonement. For a more detailed consideration of the issue, see R Girard, supra n. 2; JS Mbiti, *African Religions and Philosophy* (Heinemann Educational Books Ltd. 1969); JN Bremmer (ed), supra n 1; MA Green, supra n 1.

ATONEMENT IN ISLAM

Although atonement (*Kaffarah*) is necessary in Islam, this seems to be only as a personal act of repentance from, and satisfaction for, committed sin. Accordingly, atonement may be achieved by, among other things, doing good deeds and giving arms secretly to the poor.[6] Depending on the transgression, other acts of atonement include, reading the Quran, appeasing victims of one's wrongdoing, prayer, fasting, freeing slaves, pilgrimage to holy sites, feeding the poor, and payment of blood money to the family of a murdered believer.[7] Atonement in Islam has little to do with salvation by or through a divine being.

ATONEMENT IN JUDAISM

In Jewish religion, atonement is essential in the peoples' relationship with Yahweh. The Old Testament contains numerous prescriptions and rules for sin, guilt and burnt offerings, both for the appeasement of Yahweh, and the expiation of sins and wrongdoings.[8] There are also prescriptions on atonement for unsolved murder,[9] childbirth,[10] infectious skin diseases,[11] bodily or semen discharge, and menstruation – all of which supposedly defile the individual.[12] To this end, the Bible is replete with instances of, and references to, animal sacrifices in the form of burnt offerings, Sabbath sacrifices, and new

---

[6] See Surah 2:271, 11:114.
[7] See Surah 4:92, 5:89.
[8] See generally, Leviticus 4 – 9; 14; 16.
[9] See Deuteronomy 21.
[10] See Leviticus 12.
[11] See Leviticus 14.
[12] See Leviticus 15.

moon offerings. There are also Passover sacrifices, sacrifices on the Day of Atonement and the Feast of Tabernacles, thanksgiving offerings, and guilt offerings.[13] Essentially, many of these sacrifices are 'sin' or 'guilt' offerings, the overall purpose of which is to 'purify the guilty and to re-establish the holy bond with God through the blood of the consecrated victim'.[14] In effect, the guilt or sin of the sacrificer would supposedly transfer to the unblemished animal as his or her representative or ransom.

Jewish law prescribes sacrifices not only for individual transgressions, but also for communal or national sins.[15] The 'Day of Atonement' (*Yum Kippur*), observed on the tenth day of the seventh month of each year, is used for annual sacrifices for the cleansing of the sins of the whole nation.[16] The Jews are to observe this day in perpetuity[17] as a special Sabbath (*Shabbath Sabbathon*) in which they must abstain

---

[13] See Leviticus 1 – 9; 12-15. See also *Encyclopaedia Britannica*, http://www.britannica.com/EBchecked/topic/515665/sacrifice/66308/Divine-offerings, and Chapter 5.

[14] *Encyclopaedia Britannica,*

http://www.britannica.com/EBchecked/topic/515665/sacrifice/66313/Propitiation-and-expiation.

[15] See Leviticus 16.
[16] See Leviticus 16: 29 -34; 23: 26-32; Numbers 29:7-11. See also *The Jewish Encyclopaedia*, http://www.jewishencyclopedia.com/articles/13764-sin-offering.
[17] See Leviticus 16:31, 34. The sacrificial order in Judaism only ceased due to the destruction of the second Jerusalem temple – the designated place for the main sacrifices. See *Encyclopaedia Britannica*, http://www.britannica.com/EBchecked/topic/515665/sacrifice/66323/Religions-of-Japan.

from all work and personal pleasure.[18] The many instances of human sacrifice to Yahweh or 'foreign' gods (such as Molech and Baal) found in the Bible were ostensibly for the purpose of atonement for sins, or the appeasement of, or maintenance of good relationship with, God.[19] It seems clear that once the wrongdoer has done the prescribed act of atonement, the wrongdoing or sin concerned would be erased and would cease to count against them.

ATONEMENT IN CHRISTIANITY

In Christian theology, atonement is not obtainable through good deeds or acts of penance. Rather, 'the Atonement is the Satisfaction of Christ, whereby God and the world are reconciled or made to be at one'.[20] For Christians, therefore, Jesus Christ has atoned for the sins of humanity by his voluntary and sacrificial death, so that belief in him leads to the forgiveness of sins and divine reconciliation.[21] 1 Peter 2:24 states that Jesus 'himself bore our sins in his body on the tree, that we might die to sin and live to righteousness,' and that 'by his wounds' we have been healed'. According to Apostle Paul, Jesus 'is the propitiation for the sins of the whole world',[22] since 'all have sinned and come short of the glory of God' and require the redemptive sacrifice of Christ.[23] He goes on to articulate the necessity and benefits of Christ's atoning death as follows:

---

[18] See Leviticus 16:34.
[19] See e.g., Leviticus 18:21; 1 Kings 11:1-8; 2 Kings 23:10, 13-14; Jeremiah 19:5.
[20] See the *Catholic Encyclopaedia*, http://www.newadvent.org/cathen/02055a.htm.
[21] See Romans 4:25.
[22] 1 John 2:2. See also 1 Peter 3:18; Hebrews 13:22; Revelation 5:9.
[23] Romans 3:23-26. For the same theme, see also 1 John 4:10; Romans 4:25; Galatians 1:4; Hebrews 1:3.

ATONEMENT

For while we were still weak, at the right time Christ died for the ungodly [...] but God shows his love for us in that while we were still sinners, Christ died for us. Since, therefore, we have now been justified by his blood, much more shall we be saved by him from the wrath of God. For if while we were enemies we were reconciled to God by the death of his Son, much more, now that we are reconciled, shall we be saved by his life.[24]

The belief in the atoning sacrifice of Jesus is affirmed in the Apostles' Creed to the effect that, 'for us men and for our salvation', Jesus 'came down from heaven'.

The notion of atonement through the 'immaculate' blood of Jesus borrows heavily from the pagan and Jewish notion of atonement through the shedding of unblemished animal blood in sacrifice. The book of Hebrews observes that, as under the Mosaic Law, blood is essential for purification, and that without the shedding of blood, there would be no forgiveness of sins.[25] However, since the blood of animals or human beings could not atone for the sins of the whole world, Jesus, as God incarnate, had to come down from heaven, be born as a man, and then die in atonement for the sins of humanity. He had provided the ultimate sacrifice and furnished a new covenant of redemption.[26] This sacrifice is supposedly universal, complete and perpetual.

---

[24] Romans 5:6-11. See also 2 Corinthians 5:18; Hebrews 9:26; 10:10; Colossians 1:19-22.
[25] See Hebrews 9:22.
[26] See Hebrews 9:12-15; see also Hebrews 7:22.

The sacrifice is universal in that Jesus is the 'Lamb of God' that takes away the sins of the whole world;[27] so, anybody who believes in him would have their sins washed away. According to John 3:16, 'God so loved the world that he gave his one and only Son, that whoever believes in him shall not perish but have eternal life.' The book of Romans adds that, everyone who believes in Jesus Christ 'will not be put to shame', since 'there is no distinction between Jew and Greek; for the same Lord is Lord of all, bestowing his riches on all who call on him. For everyone who calls on the name of the Lord will be saved'.[28] The sacrifice is complete in that it suffices entirely for the purpose of atonement. Unlike Jewish and other sacrifices that are regular, periodic and continuing, this one suffices once and for all[29] and no further atoning sacrifices would be necessary or required.

Finally, the sacrifice is perpetual because Jesus had apparently laid down his life for present and future generations until the end of time. Thus, rather than people offering sacrifices to atone for the sins they had committed, Jesus had sacrificed himself for all sins, including those yet to be committed at the time of the sacrifice.[30] This raises two

---

[27] See John 1:29.
[28] Romans 10:11-13. See also Romans 10:9-10; 3:22-23; Mark 16:15-16; John 3:14.
[29] See 1 Peter 3:18.

[30] See *Encyclopaedia Britannica*, http://www.britannica.com/EBchecked/topic/515665/sacrifice/66313/Propitiation-and-expiation.

questions. The first is why human beings would need atonement for sins they have not committed. The second is how a sacrifice apparently made more than 2000 years ago would benefit people who lived after the event or who are living now. Enter the dogma of 'Original Sin'.

ORIGINAL SIN

'Original Sin' refers to the alleged sin of Adam and Eve, the supposed first human beings on earth, which subsequent human beings inherited due to their supposed descent from them. The consequences of this sinful inheritance for humans are death and separation from God. According to the book of Romans:

> *Just as sin entered the world through one man, and death through sin, and in this way death came to all people, because all sinned [...]. Nevertheless, death reigned from the time of Adam to the time of Moses, even over those who did not sin by breaking a command, as did Adam, who is a pattern of the one to come.*[31]

The Catholic Encyclopaedia notes that by sinning, Adam lost 'the complete mastery of his passions, exemption from death, sanctifying grace, and the vision of God in the next life'.[32] Because of this, 'all have sinned and fall short of the glory of God,'[33] and the human race is subject to 'privation of sanctifying grace'.[34] The rationale for this

---

[31] Romans 5: 12, 14. See also Romans 5:18-19; 1 Corinthians 15:21-22.
[32] See *Catholic Encyclopaedia*, http://www.newadvent.org/cathen/11312a.htm.
[33] Romans 3:23. See also Romans 5:18.
[34] See *Catholic Encyclopaedia*, http://www.newadvent.org/cathen/11312a.htm.

supposition is that God has the right to bestow gifts on the human race 'on such conditions as He wished and to make their conservation depend on the fidelity of the head of the family'.[35]

The death of Jesus is supposedly necessary in order to save human beings from the curse of Adam and restore us to life and relationship with God, 'for just as through the disobedience of the one man the many were made sinners, so also through the obedience of the one man the many will be made righteous'.[36] 1 Corinthians 15:21-22 re-iterates that, 'since death came through a man, the resurrection of the dead comes also through a man. For as in Adam all die, so in Christ all will be made alive'. The ultimate end of Jesus' atoning sacrifice is therefore the salvation or redemption of humankind.

Although the declaration by the Psalmist that, 'surely I was sinful at birth, sinful from the time my mother conceived me';[37] and in Exodus that, God would visit the sins of fathers on subsequent generations,[38] might appear to suggest otherwise, Jewish theology generally rebuffs the notions of inherited sin and vicarious liability for the sins of others.[39] Similarly, the Quran does not countenance the idea of inherited sin.[40] Although it tells the story of Adam and Eve (albeit with variations in detail),[41] the concept of Original Sin does not exist

---

[35] Ibid.
[36] Romans 5:18-19.
[37] Psalm 51:5. See also Ecclesiasticus 25:24.
[38] Exodus 20:5.
[39] See Chapter 6.
[40] Ibid.
[41] See Surah 2:35-37.

in Islam. According to Surah 17:15, 'whoever is guided is only guided for [the benefit of] his soul. And whoever errs only errs against it. And no bearer of burdens will bear the burden of another'.[42]

---

[42] See also Surah 6:164.

2

SALVATION

For God so loved the world that he gave his only begotten Son, that whosoever believeth in him should not perish, but have everlasting life. – John 3:16

The word salvation or redemption has both temporal and spiritual connotations. In the temporal context, it means liberation from a harmful or ruinous situation, usually by some physical act or the payment of a price or ransom. In the spiritual or eschatological sense, salvation refers to deliverance or redemption from sin and the consequences thereof. Often the person doing the delivering or redeeming is described as the saviour or messiah, which in Hebrew language, means the 'anointed one' or 'the anointed of Yahweh'. The focus here is on salvation in the eschatological sense. Judaism, Islam and Christianity all espouse the doctrine of salvation, although their perception and the means of achieving it differ.

SALVATION IN JUDAISM

References to the two types of salvation abound in the Hebrew Bible.[1] In the Jewish context, the 'anointed one' principally referred to kings

---

[1] See e.g., Exodus 13:12-13; 21: 28-32; 30:11-16; 34:20; Leviticus 25:25-28; 27:29; Numbers 18:14-17.

beginning from Saul,[2] and encompassing David,[3] Solomon[4] and all others that came after them, whom Yahweh had anointed to rule ancient Israel and save its people from their enemies. However, of all the anointed kings of Israel, the Bible singles out David and his dynasty as being specially favoured.[5] This royal lineage, it says, would eventually produce the messiah-king that would provide everlasting salvation to Israel from their national, political and personal troubles. Prophet Isaiah paints a picture of the perfect anointed king long awaited by the Jews in the following words:[6]

> *For a child will be born to us, a son will be given to us; and the government will rest on His shoulders; and His name will be called Wonderful Counsellor, Mighty God, Eternal Father, Prince of Peace. There will be no end to the increase of His government or of peace, on the throne of David and over his kingdom, to establish it and to uphold it with justice and righteousness From then on and forevermore. The zeal of the LORD of hosts will accomplish this.*[7]

However, apart from kings, the Israelites have used the title 'messiah' or 'anointed one,' for the patriarchs of the nation, the High Priest[8] and the whole people of Israel as Yahweh's chosen people.[9] Non-Jews whom the Jews perceived as their deliverers, such as King Cyrus the

---

[2] See 1 Samuel 9:16; 10:1, 23, 27; 11:13.
[3] See 1 Samuel 16:13; 17.
[4] See 1 Kings 1:39.
[5] See Psalm 2; 18:50; 20:6; 89:20; 132:10, 17; Jeremiah 33:15-16.
[6] See Daniel 9:25-26; 1 Samuel 2:10; Psalm 2:2-3.
[7] Isaiah 9:6-7. A similar picture about a great and righteous king was painted in Isaiah 11:1-5; Micah 5:3-8; Zechariah 9:9-10; Malachi 3:1-3.

[8] See Leviticus 4:3; 5; Hebrews 4:14-16.
[9] See Habakkuk 3:13; Psalm 28:8-9.

Great of Persia,[10] and Alexander the Great,[11] have also received the title. In Jewish tradition, other attributions of the title to political leaders also appear apart from the ones mentioned above.[12]

Apparently, due to changed political and social circumstances; and the cessation of the ancient nation of Israel, including the Davidic dynasty, the Jewish concept of messiah, in time, underwent a change. Now, it also incorporates a transcendental, apocalyptic and eschatological dimension. The messiah might now not be a mere human being ushering in political emancipation and dominion; he could be a divine being, emergent from heaven, who would effect a spiritual deliverance of the people at the end of time, pass judgment over sinners and rule the world from Jerusalem. According to the Jewish Encyclopaedia, 'Side by side with the traditional idea of an earthly king of the house of David,' now exists, 'the new conception of a heavenly pre-existent Messiah.'[13]

Jewish hope and craving for a messiah who would liberate them from foreign domination and rule the world, has led over time to the emergence of numerous pseudo-messiahs, some with genuine intentions and others with ulterior motives. All however, claimed a

---

[10] See Isaiah 45:1-7; *The Jewish Encyclopaedia*, http://www.jewishencyclopedia.com/articles/13236-savior.
[11] Ibid.

[12] Ibid.
[13] Ibid. See also the *Catholic Encyclopaedia*, http://www.newadvent.org/cathen/10212c.htm; IM Zeitlin, *Jesus and the Judaism of His Time* (Policy Press 1988) 38-40, 116; GF Chesnut, *Images of Christ* (Seabury Press 1984) 22-23.

divine authority to lead the people to salvation; and descent not only from David, but also from other patriarchs like Joseph and Levi. Unsurprisingly, the missions of these self-acclaimed messiahs came to naught, and many of them and their followers lost their lives in the hands of extant ruling powers.[14]

SALVATION IN ISLAM

As already noted, Islam does not entertain the ideas of original sin and the need for atonement by or through a messiah. Although the doctrine of salvation for the purpose of admittance into heaven does exist in the religion, this is dependent on the observance of Quranic edicts, the doing of good deeds, and the mercy of Allah:

> *And We place the scales of justice for the Day of Resurrection, so no soul will be treated unjustly at all. And if there is [even] the weight of a mustard seed, We will bring it forth. And sufficient are We as accountant.*[15]

Therefore, subject to the overall mercy of Allah, the Quran insists that the faithful would earn salvation by a preponderance of righteousness:

> *And those whose scales are heavy [with good deeds] - it is they who are the successful. But those whose scales are light - those are the ones who have lost their souls, [being] in Hell, abiding eternally.*[16]

---

[14] See the *Jewish Encyclopaedia*, http://www.jewishencyclopedia.com/articles/10729-messiah; http://www.jewishencyclopedia.com/articles/10730-messiah-false; F Josephus, *The Wars of the Jews (*Palatine Press 2015) 2:258-264; Antiquities of the Jews, Book 20:97-99; Acts 5:36-37. See also IM Zeitlin, supra n 51, 42-44, GF. Chesnut, supra n 13, 25-26.
[15] Surah 21:47.
[16] Surah 23:102-103.

Similarly, Surah 2:82 declares that 'they who believe and do righteous deeds - those are the companions of Paradise; they will abide therein eternally.'[17] Although Prophet Muhammad was sent to teach people the will of Allah and the way of righteousness, it is ultimately the responsibility of individuals to follow the right path. The prophet was not to sacrifice himself for anyone.[18]

SALVATION IN CHRISTIANITY

In Christianity, salvation comes only from Jesus Christ, the saviour or messiah.[19] Before his birth, an angel reportedly told his mother that he 'will be great and will be called the Son of the Most High,' who would inherit the throne of David and reign over Israel forever.[20] When Jesus asked his disciples how the Jews perceived him and Peter declared that Jesus was, 'the Messiah, the Son of the living God', Jesus approvingly replied that Peter had received the answer from heaven.[21] Further, according to the gospels, Jesus was condemned to death by the High Priest because he identified himself as the 'Messiah, the son of God', who would sit at the right hand of God in heaven.[22] Again, during his trial by Pontius Pilate, Jesus did not deny that he was the Messiah.[23] Moreover, in Titus 2:13, Jesus was described as 'our great God and saviour'. In fact, the New Testament epistles often use the

---

[17] For a similar provision, see Surah 7:42.
[18] See Surah 24:54.
[19] 'Christ' is the English translation of 'Christos', a transliteration of the word 'messiah', in Greek.
[20] See Luke 1:27-33.
[21] See Matthew 16:16-17; Mark 8:28-30.
[22] See Matthew 26:63-64.
[23] See Matthew 27:11.

title 'Christ' interchangeably with, or as a suffix to, 'Jesus' to indicate that he is the messiah'.[24]

In Christianity therefore, salvation is the deliverance of people from the bondage and consequences of sin through the blood of Jesus Christ.[25] Jesus had given his life as a ransom for the sins of humanity[26] thereby freeing it from the shackles of the devil and death.[27] In short, for Christians, Jesus Christ is synonymous with salvation.[28] Thus, the Apostles' Creed affirms the belief in the 'Lord Jesus Christ, the only begotten Son of God [...] who for us men and for our salvation came down from heaven'. The salvation wrought by Jesus Christ is supposedly exclusive and avails generally and individually. It is exclusive because according to Acts 4:12, 'there is salvation in no one else, for there is no other name under heaven given among men by which we must be saved.' On a general level, the shedding of the blood of Jesus is supposed to be a sufficient and adequate satisfaction to God for the sins of humanity – a satisfaction God has accepted for the purposes of redemption. The blood of Jesus presumably provides us with the means for the forgiveness of our sins, makes us co-heirs

---

[24] For other references to or imputations of Jesus as the saviour or Christ, see Matthew 27:22; 28:18; John 4:42; 10:11, 36; 11:4, 25, 27; 18:36; 7:38-44; Acts 10:38; Titus 2:13.

[25] See Romans 5:15-20; 1 John 2:1-2.
[26] See Mark 10:45; Matthew 20:28; John 15:13; Colossians 1:20-22; 1 John 3:16; Romans 3:24-26; 1 Timothy 2:5-6; Titus 2:14; 1 Corinthians 1:30; 6:20; Ephesians 1:7.
[27] Hebrews 2:14-16. See also 1 John 3:8.
[28] See John 1:12; 3:16, 36; 10:9; Acts 2:38; 4:12; 16:31; Romans 6:23; 8:1; 10:3; 9:10; 2 Corinthians 5:17; Acts; 1 John1: 8-9; 4:14.

of Christ,[29] the children of God and temples of the Holy Spirit,[30] among other benefits.[31] On the individual level, the salvation of Jesus Christ allegedly provides persons with the unmerited love and grace of God, which calls them to repentance from sins and enables them to do so. Repentance and abstention from sins then gain them justification, which results in the remission of sins and sanctification. By justification and sanctification, individuals become friends of God and beneficiaries of eternal life.[32] However, is the salvation of Christ compatible with the schemes of salvation in Judaism and Islam? Have human beings inherited a sinful nature that was atoned by the blood of Jesus? Does humanity indeed need salvation?

---

[29] See Romans 8:14-17.
[30] See 1 Corinthians 3:16.
[31] See the *Catholic Encyclopaedia*, http://www.newadvent.org/cathen/13407a.htm.

[32] Ibid.

3

SALVATION AND THE ABRAHAMIC COVENANT

'I will establish my covenant as an everlasting covenant between me and you and your descendants after you for the generations to come, to be your God and the God of your descendants after you.' - Genesis 17:7

In Judaism, salvation is rooted in the patriarch Abraham and the covenant the people believe God made with him. In order to deal properly with the Jewish scheme of salvation, the story of Abraham as narrated in the Bible book of Genesis needs re-visiting. Yahweh had told Abram (as he then was) to leave his native country[1] and people and migrate to another land that he would be shown. Yahweh promised to bless Abram and his descendant, to make of him a great nation, to bless or curse those who bless or curse him, and to make him the source of blessing to all peoples on earth. Abram, who was seventy-five years at this time, left his location along with his wife, Sarai and his nephew, Lot. Although, the instruction given to Abram revealed no destination, they journeyed from Haran to the land of Canaan - a land already inhabited by the Canaanites. Yahweh

---

[1] Genesis 11:28 describes this country as Ur of the Chaldeans.

appeared to Abram many times subsequently and reiterated the promise to give the land of Canaan[2] to his offspring,[3] and proceeded to seal the commitment with a covenant ceremony.[4]

When Abram was ninety-nine years old and still childless, Yahweh appeared to him again to confirm the earlier covenant and promises, at which time, Abram's name was changed to Abraham while Sarai's was changed to Sarah.[5] Abraham and his would-be descendants were ordered to keep their own part of the covenant, which required that all males, whether born in the households or bought as slaves, be circumcised from then onwards in perpetuity. Any male who fails to keep this covenant of circumcision would be 'cut off from his people'.[6] The 'everlasting' covenant with Abraham would be consolidated through Isaac and not Ishmael, who had been born to Abraham by Hagar, Sarah's servant.[7]

---

[2] Notably the land of the Kenites, Kenizzites, Kadmonites, Hittites, Perizzites, Rephaites, Amorites, Canaanites, Girgashites and Jebusites – See Genesis 15:18-21. See also Joshua 24:11; Nehemiah 9:8. This land apparently stretches from Egypt to Iraq and encompasses Sudan, Lebanon, Jordan, Syria, Palestine and parts of Turkey and Saudi Arabia.
[3] See Genesis 12:1-9; 13:14-17
[4] See Genesis 15:1-17.
[5] Genesis 17:1-8.
[6] See Genesis 17:9-14.
[7] See Genesis 17. To confirm Abraham's privileged position and friendship with God, the Bible recounts how Abraham intervened to save Lot and Sodom from the captivity of the combined armies of four kings by routing them with only 318 men of his household (Genesis 14). He also intervened to save Lot and his family from divine destruction after the angels sent by God for the mission visited him and intimated him of their mission – Genesis18 and 19.

When he was at least hundred years and Sarah at least ninety, Abraham eventually had the promised son Isaac,[8] after which Abraham sent away Hagar and Ishmael.[9] When Isaac had grown into a young man, Yahweh instructed Abraham to kill him as a sacrifice. The following day, Abraham obediently and without hesitation travelled with his son to the appointed location, tied him up, laid him on an altar, and raised his sword to slay him. At that point, Yahweh stopped him and substituted a lamb for the offering. By that act of obedience, Yahweh became convinced of Abraham's faithfulness and re-affirmed his promise to him.[10] Isaac was later to have twin sons, Esau and Jacob,[11] but it was through Jacob that Yahweh would perpetuate the covenant with Abraham. As the father of their nation and the signatory to a Divine covenant, Jews revere Abraham and boast of their descent from him.[12] There are however fundamental problems with the story of Abraham and the purported covenant he had with God.

A MYTHICAL TALE

The first problem is that the entire tale appears to be merely mythical rather that factual. The alleged call to leave his homeland could not have happened as claimed, because, even before it, Abraham's father had apparently taken him and his wife, as well as his nephew Lot,

---

[8] See Genesis 17:17; 21:1-2.
[9] See Genesis 21:8-21.
[10] See Genesis 22.
[11] See e.g., Genesis 25:21-26.
[12] See, e.g., John 8:33; 2 Cor. 11:22; Romans 11:1; 31:1; Acts 3:25; 13:26; Acts 7; Hebrews 6:13.

away from Ur on a migratory journey to Canaan. According to Genesis 11:31-32, Abraham's father:

> *Terah took his son Abram, his grandson Lot son of Haran, and his daughter-in-law Sarai, the wife of his son Abram, and together they set out from Ur of the Chaldeans to go to Canaan.*[13] *But when they came to Haran, they settled there. Terah lived 205 years, and he died in Haran.*

Therefore, rather than being called, Abraham could only have completed the migration to Canaan that his father started. Buttressing the legendary nature of the story are the claims that Pharaoh lusted after Sarai and took her away from Abraham[14]; and that Abraham defeated the armies of four nations with his 318 domestic servants.[15] Considering the size and wealth of Egypt, the highly exalted position of the Pharaoh, the number of beautiful young women at his disposal, and the fact that Sarai was already 65 years, Abraham and his immigrant family would be relatively insignificant and unlikely to draw the attention of Pharaoh or his high officials. Indeed, two similar incidents involving Sarah at 75 years old and Rebecca the wife of Isaac, also reportedly happened with Abimelech, the King of Gerar, who took Sarah into his house and coveted Rebecca.[16] The alleged defeat by Abraham of the combined military forces of Sodom, Gomorrah, Admah and Zeboiim and Bela, who had just crushed the opposing armed forces of five Canaanite nations sounds like typical

---

[13] Emphasis added.
[14] See Genesis 12:10-20.
[15] See Genesis 14.
[16] See Genesis 16:16; 20; 26:1-11

fantastic tales of national heroes.[17] As the Bible annotations to this story state:

> *Neither the battle nor any of the kings can be identified in non-biblical sources. Abraham's ability to pursue and overcome the Shemite conquerors testifies to his status as heir of Shem and recipient of Shem's blessings.*[18]

Moreover, the ancestry and humanity of Abraham and his close descendants are doubtful. Genesis 11:10-27 gives the ancestors of Abraham (the 'descendants of Shem') as Arpachshad, Shelah, Eber, Peleg, Reu, Serug, Nahor and Terah. However, rather than being the names of human beings, these names, including Abraham's supposed father, Terah and grandfather Nahor, are apparently names of places.[19] In addition, Haran, Abraham's supposed brother, appears to be the same as the town of Haran where Terah settled with Abraham, Sarai and Lot in the first leg of the migration,[20] and to which Jacob later fled.[21] The Jewish Encyclopaedia confirms that, 'Abraham's kinsfolk (Gen. xxii. 20-24) are personifications of tribes, and his predecessors and successors, from Noah to Jacob, are mythical or legendary'.[22] It further notes that the 'biography of Abraham in Genesis is probably to be regarded as legendary', having grown up 'around sacred places,

---

[17] See Genesis 14:1-17. Many such stories are replicated in the Bible book of Joshua.
[18] See the notes on Genesis 14; *The New Oxford annotated Bible* (NRSV) (Oxford University Press 2001).
[19] See the notes on Genesis 11:27-32, ibid.
[20] See Genesis 11:28.
[21] See Genesis 27:43.
[22] See http://www.jewishencyclopedia.com/articles/360-abraham. The regal period according to the Bible began with Saul, who became king very many centuries after the time of Abraham. See 1 Samuel 10:1, 17-27; 11:14-15; 13:1.

ideas, and institutions'.[23] If the ancestors and kinsfolk of Abraham were not human beings, Abraham was most probably not a human being, either.

Furthermore, there are wide discrepancies and incongruities in the Bible concerning the identity of the sons of Jacob – the great-grand sons of Abraham who apparently make up the twelve tribes of Israel. Although the identity of these people in Genesis corresponds to that given in Exodus,[24] it varies considerably from those in other books of the Bible. For example, in the list of the twelve tribes which Moses blessed in Deuteronomy 33, Simeon was missing; while in Judges 1, the tribal list does not include Reuben, Gad, Levi and Issachar. The collection of the twelve tribes in Judges 5:13-23 (in the Song of Deborah), contains three tribes that are not named after the sons of Jacob – Gilead, Machir and Meroz. It also omits five sons of Jacob contained in Genesis and Exodus – Simeon, Levi, Judah, Manasseh and Gad. With the Bible so inconsistent and contradictory regarding who or what makes up the sons of Jacob, and thus the tribes of Israel, one is not any wiser as to whether these tribal names were real people and if so who they were. As the Catholic Encyclopaedia observes:

> *Very often, where individual names are used (in the Old Testament) these names in reality refer not to individuals but to tribes, as in Genesis 10, and the names of the twelve*

---

[23] Ibid. See also WRF Browning (ed.) *Oxford Dictionary of the Bible* (Oxford University 2009)166; S Acharya, *The Christ Conspiracy: The Greatest Story Ever Sold* (Adventures Unlimited Press 2012) 141-142; 166-167.
[24] Exodus 1:1- 4.

> *Patriarchs, whose migrations are those of the tribes they represent.*[25]

Finally, the apparent barrenness of Sarah and the miraculous circumstances of Isaac's birth conform to a common biblical theme of barrenness and miraculous conception foreshadowing the birth of heroes. For example, the wives of the other Patriarchs – Isaac and Jacob – were also barren and needed divine intervention before they could conceive and establish the Abrahamic covenant.[26] The mothers of Samson, an Israelite national Judge, Prophet Samuel, and John the Baptist were also barren;[27] and Mary the mother of Jesus begot him through the Holy Spirit. These stories of barrenness and miracles sound like legends depicting the special circumstances of the birth of some of the most important people in the Bible, as well as the power of the God of Israel. Furthermore, the Bible states that Abraham was 100 years when he had Isaac; that he was too old to father a child at that point; and that the birth of Isaac was a miracle. Yet, after the death of Sarah, when Abraham was at least 137 years old and 'well advanced in years', he married Keturah and had six more children by her without any difficulty or miracle.[28] In any case, these incidences of barrenness appear inconsistent with the biblical promise that nobody in Israel would be barren or have a miscarriage.[29] It is also

---

[25] See http://www.newadvent.org/cathen/01051a.htm.
[26] See Genesis 25:21; Genesis 29:31; 30:2.
[27] See Judges 13:2; 1 Samuel 1:10; Luke 1:7. Michal, the first wife of King and the daughter of King Saul, was also barren. Although she did not eventually have a child, David went on to have numerous children through numerous women. See 2 Samuel 6:23.
[28] See Genesis 25:1-4.
[29] See Exodus 23:26; Deuteronomy 7:14.

inconsistent with the supposed injunction of God to Adam and Eve to be 'fruitful and multiply, and replenish the earth, and subdue it'.[30]

A COVENANT OF DOUBTFUL VALIDITY

The second problem is that the Abrahamic covenant, for many reasons, would be of doubtful validity even if one were to accept the biblical narrative about its occurrence. First, Abraham and his close descendants were unfit to be parties to, or beneficiaries of, the covenant, which rests on invalid suppositions. According to Jewish Law, Abraham was not eligible to be the father of Israel but along with his family, should have been ostracised or extirpated for marrying and having sexual relations with his own sister, Sarai.[31] The law decrees that anyone who has sex with his sister, 'whether the daughter of his father or the daughter of his mother' is cursed,[32] a disgrace and 'must be cut off before the eyes of their people'.[33] Thus, Isaac the son of Abraham, the father of Jacob, was a product of an incestuous relationship, in the same way as Moab and Ammon were reportedly the products of incestuous relationships between Lot, Abraham's brother, and his two daughters.[34]

Similarly, the birth of the twelve sons of Jacob contravened Jewish law by which they and their father could not have been the forebears of Israel. The twelve sons, according to the Bible, were born to Jacob

---

[30] See Genesis 1:28.
[31] See Genesis 20:8-13.
[32] See Deuteronomy 27:22.
[33] Leviticus 20:11-12.
[34] See Genesis 19:30-38.

by two sisters, Leah and Rachel, and their two servants, Bilhah and Zilpah.[35] However, the fact that Jacob married two sisters and had children by them while both were alive directly breached the biblical decree against marrying or having sexual intercourse with two living sisters.[36] This was among the laws, which the people of Israel must keep in order to avoid the fate of the original inhabitants of the land who apparently defiled it by that kind of conduct. Again, the punishment for flouting this law was that the perpetrators and their descendants, up to the tenth generation, would be cut off from the people.[37] Therefore, Jacob and his generations (up to the tenth) ought to have been extirpated, instead of being revered as the fathers of Israel.

Second, the character of Jacob, the instrument for the 'fulfilment' of the Abrahamic covenant was far from exemplary, he being a selfish and heartless man, a cheat, a trickster and a fraudster. He refused to give food to his starving brother, Esau unless the latter relinquished his right as the firstborn.[38] He connived with his mother to deceive his father and fraudulently obtain the blessings meant for his elder brother under the law and tradition.[39] He also defrauded his father-in-law,

---

[35] See Genesis 29:15-33; 30:1-13. The sons born to Jacob by Leah were Reuben, Simeon, Levi, Judah, Issachar and Zebulun. The sons born to him by Rachael were Joseph and Benjamin. Bilhah, the maid of Rachael, begot Dan and Naphtali, while Leah's maid, Zilpah, gave birth to Gad and Asher.
[36] See Leviticus 18:18.
[37] See Leviticus 18:29, Deuteronomy 23:2.
[38] Genesis 25:29-34.
[39] Genesis 27.

Laban of his livestock and grew very prosperous at his expense.[40] In addition, some of the sons of Jacob did abominable things that, according to the Bible, would have disqualified them from the assembly of the people of Israel. Reuben the first son of Jacob slept with his father's concubine Bilhah,[41] an act that carries a death sentence for both parties.[42] Furthermore, Simeon and Levi treacherously murdered all the men of the Canaanite town of Shechem and looted their women, children and properties because one of them had raped their sister Dinah whom he was desperate and offered to marry,[43] even though the prescribed punishment for the crime was marriage of the victim by the rapist.[44]

Third, the alleged covenant with Abraham relies on the absurd claim that God would base relationship with people on the removal of penile foreskin; and would only bless the nations of the earth through Abraham. However, the rite of male circumcision among the Israelites is clearly a cultural practice – a practice that is not without parallel in other parts of the world without any connection to Israel, Jewish religion, or any claim to a divine covenant.[45] The Bible confirms this by stating that:

> *The days are coming, declares the LORD, "when I will punish all who are circumcised only in the flesh – Egypt, Judah,*

---

[40] Genesis 30: 31-43.
[41] Genesis 35:22.
[42] Leviticus 20:11.
[43] See Genesis 34.
[44] See Deuteronomy 22:28-29.
[45] See the *Encyclopaedia Britannica*, http://www.britannica.com/EBchecked/topic/118439/circumcision.

> *Edom, Ammon, Moab and all who live in the desert in distant places. For all these nations are really uncircumcised, and even the whole house of Israel is uncircumcised, in heart.*[46]

Even then, the Bible gives different accounts about the origins of male circumcision. Rather than originating from Abraham, Leviticus 12:3 attributes it to the law given by God to Moses while the people sojourned in the desert after leaving Egypt. Yet, the book of Joshua credits Joshua with re-instituting and performing the rite because there had been no circumcision for males born in the desert (over a period of about forty years).[47]

A PURELY JEWISH COVENANT

The third problem is that if any covenant existed between Yahweh and Abraham, it would be a matter strictly between Abraham and his national deity and binding only on him and his descendants. It would be of no significance or consequence to people of other nations or parts of the world, just as any pact between the ancestors of other peoples and their deities would not affect the Israelites. On no rational basis would God route relationship with other peoples of the world through Abraham. If Abraham were actually the ancestor of the Jews, he would not be different from the ancestors of other nations and peoples. His migration to Canaan would be neither peculiar nor special, but consistent with the type of migration common among ancient peoples in search of new settlements and greener pastures. To this day, millions of migrants still leave their countries of birth for far-

---

[46] Jeremiah 9:25-26 (Emphasis added).
[47] Joshua 5:1-9.

away foreign lands where many of them eventually settle, have children and naturalise. Although many of such migrants would say that God blessed them in their adopted countries, they might not attribute their migration to a special call from God. That the Bible considers the migration of Abraham as special is a result of hero myth-making that elevated an otherwise ordinary activity to an extraordinary one.

4

SALVATION AND THE LAW OF MOSES

> *If you fully obey the LORD your God and carefully follow all his commands I give you today, the LORD your God will set you high above all the nations on earth .... However, if you do not obey the LORD your God and do not carefully follow all his commands and decrees I am giving you today, all these curses will come on you and overtake you [...]* - Deuteronomy 28:1-2, 15

The so-called Law of Moses is a complement to the covenant of Abraham. It is the basis of the life of the daily Jewish people, their relationship with their God, and ultimately their hope of salvation. The Law is contained principally in the Torah, which comprises the Bible books of Genesis, Exodus, Leviticus, Numbers and Deuteronomy.[1] Jews believe that God handed down these laws to them through their leader Moses and regularly spoke to them through him and other judges and prophets. They maintain that God has specially chosen them and has given them the Law and the promises arising therefrom for all eternity. However, is it true that the Jews are God's chosen

---

[1] Although rabbinic writings and interpretations of the law, such as the *Midrash* and *Talmud* are also important, those are inferior to the Torah and will not be considered here.

people? Did God give His law to Moses, and are these laws consistent with universal salvation?

ARE JEWS GOD'S CHOSEN PEOPLE?

Yahweh, who allegedly covenanted with Abraham and gave the law to the Israelites, is their own national or tribal God. The Bible initially identified this God as El,[2] and later as Yahweh, the exclusive God of the ancestors of Israel – Abraham, Isaac and Jacob.[3] This Yahweh is not the God of other nations that the Bible presumes have their own Gods, although it paradoxically describes them as idols and devils.[4] Indeed, the Bible asserts, that El, as the highest God (El Elyon) had assigned nations to different Gods, with Yahweh, one of the sons of El, getting Israel.[5] In this context, the people of Israel would be special to Yahweh in the same way as other peoples would be special to their own tribal or national deities. Because of this exclusive relationship, Yahweh would lead the Israelites to war against other nations; purport to give other nations' land and possessions to them; and order or approve the extermination of other peoples for the benefit of his own 'chosen people'. In addition, due to this relationship, Yahweh would

---

[2] Hence Elohim, El Shaddai, El Elyon, etc.
[3] Exodus 3:13-16. See also Genesis 17:1; 20:1-4; 22:1-19; 26:24; 33:20; 35:7; Ezekiel 10:5.

[4] See e.g., Psalm 96:5, 1 Chronicles 16:26; Jeremiah 10:11; 1 Corinthians 10:20; 1 Timothy 4:1.
[5] See Deuteronomy 32:8-9; Psalm 89:6-7. See also Psalm 82:1, 6-8 for further illustration that Yahweh was part of El's council. See further S DiMattei, *Are Yahweh and El the same god or different gods?* http://contradictionsinthebible.com/are-yahweh-and-el-the-same-god/; RE Friedman, *Who Wrote the Bible?* (Harper Collins 1997) 35.

be jealous of other national or tribal deities whenever his people began to transfer their allegiance or worship to them.

Nevertheless, the Bible contradicts the claim of the Israelites to an exclusive relationship with Yahweh. Ever before he became a Jewish God following Moses' encounter with him in the 'burning bush', Yahweh was apparently a Medianite deity.[6] Also contradicting that claim is the fact that Yahweh was synonymous with or related to El, the principal Canaanite deity[7] worshipped by Abraham and the other patriarchs of Israel. Exodus 6:2-3, reports God as saying to Moses: 'I am Yahweh. To Abraham, Isaac and Jacob I appeared as El Shaddai, but I did not make my name Yahweh known to them.'[8] Thus, Abraham paid homage to and received blessing from Melchizedek the Canaanite king of Jerusalem and a priest of El.[9] That the Israelites worshipped El is manifest in the nation's name. Israel means, 'Struggled with El', a name, which according to Genesis 32:28 was

---

[6] See Exodus 3.
[7] 'El' means god, while Elohim is the plural form referring to gods. See *The Illustrated Encyclopaedia of Myths and Legends (*Marshall Editions Ltd 1989) 85-86; RE Friedman, *Who Wrote the Bible?* (Harper Collins 1997) 35. See also S DiMattei, supra n 5.

[8] New Jerusalem Bible translation. See also, Genesis 14:18-22; 16:13; 17:1; 21:33; 28:3, 18; 33:20; 31:13; 32:31; 35:7, 11, 14; 48:3; 49:25; Judges 9:46. See further, S DiMattei, supra n 5.
See further FM Cross, *Canaanite Myth and Hebrew Epic: Essays in the History of the Religion of Israel* (Harvard University Press 1973); M Smith, *The Early History of God: Yahweh and the Other Deities in Ancient Israel* (Eerdmans 1990); and W Dever, *Did God Have a Wife?: Archaeology and Folk Religion in Ancient Israel* (Eerdmans 2008).
[9] See Genesis 14:17-20. Apostle Paul was later to appropriate the 'heathen' priesthood of Melchizedeck to Jesus Christ, see Hebrews 7.

given to Jacob after he wrestled with God (in the form of a man) to a stalemate. At the end of the wrestling, 'the man' said to Jacob, 'Your name will no longer be Jacob, but Israel, because you have struggled with God (El) and with humans and have overcome'.[10] This change of Jacob's name appeared to mark a switch in the nomenclature, but not the substance, of the God of Israel. The claim of Israel's specialness to God is also in conflict with the fact that the Israelites habitually worshipped other Canaanite and Mesopotamian deities such as Baal, a major deity under El,[11] Molech,[12] Tammuz,[13] Chemosh,[14] Astarte/Ashtoreth,[15] Asherah the consort of El/Baal,[16] etc.[17]

---

[10] In most Bible translations, these meanings would not be apparent because of the substitution by Bible translators of El and Yahweh with God, God Almighty or THE LORD. For the rendering of the names in their proper form, see e.g., the New Jerusalem Bible.

[11] See e.g., 1 Kings 18; 2 Kings 10:18-28. Baal means 'lord' and was a major Semitic god, inferior only to El, although the Bible subsequently describes the god as Beelzebul, the prince of devils. See *The Illustrated Encyclopaedia of Myths and Legends,*. supra n 7, 69. See also *The Encyclopaedia Britannica,* http://www.britannica.com/topic/Baal-ancient-deity.

[12] Molech, derived from MLK, which originally meant 'master' or 'king', was the Canaanite god of sacrifice. The Bible reports that the Israelites habitually sacrificed children to this god. See Leviticus 20:2-5; Jeremiah 7:32; 19:6 and p. 209.

[13] See e.g., Ezekiel 8:14.

[14] See e.g., 1 Kings 11:7, 33.

[15] See e.g., 1 Kings 11:5, 33. Jeremiah 44. Astarte or Ashtoreth was called the 'Queen of Heaven' and her worship was particularly strong in the time of Solomon. She is associated with the Akkadian goddess *Ishtar* and the Egyptian goddess *Isis*. See *Encyclopaedia Britannica*, http://www.britannica.com/topic/Astarte-ancient-deity.

[16] See e.g., Judges 6:25-30. *Asherah* was also known as *Elat* or *Baalat,* and was said to be the mother of many gods, *see* http://www.britannica.com/topic/Asherah-Semitic-goddess.

[17] See *The Illustrated Encyclopaedia of Myths and Legends* (supra) 85-86.

DID GOD GIVE MOSES THE LAW?

The veracity of the Law hinges on the claim that God personally gave them to the people of Israel on Mount Sinai, through Moses their intermediary.[18] However, the books of the law are a compilation, from different sources, of oral tradition, practices and beliefs of ancient Israelites, many centuries after the events they purport to record. The attribution of the authorship of the books of the Pentateuch to Moses is consistent with the practice of Bible compliers of attributing writings to renowned personalities in order to lend them credibility and authority.[19]

The claim that God handed down the Law to Moses on Mount Sinai also aligns with the penchant of ancient peoples to believe that gods resided on mountains from which lofty and awe-inspiring heights they came down to give laws and instructions to mortals. Therefore, just as the Israelites believed that Mount Sinai[20] was the Mountain of God,[21] the Greeks believed that Mount Olympus was the home of their own gods[22] and locals believe that Mount Everest, the highest peak in the world, is the home of the gods.[23] Similarly, different religions, including Hinduism, Buddhism and Jainism, consider Mount Kailash

---

[18] See e.g., Exodus 19 – 34; Leviticus 1:1-2; Numbers 1:1; John 5:45 – 47.
[19] See the explanatory notes on Genesis, Exodus, Leviticus, Numbers and Deuteronomy in *The New Oxford Annotated Bible* (NRSV) (Oxford University Press 2001) 81. This practice is known as pseudo-epigraphy.
[20] Alternatively, Mount Horeb.
[21] See e.g., Exodus 3:1; 18:5; 19:1-3, 10-25; 20:18-21; 24:4; Numbers 10:33.
[22] See *Encyclopaedia Britannica,* http://www.britannica.com/place/Mount-Olympus-mountain-Greece.
[23] See *Encyclopaedia Britannica,* http://www.britannica.com/place/Mount-Everest.

in Tibet as the 'Paradise of Shiva',[24] 'the cosmic centre of the universe, and the home of Lord Shiva'

Indeed, Mount Sinai appears to have derived its name from 'Sin', the Babylonian Moon god, suggesting that it had been identified as the home of that god as well. The wilderness of Sinai seems to be the same as, or around, the wilderness of Sin where the Israelites reportedly had the Manna and observed the first Sabbath.[25] As the Jewish Encyclopaedia confirms, 'it is evident that, long before the promulgation of the Law, Mount Sinai was one of the sacred places in which one of the local Semitic divinities had been worshiped.'[26] Consistent with this theme of sacredness of mountains, Jesus reportedly delivered his seminal sermon on a mountain.[27]

The tone of the narratives – references to Moses was always in the third person – confirms that persons other than Moses had written the Pentateuch.[28] In addition, the books contain accounts of events that happened after the time of Moses, including his death and burial.[29] Concerning his death, for example, the Bible reports that Moses was alone on Mount Nebo from which God showed him the Promised Land but informed him that he would not enter it. Then:

---

[24] 'Shiva' is one the three supreme Gods in the Hindu religion.
[25] See Exodus 16:1-2; 17:1; 19:1-2; Numbers 33:15.
[26] See
The *Jewish Encyclopaedia*, http://www.jewishencyclopedia.com/articles/13766-sinai-mount.
[27] See Matthew 5-7. Luke 6:17-49 records, however, that the sermon was on a plain.
[28] See e.g., Deuteronomy 1:1-2; 31:9; Numbers 12:3.
[29] See RE Friedman, *Who Wrote the Bible?* Supra n 7, 17-21.

> *Moses the servant of the Lord died there in Moab, as the Lord had said. He buried him in Moab, in the valley opposite Beth Peor, but to this day, no one knows where his grave is. Moses was a hundred and twenty years old when he died, yet his eyes were not weak nor his strength gone.*[30]

Moreover, if Moses was alone in his last days and moments as claimed above, nobody could have known where he died and where he was buried. Conversely if he was known to have died near Mount Nebo in Moab and was buried 'in the valley opposite Beth Peor', his grave would not be too difficult to discover. In short, numerous investigations over many centuries have established that, 'it is clearer than the sun at noon that the Pentateuch was not written by Moses, but by someone who lived after Moses'.[31]

It would also seem that, according to the Law, Moses was unfit to be Yahweh's spokesperson, being a product of an unlawful sexual union. His father Amram had married Jochebed, his own paternal aunt,[32] a forbidden and detestable relationship[33] the mandatory penalty for which was being 'cut off' from the people.[34] Thus, Amram, as well as Moses and Aaron, the products of that relationship, should not have

---

[30] See Deuteronomy 34:1-7.
[31] B Spinoza, *Tractatus theologico-politicus* (1670), cited in RE Friedman, *Who Wrote the Bible?* Supra n 7, 21. For a very useful and comprehensive analysis of this subject, see generally RE Friedman, supra n 7; RL Fox, *The Unauthorised Version* (Penguin Books 1991) 90-113; J Belinerblau, *The Secular Bible: Why Nonbelievers must Take Religion Seriously* (Cambridge University Press 2005) 24-29.
[32] See Exodus 6:20; Numbers 26:59; Leviticus 18:29.
[33] See Leviticus 18:6, 12.
[34] See Leviticus 18:29.

remained part of the people, not to speak of being Yahweh's chief lawgiver and priest.

The story and exploits of Moses bears a substantial resemblance to the legend of King Sargon the Great of Akkad in ancient Mesopotamia. Legend has it that this king who reigned from 2334 to 2279 BCE was secretly born by a priestess of the goddess Inanna (or Ishtar) and placed in a bitumen-sealed read basket in the River Euphrates. A gardener of the King of Kish picked the child from the river and took him home. The child found favour with the goddess Inanna, and grew to become the king's cupbearer. Sargon would later conquer Sumeria and other kingdoms in Mesopotamia to create the first recorded empire in antiquity.[35] Notwithstanding the above problems and doubts over the reality and identity of Moses, does his Law merit the description of the Law of God?

---

[35] See https://www.ancient.eu/article/746/the-legend-of-sargon-of-akkad/; See also http://www.jewishencyclopedia.com/articles/11049-moses.

5

IS THE MOSAIC LAW DIVINE?

When the LORD finished speaking to Moses on Mount Sinai, he gave him the two tablets of the covenant law, the tablets of stone inscribed by the finger of God. - Exodus 31:18

The Law contains many useful rules for the maintenance of societal order and harmony in ancient Israel. One could see some of those rules in many ancient societies. In the absence of legislatures and law enforcement agencies, ancient societies usually organised and ran their affairs through customs and traditions. These pass down orally from generation to generation, and are maintained through a system of taboos and communal sanctions. Such customs and traditions reflect the understanding and perceptions of the society at the time and the fallibilities of human beings. However, the Bible claims that God wrote and handed down these laws to Moses for the people of Israel. Is that claim justified by all the content of the Law?

THE LAW AND HUMAN SACRIFICE

In addition to prescribing the sacrifice of plant produce and animals,[1] the law prescribes the sacrifice of human beings to Yahweh. The requirement of human sacrifice is implicit in many stories in the Bible,

---

[1] See generally Leviticus 1-7; 11-17.

the first being Abraham's attempt to sacrifice his son Isaac.² Although often cited as evidence of Abraham's obedience and faith, this story³ clearly shows that the practice of human sacrifice was common or acceptable among the people of ancient Israel. If it had been otherwise, Abraham would have been taken completely aback by Yahweh's request and would not have complied so matter-of-factly. The context of this kind of human sacrifice is the decree that all firstborn offspring in ancient Israel (of both animals and human beings) and all first male offspring must be consecrated and devoted to Yahweh in appreciation for sparing the nation's firstborns in Egypt during the Passover.⁴ Israelites were to explain to their children that, the deliverance from Egypt was why they *'sacrifice to the Lord the first male offspring of every womb' and redeem each of their 'firstborn sons'*.⁵ Although, initially redemption of consecrated sons by the payment of money appeared permissible as a matter of course,⁶ it seems the law later forbade it.⁷

Abraham's willingness and attempt to sacrifice Isaac appear to reflect the tradition of his people as eventually reflected in the Mosaic Law. Isaac, as the son that 'opened the womb' of Sarah, Abraham's wife, belonged to Yahweh and was liable to be sacrificed on demand. Subsequently, the Levites, having been dedicated to the perpetual

---

² See Chapter 3.
³ See e.g., *The Catholic Encyclopaedia*, http://www.newadvent.org/cathen/01051a.htm.
⁴ See Exodus 13:2, 11-15; 22:29-30.
⁵ Exodus 13:11-16, emphasis added.
⁶ See Exodus 13:13.
⁷ See Leviticus 27:28-30.

IS THE MOSAIC LAW DIVINE?

service of Yahweh as ransom for the firstborn male offspring of both humans and animals[8] obtained the right to the firstborns as well as their redemption[9] and perpetuated Yahweh's ownership of firstborn males. The book of Micah affirms that the sacrifice of firstborns was rife among the Israelites and was acceptable to Yahweh:

> *With what shall I come before the LORD and bow down before the exalted God? Shall I come before him with burnt offerings, with calves a year old? Will the LORD be pleased with thousands of rams, with ten thousand rivers of oil? Shall I offer my firstborn for my transgression, the fruit of my body for the sin of my soul?*[10]

According to the book of Ezekiel, Yahweh had decreed this law in order to terrorise the Israelites for their rebellion against him: 'I let them become defiled through their gifts – the sacrifice of every firstborn – that I might fill them with horror so they would know that I am the LORD'.[11]

Another story of human sacrifice is that of the warrior Jephthah who sacrificed his only daughter to Yahweh in fulfilment of a vow he had made prior to going to war. Having come back victorious from the war, Jephthah killed his daughter (his only child) as promised but not before allowing her to mourn her fate for two months with the maidens of the community. Again, it is clear from this story that the practice of human sacrifice was normal otherwise; Jephthah might not have made

---

[8] See Numbers 3:11-13.
[9] See Numbers 18:14-15.
[10] Micah 6:6-7, emphasis added.
[11] Ezekiel 20:24-26, emphasis added.

the sacrifice, and the girl's mother, as well as the community would have resisted it. Even the ill-fated daughter would not have accepted her fate with equanimity, telling her father to 'do to me just as you promised, now that the LORD has avenged you of your enemies, the Ammonites'.[12]

Yet another instance of human sacrifice to Yahweh appears in the Book of Samuel. There had been a three-year famine in Israel apparently caused by the shedding of the blood of Gibeonites by King Saul. When David asked the Gibeonites how to atone for the wrongdoing of Saul, they demanded for hanging 'before the Lord' seven men from Saul's family. David duly provided the required individuals whom the Gibeonites hung on a hill 'before the Lord'. The hangings appeased Yahweh and the famine abated.[13]

It also appears normal to sacrifice foreign priests, nationals and kings to Yahweh, as demonstrated by stories involving King Josiah and Prophet Samuel. A 'man of God' had prophesied before an alter in Bethel in the presence of King Jeroboam of Israel that, a future king of Judah would sacrifice on that alter 'the priests of the high places who now make offerings here, and human bones will be burned on you.' King Josiah was later to 'fulfil' this prophecy by slaughtering 'all the priests of those high places on the altars and burned human bones on them' to the pleasure of Yahweh.[14] Prophet Samuel also

---

[12] See Judges 11:30-40.
[13] See 2 Samuel 21.
[14] 2 Kings 23:20.

sacrificed King Agag of Amalek to Yahweh, who had earlier ordered King Saul to wipe out everybody and everything in that land. Although Saul largely did as ordered, he took the king captive and brought him home with the choice livestock in order, 'to sacrifice' them to 'the Lord.'[15] Yahweh was apparently so displeased that Saul did not sacrifice Agag and the rest of the animals on the spot in Amalek that he stripped the kingship from him. Prophet Samuel then proceeded to hack Agag to pieces 'before the Lord at Gilgal'.

Native inhabitants of towns within the 'promised land' were also objects of sacrifice to Yahweh apparently because they worshipped other gods. The people of Israel must put the people to the sword and destroy everything in their lands. Then they must pile up all the human and animal corpses, as well as all the plunder, and burn them 'as a whole burnt offering to the LORD',[16] as Saul was indeed required to do in Amalek. Any prohibition of human sacrifice in the Bible seems to apply only in relation to gods other than Yahweh. Thus, Leviticus 19:1-5, forbids the offering of children to Molech because it 'defiles Yahweh's sanctuary and profanes his name'.[17] The salvation that Jesus supposedly brought rests on the same ghastly and bloody

---

[15] See 1 Samuel 15.
[16] See Deuteronomy 13:15-16.
[17] For a discussion of this practice/ritual, see the *Encyclopaedia Britannica*,

http://www.britannica.com/EBchecked/topic/515665/sacrifice/66305/Material-of-the-oblation; http://www.britannica.com/EBchecked/topic/275881/human-sacrifice.

philosophy: the shedding of his blood is the ultimate sacrifice for the atonement of the sins of humanity.

CULTURAL, AGRICULTURAL AND DIETARY LAW

The Law contains many cultural, agricultural and dietary rules that have little significance to non-Israelites. It forbids the eating of certain animals considered unclean, and prescribes many Yahweh's feasts, including the Sabbath, the Passover and Unleavened Bread, the Day of Atonement, the Feast of Weeks and the First Fruits, the Feast of Trumpets, and the Feast of Tabernacles. The law also commands the observance of the Sabbath,[18] on the pain of death or extirpation.[19] This law rests on the belief that God created the universe in six days and needed to rest, and indeed rested, on the seventh.[20] Yet, the vast majority of the world population do not observe the Sabbath and are therefore liable by virtue of that law to death or extirpation. Whereas the other festivals of Yahweh would be of no significance to people of other nations, the Feast of Passover and Unleavened Bread would be particularly repugnant to Egyptians since it celebrates the day Yahweh slaughtered all its firstborn human beings and livestock.

In addition, the law forbids the wearing of clothes woven from different materials, the cultivation of different plants on the same field, the cutting or trimming of sideburns or beards, the consumption of meat with blood in it, and of fruits from a tree in the first four years

---

[18] Exodus 20:8-11.
[19] See Exodus 31:14; 35:2-3; Numbers 15:32-36.
[20] Exodus 20:8-11.

of its life.[21] It also bans the printing of tattoos on people's bodies,[22] the eating of animal blood and fat,[23] and the wearing by women of men's clothes, and vice versa.[24] Although these laws might be culturally relevant to ancient Jews, it would be ludicrous to describe them as divine, universal or relevant to the modern world.

LAW ON ADULTERY, VIRGINITY AND SEX

The law forbids adultery[25] and decrees that its commission with 'a neighbour's wife' would result in the summary execution of both parties.[26] Similarly, the law provides that if a man sleeps with a virgin married (or betrothed)[27] to another man, both parties would be stoned to death – the man for defiling a neighbour's wife; the woman for failure to scream.[28] The killings are necessary in order to 'purge evil from Israel'. However, killing people for having sex seems unduly draconian; and the law is selective and misogynistic. It applies to men only when the sexual act is with the wife of another Israelite man, but not when it is with an unmarried woman, who cannot commit adultery with anybody. As explained by the Jewish Encyclopaedia, adultery means:

---

[21] See Leviticus 19:19, 23-27; 23:4-8; Exodus 12:1-11.
[22] Leviticus 19:28.
[23] Leviticus 7:22-27; 17:10-14.
[24] Deuteronomy 22:4-5.
[25] Exodus 20:14.
[26] See Leviticus 20:10-11; Deuteronomy 22:22.
[27] In Israelite culture, betrothal was actual marriage except that the woman would not be co-habiting with the husband until the wedding. Therefore, betrothal in this context is not a mere engagement. See *The Jewish Encyclopaedia*, http://www.jewishencyclopedia.com/articles/3229-betrothal.
[28] See Deuteronomy 22: 23-24

> *Sexual intercourse of a married woman with any man other than her husband. The crime can be committed only by and with a married woman; for the unlawful intercourse of a married man with an unmarried woman is not technically adultery in the Jewish law.'*[29]

This explanation is consistent with the punishment for adultery being applicable to a man for sleeping with his 'neighbour's' wife[30] and with the tenth commandment that outlaws coveting a neighbour's house, wife, servants, animals, or anything belonging to him.[31] Effectively, the law regards wives as properties of the husbands from which their neighbours must keep off, and which the next of kin may inherit at death.[32] However, the husbands are free to have sexual relations with as many unmarried women as they wish, in order to 'be fruitful, multiply and fill the earth'.[33] Hence, many prominent men in the Bible, such as Abraham, Jacob, Gideon, David, Solomon, Rehoboam,

---

[29] See *The Jewish Encyclopaedia*, http://www.jewishencyclopedia.com/articles/865-adultery.

[30] See Leviticus 20:10-11; Deuteronomy 22:22.

[31] Exodus 20:17.

[32] Under the levirate law, if a man dies without a male child, the surviving brother is required to take her as his wife and have children for his brother with her. If that inheriting brother dies before producing a male child, the next brother would take the woman for the same purpose. See Deuteronomy 25:5-10.

[33] See Genesis 1:28.

to name a few, had many wives as well as concubines.[34] Even the priests had concubines.[35]

Furthermore, the law against adultery does not apply when the sexual act involves foreign women, even if they are married. Accordingly, Jewish men – married or single – could take women of vanquished cities or nations as spoils of war.[36] The law also requires men, whether married or unmarried, to sleep with the wives of their brothers who died without any son in order to have children for them.[37] That this law is anti-women is demonstrated by the story of Judah and his daughter-in-law whom he slept with (and got pregnant) believing her to be a prostitute. After ordering the burning of the 'adulterous' woman, Judah had to rescind the order when he learnt that he was responsible for the pregnancy. Judah himself faced no censure for his indiscretion.[38] The test for chastity of a woman suspected of unfaithfulness by her 'jealous' husband and the treatment of victims of rape, further demonstrate the male bias of the law on adultery. A woman suspected of sexual infidelity would, in the presence of a priest, swear an oath and drink a 'bitter' concoction 'that brings a curse'. The drink would swell her stomach, rot her genitals, and make

---

[34] Abraham had at least two concubines, including Hagar and Keturah (Genesis 16:1-4; 24:1-2, 6; 1 Chronicles 1:32-33). Jacob's concubines were Bilhah and Zilpah (Genesis 20:2-14. Gideon had at least one concubine who bore him a son (Judges 8:31; 9:18). David had numerous wives and concubines (2 Samuel 5:13) while Solomon had 300 concubines in addition to his 700 wives (1 Kings 11:13). Rehoboam had 18 wives and 60 concubines (2 Chronicles 11:21).
[35] See e.g. Judges 19.
[36] See the Law and Slavery, and Law of War below.
[37] This is the so-called levirate law. See Deuteronomy 25:5-6.
[38] See Genesis 38:13-26.

her barren if she was unfaithful.[39] There is no such test for men. This kind of selective and barbaric trial by ordeal and oath taking also obtained in many primitive societies.[40]

The law regarding pre-marital sex is also anti-women and irresponsible. Under the law, a woman must remain a virgin until her wedding night when she would sleep with her husband. If on that occasion, she turns out not to be a virgin, she is liable to be stoned to death for bringing disgrace to Israel. There is no corresponding requirement or expectation that the husband should be a virgin.[41] If we were to apply this 'God's law' and kill all women discovered not to be virgins at the time of their marriage, how many women would be left in our societies or in marriage? Why, in any event, would God decree death for adult females who engage in the natural act of lovemaking? It would seem however, that if a woman remained unmarried throughout her life, she could be free from punishment for pre-marital sex since there would be no jealous husband to complain about her not being a virgin.

Further demonstrating the male-chauvinistic nature of the sexual law is the edict on rape. Deuteronomy 22:25-26 decrees that if a man rapes a woman betrothed to another, the man should be killed. However, if the woman was not married or betrothed to any man, the rapist would

---

[39] Numbers 5:11-31.
[40] See R Bartlett, *Trial by Fire and Water: the Medieval Judicial Ordeal* (Vermont: Echo Point Books and Media 2014); *The Encyclopaedia Britannica*, http://www.britannica.com/topic/ordeal;
http://mentalfloss.com/article/50161/history-trial-ordeal.
[41] See Deuteronomy 22:13-21.

only pay a fine of fifty shekels[42] of silver and must marry the woman without a right of divorce.[43] The rape victim has to marry and live with the rapist despite the physical and emotional trauma she must be going through and despite the fact that she might absolutely despise the man who might be anything from a hardened criminal to a psychopath. The fine imposed for rape might not even be up to the amount paid as bride price for a woman in normal circumstances.[44] In addition, the law allows for the distribution and rape of women, especially virgins, captured in war or civil conflict.[45] It also allows fathers to sell their daughters as sex slaves, effectively subjecting them to rapes.[46] All these rules show a scant regard for, and subjugation of, women.

LAW ON DIVORCE

The divorce law is similarly anti-women. The law gives every Jewish man freedom to divorce his wife by giving her a 'Bill of Divorce' (or 'Get'), but did not give women an equivalent right. A man who wishes to divorce his wife, need not give any reasons for it – mere displeasure with the woman, or finding 'some uncleanness' in her, would suffice.[47] Consistent with this law, Abraham summarily dismissed Hagar when his first wife Sarah eventually bore him Isaac.[48] Apart from this, a man who discovers that his new wife is not a virgin is not

---

[42] This is equivalent to about 575 grams.
[43] See Deuteronomy 22:28-29.
[44] Consider e.g., the price Isaac paid for his wife Rebekah and Jacob for his wife Rachael – Genesis 24:52-54; 29:15-20.
[45] See e.g., Numbers 31:15-18; Judges 21:10-13; 5:30; Deuteronomy 20:10-14; 21:10-14; Judges 21:20-3.
[46] See Exodus 21:7-11, and the next section.
[47] See Deuteronomy 24:1.
[48] See Genesis 21:9-14.

only entitled to divorce her, but also to return her to her family so that she would be stoned to death. Furthermore, the law requires men to divorce their wives if they are foreign woman,[49] and allows them to discard 'wives' captured in war whenever they cease to be satisfied with them.[50] There are only minor restrictions on the right of men to divorce their wives. The first arises where a husband had wrongly accused his wife of not being a virgin, in which case he loses his right of divorce.[51] The second applies where a man rapes an un-betrothed young woman, and would be required to marry her without the right of divorce.[52]

In comparison, a woman only has a right of divorce when her father had sold her as a sex slave and her purchaser gave her as a 'wife' to his own son who later marries another woman and deprives her of conjugal privileges.[53] Even when a woman's husband dies, she would, by virtue of the levirate law, not be free but must stay and be inherited by the deceased husband's brother.[54] Under this law, a woman could potentially marry many brothers if the first dies without producing a

---

[49] See Ezra 9:1-4, 18-19; 10:1-16; Nehemiah. 13:23-30; Malachi 2:11.
[50] See Deuteronomy 21:10-14.
[51] See Deuteronomy 22:13-19.
[52] See Deuteronomy 22:28-29; 24:2-4.
[53] Exodus 21:7-11. The harshness of the divorce law against women was only ameliorated by the Mishnah, which put some restrictions and qualifications on husbands' right of divorce and made the process more difficult. Men's right to divorce, without reason or the consent of the wife, was eventually abolished in the 11th Century CE by a rabbinic decree. However, divorce remains permissible where there is reason for it; or the parties agree to do, so; or the authorities imposed it for different religious, social or national policy reasons. See *the Jewish Encyclopaedia*, http://www.jewishencyclopedia.com/articles/5238-divorce.
[54] See Deuteronomy 25:5-6.

male child.⁵⁵ Although the book of Malachi claims that Yahweh hates divorce and that, 'the man who hates and divorces his wife, […] does violence to the one he should protect',⁵⁶ these statements contravene the law, and apply only to a marriage between Jewish couples. In fact, the prophet describes marriage of Jewish men to foreign women as abominable in the sight of Yahweh.⁵⁷

LAW ON HOMOSEXUALITY

The Mosaic legal code regards homosexuality as a grave sin against God and unequivocally imposes the death penalty,⁵⁸ and sometimes banishment⁵⁹ on those who engage in it. A similar attitude prevailed in many ancient cultures and still does in many today where homosexuality remains a crime. In fact, sodomy only ceased to be a criminal offence in many Western countries in the late 20th century and remained a crime in the USA until 2003.⁶⁰ However, to say that homosexuality is a grievous sin against God imputes to God rules made by human beings. Such imputation ignores the fact that homosexuality, just like heterosexuality, has existed from time immemorial, and are both autonomic and inherent inclinations. However, even people choose their sexual orientation, it is not open

---

⁵⁵ See Matthew 22:23-30.
⁵⁶ See Malachi 2:13-16.
⁵⁷ See Malachi 2:10-11.
⁵⁸ See Leviticus 20:13; 18:22; Genesis 19:1-29; Jude 1:7. Compare with the case of the men of Gibeah of the tribe of Benjamin – Judges 19, 20.
⁵⁹ 1 Kings 15:11-12
⁶⁰ In 1986, the Supreme Court in *Bowers v Hardwick* 478 U.S. 186 (1986) upheld the legality of the crime of sodomy. The case was only overruled in 2003 by *Lawrence v Texas* 539 U.S. 558 (2003). For historical trends on homosexuality, see the *Encyclopaedia Britannica*, http://www.britannica.com/topic/homosexuality.

to others to condemn or judge them as long as they do not harm anyone thereby. It is difficult to see how the sexual relationships of consenting adults could be an offence against God, when these are not offences against anybody.

Reflecting the position of Jesus on homosexuality, Apostle Paul associates it with the worship of false gods and categorises homosexuals, along with idolaters, thieves, slanderers, swindlers and drunkards, as people who would not enter the kingdom of God. Unfortunately, this kind of intolerant and prejudiced thinking prevails in many religions and societies that criminalise homosexuality and persecute or prosecute homosexuals for doing nothing other than acting in accordance with their nature, or doing with their own bodies what they liked.

LAW ON APOSTASY AND BLASPHEMY

The law commands the people of Israel to worship only Yahweh and prohibits them, on pain of death by stoning,[61] from worshipping or bowing to other gods or heavenly bodies, or making any images of, or sacrifices to, them.[62] If a prophet or seer tells the people to worship other gods, even after performing signs and wonders, that prophet or seer must be killed; and anybody who secretly entices another person to worship other gods, even if they are one's blood relations or spouses, must also be put to death.[63] The official reason for these laws

---

[61] See Deuteronomy 17:2-5.
[62] These constitute the first and second commandments. See Exodus 20:2-5; Deuteronomy 5:6-7; Leviticus 20:1-3.
[63] Deuteronomy 13.

is that Yahweh is jealous and cannot share reverence with other gods.[64] The law also decrees death for anyone who curses or blasphemes the name of Yahweh, a cause for which a certain half-Egyptian, Naboth, Jesus and Stephen were apparently executed.[65]

It is on the ground of apostasy that the law prescribes the death penalty for anyone engaging in temple prostitution,[66] since these would be devotees of their own religions,[67] hence Ezekiel's lamentations about the sexual escapades of the prostitute sisters, Oholah and Oholibah with gentile men.[68] That the law was religiously motivated is borne out by the fact that prominent men in the Bible, such as Samson (a Nazarite)[69] and prophet Hosea,[70] consorted with prostitutes. Moreover, the mother of Jephthah, another Israelite judge, was a prostitute;[71] and the two women disputing the ownership of a baby in the famed judgment of King Solomon were prostitutes.[72] More importantly, Joshua's spies on a reconnaissance mission of Jericho

---

[64] See Exodus 20:5; Deuteronomy 5:9;
[65] See Leviticus 24:15-16; Leviticus 24: 10-14, 23; See I Kings 21:8-13; Mark 14:60-62; Luke 22:66-71; Matthew 26:62-67; Acts 6:8-15; 7.
[66] Leviticus 19:29; 21:9; Deuteronomy 23:17; 23:18. However, despite this law, shrine prostitution was common in the land with Judah, one of the nation's chief ancestors, being a patron. In fact, the practice was so rife that its eradication was one of the objects of the extensive reforms credited to King Josiah – see Genesis 38; Jeremiah 2:20; See I Kings 14:24; 22:46; 2 Kings 23:7; Joel 3:3; Job 36:14; Jeremiah 5:7; Hosea 4:13-14; 6:10; Micah 1:7; Proverbs 6:25-27; Ezekiel 23; Nahum 3:4.
[67] A modern example of this practice is the *Devadasis* (or 'female servants of God') of India who served and prostitute in the temple of Krishna. See http://www.britannica.com/topic/devadasi.
[68] See Ezekiel 23.
[69] Judges 16:1-2.
[70] Hosea 1:1-9.
[71] Judges 11:1.
[72] 1 Kings 3:6-28.

patronised Rahab the prostitute who eventually shielded them from capture, and was thus instrumental in the plan of Yahweh.[73] In addition, Rahab, as well as Tamar, who acting as a temple prostitute had tricked her father-in-law Judah into sex and got pregnant by him, were named in the genealogy of Jesus,[74] even though women were not normally reckoned in Jewish ancestral trees. It was also apparently in furtherance of this law that Elijah executed 850 prophets of Baal and Asherah on Mount Carmel.[75]

The law against apostasy and the worship of other gods demonstrates religious intolerance, fundamentalism and exclusivism of the sort that have occasioned much bloodshed and suffering in human history, and still do to this day. They transgress the right of peoples and individuals to freedom of religion, irreligion and conscience.[76] Interestingly, despite these attempts to deny religious freedom, apostasy and the worship of 'foreign' gods were rife throughout ancient Israel, were blamed for most national calamities,[77] and led to lamentations by many prophets.[78]

---

[73] See Joshua 2.
[74] See Matthew 1:1-17, Luke 3:23-38.
[75] See 1 Kings 18:17-40.
[76] See Mark 3:28-29.
[77] See Exodus 32:2; 1 Kings 12:28-30; 15:26; 1 Kings 14:22-24; I Kings 18; 2 Kings 16:3 and 21:6 where Kings Ahaz and Manasseh were recorded to have sacrificed their sons to Molech.
[78] See Isaiah 1; Jeremiah 2; Amos 2:1-8; 2 Kings 23:1-30; Zephaniah 1:4-13; Micah 1:1-7; Hosea 4: 1-19.

LAW AGAINST SPIRITUALITY

The Mosaic legal code forbids Spiritism in any form, including practising as, or dealing with, mediums, psychics, witches, wizards, diviners, sorcerers, magicians and such like. According to the Law, these 'detestable' practices contributed to the removal of the Canaanites from their land by Yahweh who gave it to the Israelites.[79] Anybody who practices or engages in any of these activities is liable to death or extirpation.[80] One of the reasons given for the deposition and death of King Saul was his consultation with a medium.[81] This understanding of spiritualism aligns with the position of the New Testament on the matter. In Galatians 5:19-21, Apostle Paul includes witchcraft among the deadly sins the practitioners of which would not go to heaven. Revelations 21:8 says that those who practice sorcery or magical arts are condemned to Hell Fire, while in Acts 16:16-18, Paul considered it necessary to cast out the 'spirit of divination' from a young girl. However, the prohibition of spiritualism is more a testament to the jealousy of Yahweh than any need to prevent evil practices, since the exercise of spiritual or magical powers is acceptable when done in the name of Yahweh.[82] Yahweh promised to raise prophets for the Israelites who would only speak his mind. The people must listen to and obey only these prophets and not the

---

[79] See Leviticus 19:31; Deuteronomy 18:10-14.
[80] Exodus 22:18, Leviticus 20:6, 27.
[81] See Chronicles 10:13 (although in 1 Samuel, Prophet Samuel expressed clearly that Saul's offence and the reason for losing the kingship was his failure to wipe out the entire people and animals of Amalek as he was instructed to do – see 1 Samuel 15:16-31; 1 Samuel:28:18).
[82] See generally, SI Johnston (ed.) *Ancient Religions* (The Belknap Press, Harvard University Press 2007) 138 – 142.

prophets of Canaan. Any 'prophet, who speaks in the name of other gods, must be put to death'.[83]

All powers however, belong to the Supreme Creator of all things – not to any devil or wrong gods – a point affirmed in the Bible.[84] Although, spiritual powers may be, and have been, abused by some, it is misguided to dismiss all spiritual prowess or the practitioners of spiritual works as evil, or condemn them to death or damnation. In fact, the exercise of spiritual powers by or in the name of Yahweh was not always noble, as demonstrated by the plagues that he brought upon Egypt through Moses. Nine of the ten plagues[85] inflicted collective punishment against the whole of the Egyptian population even though they had nothing to do with the alleged refusal of Pharaoh to allow the Israelites to leave. In addition, Yahweh was responsible for the resistance of Pharaoh that led to the plagues; having hardened the latter's heart in order to demonstrate his power against the Egyptians.[86]

Yahweh also appears to have no objection to consultation with mediums when it served his purpose, as with the case of King Saul's consultation of the spirit of Prophet Samuel through the 'Witch of

---

[83] Deuteronomy 18: 14-15, 18-20.
[84] See Genesis 1:1-2, Psalm 24:1-2, 1 Corinthians 10:25-26, Exodus 19:5, Deuteronomy 8:18.
[85] These were the infestation of frogs, turning the waters into blood, the slaughter of all livestock, the infection with boils, the infection with gnats, the infestation of flies, the unprecedented hailstorm, the darkness and the infestation of locusts. Such infliction of collective punishment would be a crime against humanity in international law.
[86] Exodus 7:2-4, 10; 12:29-31.

Endor'.[87] Many of Yahweh's heroes in the Bible, such as Joseph[88] and Daniel[89] also apparently manifested prowess in clairvoyance, fortune telling and divination; and his prophets – from Samuel to Malachi – and son, Jesus, reportedly foretold the future. Is fortune telling or the ability to foretell the future, not a form of divination? Moreover, the gospel of Matthew tells of 'wise men' from Persia who saw the star of Jesus, followed it to Bethlehem, worshipped the infant Jesus, and gave him gifts.[90] There was no indication in the gospels that these men were doing anything evil, even though theirs was also a kind of divination and even though, in all likelihood, they were Zoroastrian priests. On the contrary, the Bible depicts them as being under the guidance of God to fulfil a divine purpose.

Indeed, the practice of divination, sorcery, and consultation with mediums and spiritists was prevalent throughout ancient Israel,[91] a state of affairs that led prophet Micah to prophesy to the Israelites that Yahweh would destroy their witchcraft and they will no longer be able to cast spells.[92] In addition, despite protestations to the contrary, the practice of magic in ancient Israel was in many cases similar to those of their neighbours. For example in Exodus, the magicians of Pharaoh, replicated many of the plagues wrought by Moses, the prophet of

---

[87] See 1 Samuel 28:1-25; 31.
[88] See Genesis 41.
[89] 'Wise man' was a euphemism for someone trained in astrology, magician, diviner and enchanter. See Daniel 2.
[90] See Matthew 2.
[91] See 2 Kings 17:17; 21: 6; 2 Chronicles 33:6.
[92] See also Malachi 3:5.

Yahweh.[93] Exodus also reports that Moses made a bronze snake so that those bitten by snakes (which Yahweh had sent) could look at it and receive healing, despite the fact that the Bible vilifies the serpent as a symbol of Satan.[94] Further, Jewish tradition maintains that King Solomon had a ring (the Seal of Solomon) which he received from heaven and with which he controlled demons and compelled them to build the First Jerusalem temple.[95] Although the Bible regards this ring as an instrument of Yahweh, observers could as easily describe it as an instrument of magic or witchcraft. The priests of Yahweh also discerned his will by *Urim* and *Thummim*,[96] for the benefit of Israelites and their Kings.[97] This kind of divination does not seem different from others, such as, palmistry, the use of cowrie shells or Tarot cards, etc. employed by other diviners. Similarly, the 'Ark of Covenant' revered by the Israelites as an extremely holy object that represented the presence of Yahweh,[98] could easily be seen as an object of magic by people of other nations.

---

[93] See Exodus 7-8.
[94] See Numbers 21:4-8; Revelations 12:7-9; 20:1-5; Genesis 3.
[95] See the *Jewish Encyclopaedia*,
http://www.jewishencyclopedia.com/articles/13843-solomon-seal-of.
[96] This is a method of divination by casting lots with stones or pebbles. See Exodus 28:30; Deuteronomy 33:8; Ezra 2:63.
[97] I Samuel 28:6-7. See also 1 Samuel 14:41.
[98] See Exodus 25:22; 37:1-9; Numbers 10:33; 1 Samuel 6:19; 2 Samuel 6:6-7; 12-16. However, far from being exclusive to the Israelites, the Cherubim represented on the 'Ark of Covenant' were present in the religious practices and artefacts of their 'pagan' neighbours from whom the Israelites apparently borrowed its usage and symbolism. The belief in the existence of beings, which are half-human and half-beast, such as mermaids, sphinxes, and centaurs was very common in many ancient traditional religions and mythology.

It is clear then that the blanket condemnation of spiritualism and the exercise of spiritual powers is unwarranted and unsupported by the Bible. Spiritual principles and powers are to be deployed for the good of humanity and when so used have provided tremendous benefits to peoples through the ages. The neglect or ignorance of such facilities has led to much spiritual blindness and misery in the world. Therefore, although the abuse of spiritual power by a few might make the abusers evil, it does not render the power itself or its source evil.

LAW ON REBELLIOUS CHILDREN

One of the Ten Commandments to the Israelites was to honour their fathers and mothers so that they might be blessed and live long in the land their God had given to them.[99] The death penalty awaits anyone who curses his or her parents.[100] The law further decrees that if a son is 'disobedient, stubborn, profligate and a drunkard', the parents should bring him to the elders who would stone him to death in order to 'purge the evil' from the community.[101] Therefore, the promise of long life in the commandment is literal – obey your parents, or else your life would be summarily terminated by your own parents and people. Although every parent would like their children to be respectful, responsible and resourceful, it is false to suggest that it is the will of God that parents should murder their errant children. In some cultures today parents and families still kill their sons and daughters for disobedience or bringing 'dishonour' to their families,

---

[99] Exodus 20:12; Deuteronomy 5:16.
[100] See Leviticus 20:9.
[101] Deuteronomy 21:18-21.

especially for marrying 'an unbeliever'. Surely, every decent and unprejudiced person would condemn such a barbaric practice as irresponsible and ungodly.

THE LAW AND SLAVERY

The law authorises the purchase, ownership and sale of human beings as slaves who would remain properties of the owners for use at pleasure and transferable as inheritance.[102] Although Israelites may not by this law buy their compatriots as slaves, the poor among them may sell themselves as slaves to foreigners, subject to a right of redemption whenever they or their relatives could afford the means to redeem them.[103] The law also permits Israelites to sell their own daughters as sex slaves,[104] and entitles Israelite men to take virgin girls of towns and cities defeated in wars as slaves.[105] It is this law that must have enabled men, especially the kings, to amass concubines – sometimes in their hundreds. God could not have decreed these heinous and reprehensible practices. Yet, Jesus endorsed slavery in his parable on watchfulness in expectation of his second coming:

> *The master of that slave will come on a day when he does not expect him and at an hour he does not know, and will cut him in pieces, and assign him a place with the unbelievers. And that slave who knew his master's will and did not get ready or act in accord with his will, will receive many lashes, but the*

---

[102] Exodus 21:2- 6, 20-21; Deuteronomy 15:12-17; Leviticus 25:44-46.
[103] Leviticus 25:47-49.
[104] Exodus 21:7-11.

[105] See Numbers 31:17-19; see also Genesis 34:29; Deuteronomy 21:11-14.

> *one who did not know it, and committed deeds worthy of a flogging, will receive but few.*[106]

Similarly, Apostle Paul unequivocally supported slavery as consistent with the gospel of Jesus Christ. He enjoined slaves to remain fully submissive and respectful to their 'earthly' and Christian masters and serve them with fear, trembling and sincere heart.[107] In fact, when the slave (Onesimus) of a prominent Christian (Philemon) escaped and ran to Paul, the apostle sent him back to his master, whom he admonished to forgive and re-accept the slave. As for slave owners, Paul only advised them to treat their slaves 'justly and fairly'.[108] In the light of these comprehensive endorsements of slavery, Paul's assertion that in the church all are one in Christ and that, 'there is no longer Jew or Greek, there is no longer slave or free, there is no longer male and female',[109] sounds hollow indeed.

LAW OF WAR

The prescriptions of the Law for dealing with people and cities vanquished in war will horrify most people. When the Israelites invade any distant city (i.e., those not part of the 'Promised Land'), they are required to make to the people of that city an offer of peace. 'If they accept and open their gates, all the people in it shall be subject to forced labour and shall work for you'.[110] If the people refuse this offer, every male – from adults to infants – in that city must be killed

---

[106] Luke 12:46-48.
[107] See Ephesians 6:5, Titus 2:9-10; Timothy 6:1-2.
[108] Colossians 4:1.
[109] Galatians 3:28.
[110] Deuteronomy 20:10-11.

while the women (especially the virgins), children, livestock and everything else of value should be taken and shared as spoils.[111] An example of the implementation of this law was the Israelites' vengeful war against the Midianites.[112] Where the invasion involves any of the cities of the 'Promised Land', the Israelites must make no offer or treaty of peace and must 'not leave alive anything that breathes'. They must 'completely destroy them – the Hittites, Amorites, Canaanites, Perizzites, Hivites and Jebusites'.[113] Apparently, pursuant to this 'divine' injunction, the Israelites conquered and destroyed the cities of Canaan and largely wiped out their inhabitants.[114] It was for breaking this law that Achan and his children were stoned to death and all his possessions burned.[115] It was also because King Saul failed to wipe out the entire people and livestock of Amalek that he lost his throne, life and dynasty.[116]

To claim that these decrees are divine is falsely to allege that God orders or aids the destruction, annexation or expropriation of nations, and is thirsty for the blood of human beings.[117] At best, this claim

---

[111] Deuteronomy 20:12-14. A classic example of the implementation of this law was the Israelites' war against the Midianites (for which, see Numbers 31). For other instances, see Genesis 34:28; Exodus 12:36; Deuteronomy 2:35; 13:16; 3:3-7; Numbers 21:27-35; 1 Samuel 14:32; 17:53; 2 Samuel 3:22; 2 Kings 7:16.
[112] See Numbers 31
[113] Deuteronomy 20:15-17. See also Deuteronomy 7:1-2. The reason given for these wicked commands was the need to ensure that the people of those cities did not influence the Israelites into worshipping their gods.
[114] See Joshua 6-12.
[115] Joshua 6-7.
[116] See 1 Samuel 15:16-31; 1 Samuel: 28:18.
[117] See for example Deuteronomy 20:3-4, which states that when the Israelites go to war against other nations, the commander of the armed forces should declare: 'Hear, O Israel, today you are going into battle against your enemies. Do not be fainthearted

arose from the belief that different nations have different gods who are constantly waging proxy wars of superiority against one another. At worst, it is an attempt to justify aggression, ethnic cleansing, genocide, war crimes and crimes against humanity by the authorities of the day.

In contrast to Yahweh, some of the so-called pagan nations around ancient Israel appeared to have laws of war that are more humane. The Bible recounts that on many occasions armies of neighbouring nations had invaded and defeated the Israelites. However, these invading armies did not annihilate the Israelites and their livestock; neither did they single out their males for extermination, nor appropriate their virgin girls as concubines. Instead, they ruled the land and carried most of its people into exile from which they sometimes returned.[118] At times, the exiles occupied privileged positions, such as when Daniel became the governor of Babylon;[119] and Esther the queen of Persia and Media, with Mordecai the second in command to the king.[120] The privileged positions of these exiles meant that the Israelites were well protected and looked after. What would have been the fate of the Israelites if the nations that conquered them followed Yahweh's laws of war and completely destroyed them?

---

or afraid; do not be terrified or give way to panic before them. For the LORD your God is the one who goes with you to fight for you against your enemies to give you victory.'

[118] See 2 Kings 17; 2 Kings 24, 25; Ezra 1 – 8; Nehemiah 2-8.
[119] See Daniel 2:48-49.
[120] See Esther 10.

OTHER LAWS

The Mosaic code contains other sundry laws that are detestable. These include those forbidding disabled people or those with any deformity from being part of the priesthood: According to Leviticus:

> *No man [...], who has any defect, may approach to offer the bread of his God. For any man who has a defect shall not approach: a man blind or lame, who has a marred face or any limb too long, a man who has a broken foot or broken hand, or is a hunchback or a dwarf, or a man who has a defect in his eye, or eczema or scab, or is a eunuch. No man of the descendants of Aaron the priest, who has a defect, shall come near to offer the offerings made by fire to the LORD.*[121]

The reason for this prohibition is that such persons would 'profane the sanctuaries' of their supposed creator.[122] The law prohibits so-called illegitimate children and their descendants, as well as people 'emasculated by crushing or mutilation', from attending places of worship.[123] It also encourages cannibalism,[124] cruelty,[125] and tyranny.[126] Although one might excuse some of the above laws as a product of the prevailing circumstances and ignorance of the people of old, one cannot reasonably claim that they are laws of the universal God, or that they are applicable in the present age.

---

[121] Leviticus 21:16-23.
[122] Leviticus 21:23.
[123] Deuteronomy 23:1-2.
[124] See e.g., Leviticus 26:29; 2 Kings 6:28-29; Jeremiah 19:9; Lamentations 2:20.
[125] See e.g., Numbers 16; 23-35; Hosea 13:16; Psalms 137:8-9.
[126] See numbers Numbers 12, 16.

IS THERE SALVATION IN THE LAW?

The salvation promised to the Jews is conditional on their meticulous observance of even the smallest detail of the Law, with infractions attracting severe retributions. However, given the nature and severity of many of these laws, no one is likely to achieve that salvation. The Old Testament is replete with instances of gruesome personal and national calamities attributed to the failure of the Israelites to keep the laws of Yahweh.[127] It is no wonder that the people of Israel habitually went after other gods; and that some Christian authorities fancifully sought to distinguish Yahweh from the loving and kind God they claimed Jesus represented.[128] It is also not surprising that Apostle Paul had insisted that the Law is a curse, and that salvation no more depends on its observance.[129]

The fact that the observance of the Abrahamic covenant and the Mosaic Law has not saved the Israelites from individual and national calamities within and outside Israel is a testament to the fact that they do not provide salvation. In addition, in as much as they are tribal and national in orientation and character, neither the Abrahamic covenant nor the Mosaic Law is likely to furnish a basis for the salvation of humanity, even if such salvation were to be necessary.

---

[127] See Chapter 8, and Lamentations 2:20-22.
[128] For example, the Bible of the Marcionites - an early sect of Christianity- does not include the Old Testament at all. See,
http://www.earlychristianwritings.com/info/marcion-layman.html.
[129] See Galatians 3.

6

SALVATION THROUGH JESUS CHRIST

Salvation exists in no one else, for there is no other name under heaven given to men by which we must be saved. -
Acts 4:12

Assuming his story in the New Testament to be factual and accurate, has Jesus indeed furnished humanity with salvation by shedding his blood on the cross? For this to be the case, human beings must be so inherently and helplessly soiled and disconnected from God as to necessitate an atoning sacrifice. Then, the shedding of the blood of Jesus must be capable of removing this dirt and restoring the connection between humans and God. In Christian theology, the atoning sacrifice of Jesus was essential for salvation because of the sin originally committed by the first humans, which we as their offspring, inherited. This sin, it says, had cut humans off from the sanctifying grace of God and rendered them unjust. The shedding of the blood of Jesus was supposed to sanctify and restore human beings to divine grace. Are these claims true?

DID ADAM AND EVE COMMIT ORIGINAL SIN?

According to the Bible, the sin of Adam and Eve that led to the 'fall' of human beings from grace was disobedience, and the account of this is in Genesis 3. By this account, God having created Adam and his companion Eve placed them in the Garden of Eden, which contained all they needed for sustenance and happiness. However, God had forbade them from eating the fruits of the 'Tree of knowledge' of good and evil and warned that if they disobeyed this command, they would 'certainly die'. However, a serpent convinced Eve that eating the fruit would not kill but would instead make them God-like, with knowledge of good and evil. She ate the fruit and gave some to Adam who also ate. After eating the fruit, instead of dying as forewarned, the eyes of the couple 'were opened' and they realised they were naked.

Subsequently, God came down to the garden and having discovered what transpired, imposed punishments to all concerned. For the serpent, it would thenceforth have no limbs, crawl on its belly and eat dust, and be in perpetual enmity with Eve and her offspring. The punishment for Eve was pain during labour and childbirth, and subjugation to her husband. Adam's punishment was that he would thenceforth earn his livelihood with hard labour, as the ground would not yield food for him without painful toiling. God told Adam that these punishments would subsist until he returned to the ground, since he came from it. Having pronounced the punishments, God, while noting that, 'the man has now become like one of us, knowing good and evil', dismissed the couple from the Garden of Eden. In order to prevent them from returning and eating the fruits of the 'Tree of Life' that would make them immortal, God stationed at the east side of the Garden, cherubim and a flaming sword.

However, the world did not begin at the Garden of Eden, and Adam and his wife were not the first human beings on earth. The story of their creation and fall are instead reflective of common mythology. As observed by the Encyclopaedia Britannica, myths of humans 'falling' from a pristine condition due to sin or misbehaviour and being subsequently subjected to suffering existed in many ancient societies and religions as explanations of the human condition.[1] If Adam was not the first human or forbearer of the human race, humanity could not have inherited a sinful nature from him, could not have fallen from the grace of God, and would not need any atoning sacrifice in justification. Moreover, 'Adam' was not originally the personal name of anybody but the Hebrew generic name for man or earth. Thus, Adam could not have committed the mortal sin attributed to him.

HAVE HUMAN BEINGS INHERITED ORIGINAL SIN?

Assuming that Adam and Eve were indeed human beings and the first on earth, they could not by the Bible's reckoning, have passed on any sins or their repercussions to subsequent human beings.

First, the Bible makes it clear that God had already completely punished Adam and Eve for their so-called sin in their lifetime. The

---

[1] See *The Encyclopaedia Britannica,* http://www.britannica.com/topic/salvation-religion. See also D Rosenberg, *World Mythology: An Anthology of the Great Myths and Epics* (McGraw Hill Companies Inc. 1994).

labours of food production and childbirth were to subsist until the death of the couple. Therefore, apart from these punishments, there is no indication in the Bible that God's relationship with the couple changed: God made garments for them to cover their nakedness and still came down to speak to them as before.[2] Ironically, the only other consequence of the 'disobedience' was that Adam and Eve 'became like God, knowing good and evil', as the serpent had assured.[3] In other words, by eating the forbidding fruit, Adam and Eve became wise and knowledgeable, having snapped out of the apparent ignorant hypnosis in which God had supposedly placed them.

Second, although God had reportedly assured that he would certainly die if he ate the forbidden fruit, Adam apparently lived to be 930 years.[4] Generations after him also lived incredibly long lives,[5] including Methuselah, who lived to be 969 years.[6] Moreover, the Bible reports that many generations after Adam, God reduced human lifespan to a maximum of 120 years, not because of the sin of Adam, but due to the wickedness of the people of that time, including sexual relationships between the 'sons of God' and 'daughters of men'.[7] However, despite this apparent curtailment of the human life span, many notable figures in the Bible subsequently lived well beyond 120

---

[2] See Genesis 3:21; 4.
[3] See Genesis 3:4-7, 21.
[4] The Bible does not say how long Eve lived, but since she continued to reproduce with Adam even when he was well advanced in years, she presumably had an equivalent lifespan. See Genesis 5:4-5.
[5] See Genesis 5.
[6] See Genesis 5:25.
[7] See Genesis 6:1-3.

years, including Abraham (175 years),[8] Isaac (180 years),[9] and Jacob (147 years).[10]

Third, the claim that death came to the world through Adam is unfounded given the fact that all animals die and that God never intended humans to be immortal, according to the Genesis narrative. Recall that after the couple had eaten of the knowledge tree, the Bible reports that God became afraid that they might eat also of the Tree of Life and become immortal like God. To avert this danger, God expelled them from the Garden and installed security to prevent their re-entry. If one assumes that God had planned immortality for humans, the implication would be that in a relatively short period after creation, the serpent and the first humans succeeded in frustrating the plan. Considering the information that the Tree of Knowledge stood tantalizingly in the garden, this story also suggests that God set elaborate traps to ensnare and damage human beings after creating them.

Fourth, the so-called punishments of Adam and Eve are not punishments at all, as labour, including farming, is not attributable to any sin. Historically and archeologically, human beings began life as hunter-gatherers, and only started cultivating their own food much later in their development. The couple could not have moved from hunter-gatherers to farmers within the short space of time indicated in

---

[8] See Genesis 25:7.
[9] See Genesis 35:28.
[10] See Genesis 47:28.

the Bible. As for painful labour before and during childbirth, women bear children in the same way and suffer similar pains as other mammals that neither sinned nor received any punishment. The so-called sin and punishments of Adam and Eve were apparently attempts to explain the phenomenon of farming, the painful process of childbirth, and the process of human development and civilization. It was also an attempt to explain the fact that snakes, unlike most terrestrial animals, have no legs. This is reminiscent of folktales that abound in many traditional societies. The notion that the snake deceived Eve is consistent with the perception in that part of the world of the snake as a mythological and crafty animal, in the same way other cultures perceive tortoise, fox, coyote, jackal, etc.[11] Conversely, the 'Original Sin' implies that human beings suffer double jeopardy for the same offence. This is because although they inherited labour – in terms of both livelihood and childbirth – from Adam and Eve as punishment for their sin, they remain cut off from the grace of God because of the same sin.

Fifth, the generations of people nearest to Adam perished in the flood with only Noah and his family surviving. Thus, according to the Bible, the Adamic race had ceased to exist and the present human race, descended from Noah whom it described as 'a righteous man, blameless among the people of his time, and [...] walked faithfully

---

[11] See e.g., M Hoffman, *A Twist in the Tale: animal Stories from around the World* (Frances Lincoln Ltd. 1998); H Ward, *Unwitting Wisdom: an Anthology of Aesop's Fables* (Chronicle Books 2004); M Green, *Animals in Celtic Life and Myth* (London and New York: Routledge 2002).

with God'.[12] God made a new covenant with Noah through whose sons, Shem, Ham and Japheth the earth was supposedly repopulated.[13] Therefore, the current human race could not have inherited the sin of Adam – a point well illustrated by the fact that the Jews of the Old Testament did not suffer from the sin of Adam and did not require any atonement for it. Yahweh apparently made a covenant with Abraham and his descendants by which he would be their God, and they, his chosen people.[14] Throughout the Old Testament, Yahweh continued this special relationship with the people of Israel and apparently spoke to and dealt with them through various leaders, judges, prophets, and kings.[15] The only obstacle between the Israelites and Yahweh was their constant disobedience and worship of foreign Gods rather than the sin of Adam. Even then, Yahweh regularly forgave them when they repented.

Sixth, the transmission of sins and punishment to endless generations[16] of the human race is an unethical notion that has no basis in reality. The fact is that human beings bear personal responsibility for their own wrongdoings, and guilt is not transferable from parents to their offspring who did not adopt those wrongdoings. In fact, the Bible in a number of places rejects the notion of vicarious liability for the sins of other people. According to Deuteronomy 24:16, 'Parents

---

[12] See Genesis 6:9.
[13] See Genesis 9:19; 10.
[14] See Chapter 3.
[15] See Chapter 4 and 5.
[16] See Exodus 20:5; 34:7; Deuteronomy 5:9; Numbers 14:18; 2 Samuel 12:14. See also Genesis 9:21-25; Deuteronomy 28:18; 1 Samuel 3:12-13; Jeremiah 16:10-11; 29:32; 32:18; Isaiah 14:21; 1 Kings 2:33; 2 Kings 2:23; 5:27

are not to be put to death for their children, nor children put to death for their parents; each will die for their own sin'.[17] Jeremiah 31:30 affirms this principle by stating that parents would not eat sour grapes only to set their children's teeth on edge; 'instead, everyone will die for their own sin; whoever eats sour grapes—their own teeth will be set on edge'.[18] The book of Ezekiel comprehensively rubbishes the notion of vicarious liability for the sins of others, stating that it would be unjust and unethical to punish a son for the sins of the father, and vice versa.[19] As to why this should be the case, Ezekiel insists that those who have been careful to do the right thing and keep the laws of Yahweh must live, but those who sin must be the ones to die. A child, it says, 'will not share the guilt of the parent, nor will the parent share the guilt of the child. The righteousness of the righteous will be credited to them, and the wickedness of the wicked will be charged against them'.[20] Transferring the sin of Adam to all succeeding generations of humanity is therefore also a contravention of the Bible.

Finally, the notion of 'Original Sin' wrongly depicts God as unduly vindictive and unforgiving. God did not afford Adam and Eve any opportunity to repent and make amends even though they had only made one transgression. Yet, the Bible promises that:

> *If a wicked person turns away from all the sins they have committed and keeps all my decrees and does what is just and right, that person will surely live; they will not die.*[22] None of

---

[17] See 2 Kings 14:6 for an implementation of this decree.
[18] See Jeremiah 31:29-30.
[19] See Ezekiel 18.
[20] See Ezekiel 18:19.

the offenses they have committed will be remembered against them. Because of the righteous things they have done, they will live. Do I take any pleasure in the death of the wicked? Declares the Sovereign LORD. *Rather, am I not pleased when they turn from their ways and live?*[21]

Similarly, the Bible declares that God:

> *[...] does not deal with us according to our sins, nor repay us according to our iniquities. For as high as the heavens are above the earth, so great is his steadfast love toward those who fear him; as far as the east is from the west, so far does he remove our transgressions from us. As a father shows compassion to his children, so the Lord shows compassion to those who fear him. For he knows our frame; he remembers that we are dust.*[22]

The Bible also states that, if we confess to God, 'he is faithful and just to forgive us our sins and to cleanse us from all wickedness'.[23] Numerous other passages in the Bible attest to the forgiving nature of God and the necessity for us to forgive one another.[24] The suggestion that God would hold the one isolated sin of Adam and Eve against them for their entire life and thereafter against humanity as a whole is repugnant and makes a mockery of divine justice. Since all these provisions (and others like them) on the transience of repented sins and the willingness of God to forgive them, came much later than the events in Genesis, it would follow that they have repudiated the notion

---

[21] See Ezekiel 18:21-23.
[22] Psalm 103:10-14.
[23] 1 John 1:8-9.
[24] See e.g., Proverbs 28:13; Luke 6:37; Ephesians 4:32; Mark 11:25; 1 John 1:9; Matthew 6:14-15; 18:21-22; Colossians 3:13.

of Original Sin, even if it had any merit in the first instance. Also repudiating the notion is the assertion by the Psalmist that human beings are 'fearfully and wonderfully made'.[25] Clearly, the concept of Original Sin provides a false foundation for the doctrines of atonement and the salvation of Jesus Christ.

DOES BLOODLETTING ATONE FOR SIN?

Another basis for the concept of salvation is the belief that the shedding of human or animal blood is required for the expiation of sins. Thus, the shedding of the blood of Jesus Christ would wash away the sins of everybody who believes in him and turn them into 'born again' new creations of God.[26] The Bible claims that Jesus instituted the 'Eucharist' or Holy Communion as a memorial in honour of his sacrifice at the 'Last Supper' with his disciples. On that occasion, he purportedly gave the disciples bread and wine to represent his body and blood that he was soon to give up for their sins. They were to repeat this ritual in celebration of the 'new covenant' he had brought about.[27] The gospel of John goes as far as suggesting that the bread and wine were actually the flesh and blood of Jesus, and are indispensable for salvation:[28]

> *Jesus said to them, "Very truly I tell you, unless you eat the flesh of the Son of Man and drink his blood, you have no life in you. Whoever eats my flesh and drinks my blood has eternal life, and I will raise them up at the last day. For my flesh is*

---

[25] Psalm 139:14.
[26] See 2 Corinthians 5:17; John 3:3.
[27] See Luke 22:19-20; 1 Corinthians 11:23-26.
[28] John 6:51.

> *real food and my blood is real drink. Whoever eats my flesh and drinks my blood remains in me, and I in them.*[29]

The above passage (which caused many disciples of Jesus other than the twelve to desert him)[30] must have inspired the Roman Catholic dogma of transubstantiation – the presence of Jesus bodily in the sacrament of Eucharist and the teaching that the Eucharist is essential 'food and medicine' necessary for sustaining spiritual and supernatural life and for the salvation of the soul.[31] However, the notion of Eucharist, as well as the indwelling of deity in it, was also obtainable in some more ancient religions where blood sacrifice played an important part:

> *The communion sacrifice may be one in which the deity somehow indwells the oblation so that the worshippers actually consume the divine—e.g., the Hindu soma ritual. The Aztecs twice yearly made dough images of the sun god Huitzilopochtli that were consecrated to the god and thereby transubstantiated into his flesh to be eaten with fear and reverence by the worshippers.*[32]

It may also be noted, that in Genesis, Melchizedeck, the 'pagan' king of Jerusalem and the high priest of El, a Canaanite deity, performed the Eucharist with Abraham, before the latter gave him a tenth of his war booty.[33] Blood communions or covenants, including the idea of

---

[29] John 6:53-56.
[30] See John 6:60, 66.
[31] See http://www.newadvent.org/cathen/05584a.htm.
[32] *Encyclopaedia Britannica*, http://www.britannica.com/EBchecked/topic/515665/sacrifice/66317/Building-sacrifices.
[33] See Genesis 14:18.

transubstantiation, is also common among occult and cannibalistic groups as an act of fellowship, rite of passage or ritual.[34] It is appalling to input to God a barbaric practice that has led to the slaughter of untold number of human beings around the world.

To suggest that the blood of animals, human beings or gods, would wash away people's wrongdoings and save them from their effects is to lampoon divine justice as set down in the immutable law of nature. For every cause, there is a consequence – positive or negative – and everybody is responsible for his or her wrongdoings. The blood of animals, human beings or gods would not wash away the sins of anybody; and an innocent person or animal would not bear the sins of another, in order to set the sinner free. Even if one were to take the so-called sin of Adam as a metaphor for the inclination of human beings to do evil, the shedding of the blood of animals, human beings or gods cannot vicariously remove such evildoing.

IS THE SACRIFICE OF JESUS REAL?

Even if a blood sacrifice could wash away sins, it is doubtful that Jesus has paid the price for the sins of humanity. This is because, according to the gospels, after Jesus' crucifixion and burial, he resurrected on the third day and subsequently ascended to heaven where he sits on the right hand of God. Did Jesus really give his life when his 'death' was only temporary, and he knew from the beginning that it would be so? The unfortunate human beings sacrificed to gods could be said to

---

[34] See L Spence, *An Encyclopaedia of Occultism* (New York: Cosimo Inc. 2006), 283-284; HC Trumbull, *The Blood Covenant* (Literary Licensing LLC 2014).

have given their lives for their communities in that they were truly dead. Similarly, animals slaughtered in sacrifice remain forever dead, often eaten and digested by people. They do not have the liberty of giving their lives and having it back. By purporting to give his life for sins and then getting it back in less than seventy-two hours, Jesus could not in truth be said to have sacrificed his life as ransom for any one.

The claim that Jesus gave his life to save humanity is analogous to a situation where kidnappers snatch someone's son and demand a sum of money as ransom to free him. The victim's father agrees to pay the ransom; but unknown to the kidnappers, arranges with the police who promise to recover the ransom money in three days after he has paid it. The father goes to the kidnappers and pays the money while the police, who had marked all the notes, monitor the whole transaction and observe the hideout of the kidnappers. After the money has exchanged hands and the kidnappers have released the victim, the police move in, arrest the kidnappers, and recover the cash, which they duly return to the victim's father. Meanwhile, throughout the kidnap saga, the 'victim' had foreknowledge that he would certainly be free after three days, and of the exact sequence of events. Would the victim's father have paid the ransom to save his son? Would the kidnappers have really received a ransom? Would the 'ransom payment' not have been a charade?

The payment of ransom for the sins of humanity also begs the question who the recipient of the ransom was. If the ransom were to God in satisfaction for the sins of humans – the so-called substitutionary doctrine - it would mean that God sacrificed an 'only begotten son' for self-gratification. This would be akin to kidnappers demanding a ransom from themselves, and proceeding to pay it from their pockets, before they could release their victim. Such a ransom is pointless and is no ransom at all. However, Psalm 49:7-9 declares that, 'No one can redeem the life of another or give to God a ransom for them – the ransom for a life is costly, no payment is ever enough so that they should live on forever and not see decay'. If on the other hand, the ransom were to the devil for the release of humans from the hold of sin and bondage,[35] it would mean that God is beholden to the devil and needed to give satisfaction to it.[36] This is utterly nonsensical. Moreover, since the devil does not exist,[37] any ransom payment to it would be completely meaningless.

EXCLUSIVELY JEWISH SAVIOUR

Even if one were to accept that Jesus died to atone for sins, a claim that is demonstrably without substance, his sacrifice cannot be for everybody but only probably for the people of Israel. Matthew's gospel tells us that Jesus received that name because, 'he will save his people from their sins'.[38] Moreover, the gospels insist that Jesus was from the lineage of King David and had inherited the throne on which

---

[35] See Mark 10:45; Matthew 20:28; John 15:13-15; Romans 4:25; 5:8-10; Colossians 1:13-14; Hebrews 2:14; 1 Peter 2:24; 3:18.
[36] For a discussion of the Christian rationales for the doctrine of atonement, see GF Chesnut, *Images of Christ: An Introduction to Christology* (Seabury Press 1984) 1-19.
[37] See Chapter 13.
[38] See Matthew 1:21.

he was supposed to reign forever.³⁹ They also make it clear that he had come to save and deliver the lost sheep of Israel.⁴⁰ Therefore, not only did Jesus not preach to gentiles, he expressly forbade his disciples from doing so.⁴¹ He did not plan or envisage that his gospel would reach people outside Israel.⁴² Even after his purported resurrection, the disciples of Jesus still believed that Jesus 'was the one who was going to redeem Israel'.⁴³ The ideas that Jesus came to save the whole world and wanted his gospel to reach a global audience for that purpose were the creations of Apostle Paul and the gospel writers.⁴⁴

Furthermore, since Yahweh is exclusively the God of the Jews,⁴⁵ if he had sent his son Jesus to die for people's sins, the relevant people could only be his people of Israel and not the people of the world for which he never cared and of whose Gods he was jealous. Therefore, any salvation wrought by Jesus would be a salvation for the Jews. This though, is untenable given that the Jews do not believe that Yahweh had a son and do not accept Jesus as their messiah. Throughout the Old Testament, the Bible designates THE LORD (Yahweh) unequivocally as the only saviour of individuals and the whole nation of Israel. For example, in Isaiah 43:11, Yahweh declares that, 'I even I, am Yahweh, and apart from me there is no saviour'.⁴⁶ In Psalm 27:1,

---

[39] See Luke 1:30-33; 3:23-37; Matthew 1; 9:27; 15: 22; 20:30; 21:15; Mark 10:47.
[40] Matthew 2:1-6; 15:24.
[41] Matthew 10:5-7.
[42] See Chapter 11.
[43] See Luke 24:21.
[44] See Chapter 10.
[45] See Chapter 4. See also Matthew 15:21-28; Mark 7:24-30.
[46] See also Isaiah 45:15, 17, 21-25.

the psalmist declares that, 'Yahweh is my light and salvation whom shall I fear? Yahweh is the stronghold of my life – of whom shall I be afraid?' Isaiah 44:24 describes Yahweh as the redeemer of Israel, while Hosea 13:4 quotes Yahweh as saying to the Jews: 'But I have been the Lord your God ever since you came out of Egypt. You shall acknowledge no other God but me; no saviour except me'. Finally, Psalm 107 makes it clear not only that redemption comes from Yahweh, but also that only he is entitled to gratitude for it.

Apart from Yahweh, other persons regarded as saviours by Jews have been kings chosen and anointed by Yahweh to rule over them or persons who have saved them from their enemies.[47] For the Jews, it is clear that the Lord and saviour is, and will remain, Yahweh, not Jesus Christ. The messiah to come from Yahweh would expectedly vanquish Israel's enemies, restore the nation's glory, and ensure its domination over the nations of the world.[48] Any purported messiah who could be arrested and killed by the enemies of Israel without accomplishing the above objectives, would for them, be a false one, more so if that person suffered such a shameful and accursed death as crucifixion.[49] Nevertheless, even if Jesus Christ were to be the saviour of humanity, it is doubtful that the salvation he supposedly brought

---

[47] See 1 Samuel 9:16; 10:1, 23, 27; 11:13; 1 Samuel 16:13; 17; See 1 Kings 1:39; Leviticus 4:3; 5; Hebrews 4:14-16; Habakkuk 3:13; Psalm 28:8-9; Isaiah 45:1-7; *The Jewish Encyclopaedia,* http://www.jewishencyclopedia.com/articles/13236-savior.
[48] See *The Jewish Encyclopaedia,* http://www.jewishencyclopedia.com/articles/10729-messiah.
[49] See Deuteronomy 21:23; Galatians 3:13; *The Jewish Encyclopaedia,* http://www.jewishencyclopedia.com/articles/10730-messiah-false.

would be within the reach of many people.[50] That supposed salvation would also be inconsistent with the one Yahweh had already apparently instituted through Abraham and Moses.[51]

---

[50] See Chapter 7.
[51] See Chapters 3 and 4.

7

THE PRICE OF CHRIST'S SALVATION

When the disciples heard this, they were greatly astonished and asked, "Who then can be saved?" Jesus looked at them and said, "With man this is impossible, but with God all things are possible. - Matthew 19:25-26

Even if Jesus were to be the source of human salvation, it is unlikely that many people, including his supposed core followers, would benefit from it. This is because few believers would be able to do what it takes to gain that salvation and a place in heaven. The major impediments are the unreasonable and virtually impossible demands of being a disciple or follower of Jesus on many areas of human existence, including life itself, family, career, sex and wealth.

NO CAREER, FAMILY OR LIFE

True followers of Christ must be prepared to forgo their careers, spouses, children, parents, and even their lives for him. Jesus made his disciples to leave their occupations,[1] and taught that nobody could

---
[1] See Luke 5:1-11; Mark 1:16-20; Matthew 4:18 -22.

be his disciple unless he hates his own life, parents, and family.[2] He demonstrated his scant regard for family when he forbade would-be followers from burying their fathers or saying goodbye to members of their families.[3] He also made it clear that discipleship equals suffering and death, declaring that anyone who wants to be his disciple must deny himself, take up his cross daily and follow him, with a readiness to die. According to him, 'whoever wants to save their life will lose it, but whoever loses their life for me will save it. What good is it for someone to gain the whole world, and yet lose or forfeit their very self?'[4]

Jesus' teaching that his followers must hate self, parents, spouses and families, and love him instead, seems unduly possessive and self-serving. He appeared jealous of sharing believers' love with anyone, not even the believers themselves. This teaching aligns with the Old Testament teaching that Yahweh is jealous of other Gods when they get the reverence of the Israelites.[5] Yet, the universal God would not crave our love or be jealous that we might love others or family more, a point Jesus apparently recognised when he observed that whatever we do to the least among us, it is to God that we do it.[6] Indeed, the teaching to hate ones' life in favour of Jesus might encourage believers to commit religiously motivated suicide in order to show their devotion to, or be with, 'the Lord,' as has in fact been the case

---

[2] See Luke 14:26-33; Matthew 10:37-39.
[3] See Luke 9:57-62.
[4] Luke 9:23-26.
[5] See e.g., Exodus 20:4-5; 34:12-14; Psalm 78:58; Ezekiel 39:25; Isaiah 42:8.
[6] Matthew 25:40.

with many suicidal Christian sects.[7] Besides, hating one's life or self, as Jesus taught, is inconsistent with loving one's neighbours, since in order to transmit love to others, a person must first love himself or herself. Moreover, if people were to leave or completely neglect their parents, spouses or families in the observance of Jesus' instructions, would this not indicate a wanton lack of love and abdication of responsibilities? How many Christians are prepared to follow the above instructions for the salvation of Christ?

NO SEX

A candidate for the Kingdom of Christ may have to give up sex completely. This is because Jesus encouraged his followers to become celibate or eunuchs, or otherwise, to leave any spouses they already have. According to him, although some were born or made eunuchs, 'others have renounced marriage because of the kingdom of heaven.'[8] Apostle Paul expressed a similar view when he stated that, it is better for a man not to touch a woman and for people not to marry, but to remain celibate like him.[9] Apparently, these instructions led to the doctrine of celibacy among Catholic priests and nuns – a vow many appear unable to keep giving the pervasive sexual abuse scandals involving the clergy.[10] It also explains why devout men would opt for

---

[7] For an account of this and other apocalyptic movements, see *the Encyclopaedia Britannica*, http://www.britannica.com/topic/Apocalyptic-Movements-1891921.
[8] Matthew 19:12.
[9] I Corinthians 7:1-3, 6-9.
[10] See https://www.nytimes.com/topic/organization/roman-catholic-church-sex-abuse-cases; https://www.bbc.co.uk/news/world-44209971.

castration in order to serve Jesus better.[11] As Jesus had taught, people should cut off any part of their body that would make them to sin and enter Hell Fire, since it would be better to go to heaven deformed than to go to hell whole.[12] Interestingly, the practice of castrating males was common in many so-called pagan religions and imperial kingdoms where priests and palace guards were often eunuchs.[13] One wonders what would become of Christians, as well as the entire human race, if everyone had followed the advice of Jesus and Paul and became eunuchs or celibate 'for the kingdom'.[14]

Jesus also proclaimed that, 'sexual immorality', including fornication or sex outside marriage,[15] was one of the evil things coming from within to defile an individual.[16] In reiteration of this point, the New Testament, especially the Pauline epistles, prescribes sex only for spouses, with intercourse between unmarried people, deemed sinful.[17] The condemnation of pre-marital sex as sinful and immoral pre-supposes that everybody must get married, when this is not always possible or desirable. People might remain single out of personal choice or due to circumstances beyond their control, including

---

[11] The most prominent being Origen, one of the foremost Christian theologians and church fathers, and the Valesii, a 3rd Century Christian sect who believed that castration was essential for serving Christ. See *Encyclopaedia Britannica*, http://www.britannica.com/EBchecked/topic/195333/eunuch.
[12] Mark 9:43-47; 5:29–30.
[13] See *The Encyclopaedia Britannica*, http://www.britannica.com/topic/eunuch; the *Ancient History Encyclopaedia*, at http://www.ancient.eu/Cybele/.
[14] See U Ranke-Heinemann, *Eunuchs for the Kingdom of Heaven: Women, Sexuality and the Catholic Church* (Penguin Books Limited 1991).
[15] See 1 Corinthians 7:2; 6:18-20; Galatians 5:19-21.
[16] See Matthew 15:19-20; Mark 7:20-23.
[17] See 1 Corinthians 7:2. See also See 1 Corinthians 6:13-20; Galatians 5:19-21.

inability to get spouses. There is no reason why such people must remain virgins or celibate for life. Moreover, the condemnation erroneously portrays as sinful a natural activity that injures nobody. There is no rational reason why consensual lovemaking between adults outside a marital set-up should be immoral since marriage is only a socio-cultural and mundane arrangement, rather than a divine institution. Although there are good reasons for parents and societies to be concerned about sexual activity between minors, these should be more about the emotional, physical and social fallouts of pre-mature sex than any conception of sin as such. Moreover, sex has many healthful benefits – emotional, physical and biological. To deprive adults of it simply because they have no husbands or wives is unnatural and inhuman. It is no wonder that people largely do not observe this edict.

Furthermore, Jesus applied a very harsh and unrealistic interpretation of the Mosaic Law on adultery. He taught that aside from committing the physical act, a person could commit adultery by mere thought or state of mind in that, 'anyone who looks at a woman lustfully has already committed adultery with her in his heart.'[18] Jesus further taught that divorcees (except those who divorce due to infidelity) who failed to remain celibate for the rest of their lives would be committing adultery, even if they had re-married. In Jesus' view, adultery and lust are evil and defiling of the persons who engage in them.[19] In addition,

---

[18] Matthew 5:27-28.
[19] Matthew 15:19-20.

he reiterated the position of adultery as one of the Ten Commandments which must be kept as a pre-condition for eternal life.[20] However, there is no sensible reason for condemning a person for desiring a woman but refraining from acting on the desire. Feeling a sexual desire for somebody of the opposite gender is a natural thing, while refusing to act on every sexual desire or impulse is a commendable act of self-control. If men could commit adultery in this way and therefore miss salvation, it is unlikely that many men would gain admission into heaven. One also wonders what would happen to women who look lustfully at men. Would they suffer the same fate? On what reasonable ground should divorcees be required to remain celibate for life, or otherwise be guilty of adultery? How many believers observe these teachings?

NO DIVORCE EXCEPT FOR INFIDELITY

On the matter of divorce, as with adultery, Jesus attempted to re-interpret the Mosaic Law in a more onerous and unreasonable way. According to him, divorce was permissible – for men and women – only on the ground of sexual immorality or unfaithfulness. Anyone who divorces other than on this ground and marries another person commits adultery.[21] Jesus rationalised this teaching on the ground that, no one should 'put asunder' what God had joined, having from the beginning created human beings as male and female. It was for this reason, he said, that a man would leave his parents and unite with

---

[20] See Luke 18:18-20.
[21] See Mark 10:11-12; Matthew 19:9.

his wife as one flesh.[22] Jesus also insisted that the Mosaic Law allowed men to divorce their wives only because of the hardness of the people's heart, even though this was not originally the divine plan. One may however fault this teaching on a number of grounds.

First, as no one was there at the time of creation, no one could say what the intentions of God in relation to men and women were. The primordial creation of male and female human beings, even as narrated in Genesis, does not logically lead to a conclusion that the creator intended marriage or forbade divorce. The narrative in Genesis chapter 1 does not claim that Yahweh joined Adam and Eve in marriage neither did it claim that he pronounced their relationship permanent until death. It merely stated that having created the first human beings concurrently in the divine image, the creator enjoined them to be fruitful, multiply and fill the earth, exercising dominion over other living creatures. Genesis Chapter 2, though, has a different creation story, making animals and man products of earth, and the woman a product of the man's rib. Because the woman was purportedly taken from a man's rib – an apparent incestuous fiction apparently used to highlight the perceived inferiority of women to men – the man felt able to declare, 'that is now bone of my bones and flesh of my flesh; she shall be called woman for she was taken out of a man.' However, the practice and rites of marriage differ from place to place, and in many instances, are far from savoury, involving as it

---

[22] Matthew 9:4-6. See also Mark 10:6.

were children, force and enslavement.[23] Many also marry for different reasons – money, power, position, culture, indebtedness, desperation, etc., and sometimes love. It is also a notorious fact that many have been victims of murder, attempted murder or other serious crimes perpetrated by their spouses.

Second, Yahweh, the creator Jesus was apparently referring to, does not seem to mind polygamous marriages or men having many sexual partners. From the beginning of Biblical times, men, including the Hebrew patriarchs Abraham and Jacob, had multiple wives and concubines. Moses, the lawgiver, had more than one wife, while many prominent men after him, including the Judges and kings of Israel, had numerous wives and concubines. In short, the norm for men[24] was to have multiple women; and there was no indication in the Bible that this displeased Yahweh, who in fact approves it by authorising men, single and married, to take foreign virgins as spoils of war.[25]

Third, Jesus' position makes remaining in marriage a matter of compulsion. However, if marriage is voluntary, there is no reason why parties who do not wish to continue with it should be compelled to do

---

[23] For a discussion of the institution of marriage around the world, see the *Encyclopaedia Britannica,* http://www.britannica.com/topic/marriage.
[24] Abraham had at least two concubines, including Hagar and Keturah (Genesis 16:1-4; 24:1-2, 6; 1 Chronicles 1:32-33). Jacob's concubines were Bilhah and Zilpah (Genesis 20:2-14. Gideon had at least one concubine who bore him a son (Judges 8:31; 9:18). David had numerous wives and concubines (2 Samuel 5:13) while Solomon had 300 concubines in addition to his 700 wives (1 Kings 11:13). Rehoboam had 18 wives and 60 concubines (2 Chronicles 11:21. See further Judges 19.
[25] See Deuteronomy 2:35; 3:3-7; 13:16; 20:12-14; Numbers 21:27-35; 31; Genesis 34:28; Exodus 12:36; 1 Samuel 14:32; 17:53; 2 Samuel 3:22; 2 Kings 7:16.

so or sentenced to a lifetime of celibacy for quitting. Insisting that people must remain in marriage against their will and in all circumstances, except for infidelity, is unreasonable and could lead, and has led, to some married people seeking violent or other unwholesome means of exit. Why should spouses of killers, rapists or other criminals have to stay in the marriage against their wish? On what rational grounds should victims of forced, child or abusive marriages be made to remain in such so-called unions? Consider also people who discover that their spouses now prefer to be with people of the same sex; or couples who are not in love with, or even hate, each other. Jesus' anti-divorce sentiments have the potential of compelling many, especially women, to remain in abusive, painful and unworkable marriages for life – a very inconsiderate proposition that many Christians rightly ignore.

Fourth, Jesus' position on divorce contradicts other biblical texts. Although it seems to accord with the statement in Malachi,[26] that Yahweh hates divorce and that married couples should stay together, the same Yahweh allows divorce freely[27] and does not object to divorced people re-marrying.[28] Furthermore, Ezra and Nehemiah, a priest and a prophet of Yahweh respectively, made Israelite men to divorce their foreign wives – a course of action also favoured by Malachi.[29] Moreover, Apostle Paul, while insisting like Jesus that

---

[26] See Malachi 2:15-16.
[27] See Deuteronomy 24:1
[28] Deuteronomy 24:2
[29] See Ezra 10:10-14; Nehemiah 13:23-27; Malachi 2:11-12.

marriage is for life and that divorcees must remain single, permits divorce in a marriage between a believer and an unbeliever, even in the absence of sexual unfaithfulness.[30] Jesus also contradicted his own teaching by prescribing celibacy and spousal abandonment to his followers – prescriptions that would if followed likely lead to *de jure* or *de facto* divorces.

NO WEALTH

Jesus' position on wealth was largely negative and could if followed to the letter, lead to the perpetuation of poverty and hardship among his followers. He insisted that people must sell all their possessions and give away the proceeds before they could truly be his disciples.[31] Jesus then assured that, 'everyone who has left houses or brothers or sisters or father or mother or wife or children or fields,' for his sake 'will receive a hundred times as much and will inherit eternal life.'[32] The early Christians apparently took these teachings to heart in their adoption of a communal lifestyle in which believers sold their properties and brought the proceeds to the church.[33]

Jesus also advised against the acquisition of wealth in the first place. In Matthew 6:19-21, he said that people should refrain from storing treasures on earth 'where moth and rust destroy and where thieves break in and steal'. Instead, they should store treasures in heaven

---

[30] See 1 Corinthians 7:15.
[31] See e.g., Matthew 19:21; Luke 12:33; 18:22.
[32] Matthew 19:29.
[33] See Acts 4:32-37; 5:1-10. Thus, Ananias and his wife Sapphira were apparently killed for keeping part of the proceeds of the sale of their land while claiming to bring all of it to the church.

'where moth and rust do not destroy, and where thieves do not break in and steal'. He also pronounced curses on those who are rich, fulfilled and happy; suggested that the kingdom of God is for the poor,[34] and insisted that it would be virtually impossible for a rich person to enter it.[35] The Epistle of James expresses a similar sentiment when it states that, God has 'chosen those who are poor in the world to be rich in faith and heirs of the kingdom, which he has promised to those who love him.'[36] Apparently, Jesus and the writer of James' Epistle seemed to think that wealth comes from the devil who owns and dispenses it on earth. Therefore, Jesus insisted that, 'no one can serve two masters; for either he will hate the one and love the other, or else he will be loyal to the one and despise the other.' No one could 'serve God and mammon.'[37] In addition, the devil allegedly tempted Jesus by offering him the world and all its riches in return for worship.[38] Yet, all wealth comes from God who has given people the ability to acquire it.[39] The bible even observes that money answers everything.[40]

Jesus's apparent opposition to the acquisition and accumulation of wealth is illustrated by his teaching that, we should 'take no thought' for our life, what we should eat, drink or wear since life is more

---

[34] See Luke 6:24-26.
[35] See Mark 10:25; Matthew 19:23-24; Luke 18:25.
[36] James 2:5.
[37] Matthew 6:24 (NKJV).
[38] See Matthew 4:1-11; Luke 4:1-13, and Luke 16:13.
[39] See Psalm 24:1-2 Deuteronomy 8:18; Proverbs 10:22; I Corinthians 10:25-26; Exodus 19:5.
[40] See Ecclesiastes 10:19.

important than food and the body more important than clothing.[41] Although, this teaching is often interpreted as an advice against worrying about material things, it fits more accurately into Jesus' overall advice against the acquisition of wealth. Jesus in fact further went on to state that we should emulate the birds of the air, which 'neither sow nor reap nor gather into barns' yet God feeds them.[42] By the above teachings, we are apparently supposed to stay idle and wait for God to feed us and take care of our needs. However, not worrying about material acquisitions is different from indolence and lack of vision or planning. It is difficult to see how one could sustain life without food; and it is clear from the Bible that following Jesus did not obviate the need for material sustenance. Indeed, the Bible reports that upon Jesus' death and ascension, his disciples quickly went back to their occupations,[43] while early Christians relied on donation of their assets to maintain their material existence.[44]

Although many people do and have done terrible things in the pursuit and use of wealth, the assumption that wealth is inherently wrong or from the devil cannot be correct. Like any other thing, wealth can be well used or abused. Wealth could also be well gotten or ill gotten. The problem is not with wealth, as such, but with the process of its acquisition and the manner of its use. Even if one assumes that Jesus did not condemn wealth itself but the love thereof,[45] that cannot still

---

[41] See Matthew 6:25.
[42] See Matthew 6:26.
[43] See John 21.
[44] See Acts 4:32-36; 5:1-11.
[45] See for example, 1 Timothy 6:10; Ecclesiastes 5:10.

be correct. If wealth is good, it cannot be wrong to love it. If a person does not love money, how could he or she endeavour to make or attract wealth? If God gives wealth or the ability to make it, there will be no contradiction in loving God and wealth at the same time. In any case, wealth is essential for the doing of good deeds, including providing service to people and helping those in need.[46] It has also been indispensable in the spread of the gospel of Jesus. The church and its congregation certainly love it.

Jesus himself understood that following his advice would only be possible 'with God'. It is however difficult to see why God would want to help people to live in poverty. Although, Jesus' instructions on the non-acquisition of wealth might have been meaningful for early Christians who anticipated the imminent end of the world, it is totally unrealistic and impracticable in an enduring world. It is clear that if a rich person cannot enter the kingdom of God, a huge number of Christians, including the leaders, would be certain to miss out. It is also clear that few believers would be able to comply with the other requirements of following Christ and therefore benefiting from his salvation. Merely believing in him as lord and saviour would clearly not suffice.[47]

---

[46] See 2 Corinthians 9:7; Proverbs 14:31; 28:27; Ephesians 4:28.
[47] See Chapter 12.

8

IS JUSTIFICATION BY LAW OR CHRIST?

But that no one is justified by the law in the sight of God is evident, for "the just shall live by faith [...] Christ has redeemed us from the curse of the law, having become a curse for us. – Galatians 3:11, 13

As has been demonstrated,[1] Jews still steadfastly believe in the relevance and efficacy of the Abrahamic Covenant and Mosaic Law for their salvation, and reject any salvation through Jesus Christ. Meanwhile, Christians profess salvation through Jesus Christ and lay claim to the covenant of Abraham whose children they purport to be by faith. Paradoxically however, Christians seek to distance themselves from the Mosaic Law, the indispensable counterpart to the covenant. Yet, the New Testament claims that Jesus Christ was the fulfilment of the Law and bases his ministry on Jewish prophecies. So, is the conflict between the salvation supposedly brought by Jesus Christ reconcilable with the salvation allegedly rooted in Abraham and the Law?

---

[1] See Chapters 3, 4 and 8.

JESUS AND THE ABRAHAMIC COVENANT

The Bible's New Testament designates Jesus as Abraham's seed and traces his ancestry to the patriarch.[2] It also claims that the mission of Jesus Christ was in line with the Abrahamic covenant. In a song attributed to Mary the mother of Jesus after the visitation to her by Angel Gabriel prior to the conception of Jesus, she declared that God 'has helped his servant Israel, remembering to be merciful to Abraham and his descendants forever, even as he said to our fathers'.[3] Similarly, Zechariah, the father of John the Baptist, sang praises[4] to the God of Israel because he had come to redeem his people by raising up Jesus of the house of David, as 'a horn of salvation', thereby showing mercy to their fathers in remembrance of the covenant with Abraham.[5]

In his own statements, Jesus not only recognised the people of Israel as the descendants of Abraham, he identified the benefit apparently associated with that relationship.[6] In the parable of the rich man and Lazarus, Jesus claimed that, 'father' Abraham was in heaven when Moses was still on earth as the prophet of God.[7] He also affirmed that the Jews receive salvation due to their decent from Abraham[8] - a claim endorsed by several other passages in the New Testament.[9] Jesus' acceptance and endorsement of the Abrahamic tale and its purport

---

[2] See Matthew 1:1-17; Luke 3:21-38.
[3] See Luke 1:54-55.
[4] The song is commonly known as *The Benedictus*.
[5] See Luke 1:67-73.
[6] See John 8:37.
[7] Luke 16:19-31.
[8] See Luke 19:9; John 4:22; 8:1-59.
[9] See e.g., Acts 3:25; Hebrews 6:13-14; Romans 11: 1-22, 25-32; Acts 7.

indicates that he was a bona fide Jewish man with a worldview shaped by the religion and culture of his people. It however raises the profound question whether he or Abraham is the source of salvation, because unless validly displaced, the covenant of Abraham would negate the salvation of Jesus Christ.

SALVATION THROUGH ABRAHAM OR JESUS?
Christians believe that the blessings of Abraham avail them, and that they are the children of Abraham by virtue of their faith in Jesus Christ. In this connection, the New Testament has modified the phrase, 'the seed of Abraham' to include gentiles who believe in the gospel of Jesus.[10] It also claims that the declaration that God would bless all nations through Abraham was a prior announcement of the gospel of Jesus to Abraham and meant that, 'those who have faith are blessed along with Abraham, the man of faith'.[11] According to the New Testament, faith in Jesus Christ not only makes believers part of the Abrahamic Covenant; it gives them a superior key to salvation. For Jews, it insists that descent from Abraham would no longer suffice for salvation; belief in Jesus is essential.

This re-interpretation aligns with some of the teachings of Jesus. Although he endorsed the Abrahamic story and covenant, he had also insisted that being a descendant of Abraham does not guarantee salvation, and that non-Jews who accept his message would be saved while the Jews might miss out in spite of their Abrahamic

---

[10] See Galatians 3.
[11] Galatians 3:7-9. See also Romans 4; 9:6.

connections.[12] He also told the Jews that they should not rely for salvation on mere descent from Abraham since God could raise children to Abraham from stones. Jesus even referred to Jews as children of the devil,[13] and claimed to have pre-existed Abraham.[14] That the Jews would not be saved merely because of their Abrahamic ancestry was clearly spelt out by Peter, the chief disciple of Jesus, who told them that they must repent and turn to God through Jesus, the Christ.[15]

Could Jesus or his followers change or re-define the Abrahamic covenant or its significance? The answer according to the Bible is in the negative. The Bible makes it clear that the covenant with Abraham and his descendants is everlasting and not liable to change as long as the people of Israel kept their side of the deal.[16] Yahweh would cut off from the people, any person not circumcised in conformity with the covenant.[17] In fact, he almost killed Moses because of a delay in the circumcision of his son, a consequence averted only by the swift and improvised circumcision of the boy by his mother.[18] If Yahweh would not spare Moses, the chief custodian of his law, for a mere delay in observing the covenant, it is unlikely that he will spare anybody else for breaking it. For the Jews, not only is the covenant permanent, it is

---

[12] See Luke 13:28-30. See also Matthew 8:10.
[13] See Luke 3:8; John 8:44.
[14] John 8:1-59.
[15] See Acts 3:9-20.
[16] Genesis 17:8-9.
[17] Genesis 17:14.
[18] See Exodus 4:24-26

the lynchpin of their salvation. It does not envisage any change and no one is authorised to change or modify it. The Abrahamic tale severely damages the story of Jesus: If the same God had made a perpetual covenant to bless and save the Israelites and the world through Abraham, it would follow that, there would be no need for salvation through Jesus Christ.

JESUS AND THE LAW

Salvation through Jesus Christ would also be untenable unless he had effectively displaced the Mosaic Law. The gospels insist that Jesus, his ministry and his status as the messiah were rooted in the Jewish law. They claim that the key events surrounding him and his life – conception, birth, resurrection etc., were in fulfilment of Old Testament prophecies. Early in his ministry, Jesus reiterated the Jewish foundation of his ministry and made it clear that, far from abolishing the law, he had come to fulfil it and its associated prophecies. Insisting that 'not the smallest letter or the least stroke of a pen' in relation to the law would go unaccomplished,[19] Jesus asserted that anyone who breaks any of the laws or teaches others to do so, would be among the least in heaven. Those who practice the law and teach others to do so would be the greatest in heaven.[20] Thus, as far as Jesus was concerned, the Mosaic Law and the concomitant regime of the prophets are valid and vital for salvation.

---

[19] Matthew 5:17-18.
[20] Matthew 5:19.

Consistent with the above position, Jesus reportedly observed the law and lived according to its tenets throughout his life. He was consecrated and circumcised as required by the law.[21] He was a pious Jew and observed its festivals, including the Passover.[22] Jesus was also educated in the Jewish law,[23] was addressed as rabbi (a learned teacher of the law),[24] and dressed as such.[25] He revered the Jewish temple and synagogues, regularly preached in them[26] and chased away those trading in the temple.[27] If Jesus were a religious renegade, the Jewish authorities would not have allowed him free use of the temple and synagogues.[28] Jesus also taught faithful compliance with the law as illustrated by his advice that keeping the Ten Commandments is a pre-requisite for eternal life.[29] In fact, Jesus' statement of the 'greatest commandment'[30] was a re-statement of Jewish faith contained in Deuteronomy 6:4-5, and the need to love fellow Jews as decreed in Leviticus 19:18. The former declares, 'Listen, Israel: Yahweh our God is the one, the only Yahweh. You must love Yahweh your God with all your heart, with all your soul, with all your strength.'[31] The latter

---

[21] Luke 2:21-24.
[22] Luke 2: 41-49; 22:7-21; Mark 14:12-26; Matthew 26:17:29.
[23] See Luke 2:46-47.
[24] See Matthew 22:15-33; Mark 10:17-22.
[25] See Mark 6:56.
[26] See e.g., Luke 4:16-30; 20:1; Mark 11:15-17; John 2:13-17; 18:20.
[27] See John 2:13-17.
[28] See e.g., Luke 4:14-30, 44; 20:1.
[29] Mark 10:17-21.
[30] See Matthew 22:37-38.
[31] Deuteronomy 6:4-5 (New Jerusalem Bible). This is known as the *Shema*.

enjoins Jews not to 'seek revenge or bear a grudge against anyone among your people, but love your neighbour as yourself'.

Although Jesus reportedly disputed with the Pharisees,[32] such disputations appear largely to concern the interpretation of the law and their hypocrisy – the kind of disputations frequently seen among different sects of other religions.[33] For example, when the Pharisees accused his disciples of eating without washing their hands as required by tradition, Jesus re-affirmed the veracity of the law (in particular the law to honour one's parent and to kill disobedient sons) but insisted that the Pharisees had abandoned God's law in favour of traditions.[34] In fact, Jesus enjoined his listeners to listen to the teachers of the law and the Pharisees and do their bidding since they 'sit in Moses' seat'.[35]

Thus, from the utterances and actions attributed to Jesus, it is clear that he never intended a dethronement of the law but its better, and sometimes stricter, observance. It would also seem that the New Testament's negative characterisation of the Pharisees and their apparent condemnation by Jesus are reflective of the animosity between them and the early church.[36] However, although Jesus appeared fully to have observed and lived in accordance with the law, he would have done so as other Jewish men of his day. The Bible does

---

[32] The pharisaic group was one of the most popular and dominant of the schools of Judaism at the time.
[33] For a discussion of this, see IM Zeitlin, *Jesus and the Judaism of His Time* (Policy Press 1988) 11-21.
[34] See Mark 7:7-10; Matthew 15:1-9.
[35] Matthew 22:1-3.
[36] See WRF Browning (ed.) *Oxford Dictionary of the Bible* (Oxford University 2009) 288.

not support the claim that he was the fulfilment of Old Testament messianic prophecies as none of them cited in the gospels referred to him. Therefore, the Jews still observe the law, or as much of it as possible in the present time and circumstances, and continue to wait for their messiah. If Jesus was not the fulfilment of these prophecies, he could not be the fulfilment of the law.

Just like Jesus, the Bible reports that his disciples continued to practice Judaism after his death. In fact, all the Jewish 'converts' to Christianity in Israel remained 'zealous for the law', and complained that Paul was teaching the Jews in diaspora not to keep it.[37] They insisted that gentile converts must observe the Abrahamic covenant and the Law as pre-conditions for acceptance. It was such insistence that caused the quarrel between Paul and Peter and the former's admonition of the Galatians against the Law.[38] The insistence of Jesus' disciples on the validity and compulsion of the Mosaic Law was reasonable and understandable. Having apparently followed their master in his own observance of that law and having observed and listened to him first hand, they could find no need or justification for abandoning it.

Indeed, a description of the life of the early Christians in Acts[39] is identical to a description of the Essenes, a sect of Judaism, provided by the Jewish historian Josephus. According to Josephus, the Essenes

---

[37] Acts 21:20-21.
[38] Galatians 2:11-21; 3.
[39] See Acts 4:32-36; 5:1-11.

were the most devout, virtuous and righteous of the Jewish sects. These attributes were:

> *demonstrated by that institution of theirs, which will not suffer any thing to hinder them from having all things in common; so that a rich man enjoys no more of his own wealth than he who hath nothing at all. There are about four thousand men that live in this way, and neither marry wives, nor are desirous to keep servants, as thinking the latter tempts men to be unjust, and the former gives the handle to domestic quarrels; but as they live by themselves, they minister one to another. They also appoint certain stewards to receive the incomes of their revenues, and of the fruits of the ground; such as are good men and priests, who are to get their corn and their food ready for them [...].*[40]

It would seem therefore, that the early Christians were essentially a sect of Judaism.

DID JESUS DISPLACE THE LAW?

Despite the above facts and although Jesus had insisted that people must observe even the smallest letter and the smallest aspect of the law, Apostle Paul gave a different message. He taught that Christians should not observe the law; that Jesus has done away with it; and that justification now comes by faith in Jesus Christ rather than by the observance of the covenant and the law. According to Paul, 'neither circumcision nor un-circumcision means anything; what counts is the new creation'.[41] Declaring the 'old covenant' obsolete in the wake of

---

[40] See F Josephus, F Josephus, *Antiquities of the Jews* (Acheron Press 2012) Book 18, Chapter 1:5. See also WRF Browning (ed.) supra n 36, 103-104.
[41] Galatians 6:15.

Jesus,[42] Paul called the Galatian Christians fools for attempting to follow the Mosaic Law rather than relying on faith in Jesus. According to him, those striving to observe the law are under a curse, because justification does not come from it, but 'the righteous will live by faith'.[43]

Paul's position is understandable. As we have seen, many of the Mosaic edicts do not commend themselves to civilised or non-Jewish societies. Perhaps then, Jesus' coming was a way of freeing people from that draconian legal system. Many early Christians in fact believed that the vengeful and harsh God of the Old Testament was different from the God of love and grace apparently represented by Jesus and espoused by Paul. Accordingly, the first Cannon of Christian scripture put together by Bishop Marcion of Sinope,[44] the foremost advocate of this position, did not have the Old Testament, but comprised only ten epistles of Paul and an abridged version of the gospel of Luke.[45] The church eventually declared Marcion a heretic, and in 144 CE, excommunicated him although he was able to establish a parallel church that rivalled the orthodoxy for hundreds of years.

---

[42] See Hebrews 8:3.
[43] See Galatians 3:10-13. Deuteronomy 27:26 confirms that, 'Cursed be anyone who does not confirm the words of this law by doing them.' And all the people shall say, 'Amen'.
[44] Sinope (Sinop) is in present day Turkey.
[45] The Marcionite Bible comprises a shorter Gospel of Luke, and the following letters of Paul: Galatians, 1 and Corinthians, Romans, 1 and 2 Thessalonians, Ephesians, Colossians, Philemon, and Philippians. For more information, see http://www.earlychristianwritings.com/info/marcion-layman.html.

IS JUSTIFICATION BY LAW OR CHRIST?

However, the claim that the Mosaic Law is defunct and that faith in Jesus has supplanted it is untenable. This is because the Law is supposed to be binding on the Israelites forever, without any freedom on their part to abandon or change it. The people indeed swore, under a curse, to abide forever by the law in their individual and collective capacities[46] - a vow Moses sealed by a blood covenant.[47] As already discussed, individual laws attract draconian penalties for non-compliance, while a plethora of national punishments follow collective contravention, as against blessings for compliance. The Jews indeed believe that the life of the people and their nation depend on compliance with the Law.[48] The Bible records that on many occasions, calamities, including defeats in wars and deportations, had befallen the people of Israel due to their disobedience of Yahweh's laws and covenants.[49] There is little wonder then that the book of Joshua admonishes the Jews that:

> *This Book of the Law shall not depart from your mouth, but you shall meditate on it day and night, so that you may be careful to do according to all that is written in it. For then you will make your way prosperous, and then you will have good success.*[50]

Moreover, to suggest that apparently immutable laws handed down by God, and requiring obedience at the pain of serious punishments,

---

[46] See Deuteronomy 27:26.
[47] See Exodus 24:7-8.
[48] See e.g., Deuteronomy 11; 28; 1 Samuel 12:14-15.
[49] See e.g., 2 Kings 17: 13-20; 2 Kings 24; 2 Chronicles 36:15-20; Isaiah 3:8; 42:24-25; Joshua 5:6; Nehemiah 9:32-33; Daniel 9:10-11.
[50] Joshua 1:8.

including death and national destruction, are no longer valid, useful or acceptable implies that God is prone to mistakes and errors of judgment.

In any event, Paul never met Jesus, was not a follower of his, and did not learn from him or any of his disciples and followers. By his own admission, the gospel he preached was 'not of human origin', and was not received from or taught by any man. Instead, he supposedly received the gospel 'by revelation from Jesus Christ'.[51] Paul was not in a position to know first-hand what Jesus felt or taught about the law; and the alleged revelation he received was not verifiable. It is therefore doubtful that Paul could speak for, and in effect, overrule Jesus and his disciples in their endorsement and observance of the law.

Moreover, Paul did observe the law and expressed his full endorsement of its tenets, as well as those of the prophets.[52] For instance, while answering the charge that he was a ringleader of the Nazarenes, Paul declared that, 'I worship the God of our ancestors as a follower of the Way, which they call a sect. I believe everything that is in accordance with the Law and that is written in the Prophets.'[53] Thus, although Paul insisted that there was no need for gentile Christians to observe the law, he did not mind that the Jewish Christians observed it. He observed it himself.[54]

---

[51] See Galatians 1:11-24.
[52] See Acts 24:14-15; 1 Corinthians 9:20-21; Acts 16:3.
[53] Acts 24:14.
[54] See, in addition, Acts 18:21; 25:8.

Paul suggested that Jewish Christians would be judged according to the tenets of the law, since 'it is not those who hear the law who are righteous in God's sight', but those who obey it.[55] Paul believed that the Jews, being under the covenant and law of God, have much advantage because 'they have been entrusted with the very words of God'.[56] He regarded it as a dishonour to God for those who have the law not to fully observe it.[57] Therefore, faith in Christ does not nullify but upholds the Mosaic Law.[58] Paul's discountenancing of the law for non-Jews appears to be a clever and cynical strategy to win converts for his church. As he pointed out:

> *To the Jews I became like a Jew, to win the Jews. To those under the law I became like one under the law (though I myself am not under the law), so as to win those under the law. To those not having the law I became like one not having the law (though I am not free from God's law but am under Christ's law), so as to win those not having the law.*[59]

Paul's position on whether there is need to observe the law appears hypocritical - a case of blowing hot and cold, or eating one's cake and purporting to have it.

Although Apostle Paul masterminded the separation of Christianity from the Mosaic Law, this separation is untenable since the superstructure of Christianity rests on the foundation of Judaism and the law. Were this foundation to be undermined, the superstructure

---

[55] Romans 2:13.
[56] Romans 3:1-2.
[57] Romans 2:23.
[58] Romans 3:31.
[59] 1 Corinthians 9:20-21.

would certainly collapse. For this reason, the entire Jewish scriptures remain an integral part of the Christian Bible in conjunction with the New Testament.[60] In fact, the so-called Old Testament is 'old' only as far as Christianity is concerned. In Judaism and for Jews, it remains very much a current and abiding testament. It would seem therefore that Jesus, even if he existed, did not bring a new wine but had served an old one from a new bottle. However, Jesus' attitude to and relationship with the parochial and nationalist Mosaic Law is wholly inconsistent with the belief that he is the saviour of humanity, even if such a saviour were to be needed.

DISCIPLES OF JESUS AND THE GOSPEL

If Jesus had sought to overthrow the law and had trained disciples to propagate a new salvation paradigm to the world, one would expect them to be pivotal in the spread of Christianity. However, most were irrelevant in this project, as they had no distinct act or role. The few who appeared to be active seemed to concentrate their ministry within Israel and vanished from biblical records very early in the life of the church. However, they appear to have made little impact with their evangelisation given the almost total rejection of the gospel and Christianity by Israelites. This state of affairs reinforces the observation that the early Christians were simply of the Essene sect of Judaism. The claims that the disciples were active missionaries in Asia and Europe; that they suffered martyrdom for the cause of Christ; and that Peter was the first bishop of Rome rests only on church tradition

---

[60] For an attempt to rationalise this paradox, see GF Chesnut, *Images of Christ: An Introduction to Christology* (Seabury Press 1984) 30-32.

rather than historical fact. Similarly unfounded is the claim that the disciples or their companions wrote the gospels of Matthew and John; the epistles of Peter, James, Jude and John; and Revelation. The church merely ascribed authorship of the books to the disciples or brothers of Jesus in order to make them seem authoritative.[61]

Rather than the disciples of Jesus, the message of Christianity as we have it today is attributable to the dictates of church leaders and the exploits of Paul and his associates - people who were neither followers of Jesus nor witnesses of his ministry. It seems curious that the untrained Paul would be the one to take the gospel to the world when Jesus had apparently trained his twelve and other disciples, and commissioned them to do so. It would be no exaggeration to suggest that there would have been no gospel of Christ were it not for Paul and the political forces in the Roman Empire.[62] The 'conversion' of Paul (a Roman citizen) and the intervention of Emperor Constantine led to the formulation of the Christian credo as we have it today. The intervention of Constantine and successor emperors (especially Theodosius who in 380 CE decreed Christianity the official religion of the empire) provided the political, economic and military impetus that transformed a relatively minor sect into a global religion.

---

[61] See the Introduction to the respective books in *The New Oxford Annotated Bible (NRSV)* (Oxford University Press 2001). See also, the *Catholic Encyclopaedia*, http://www.newadvent.org/cathen/08435a.htm; http://www.newadvent.org/cathen/08542b.htm; http://www.newadvent.org/cathen/11752a.htm; http://www.newadvent.org/cathen/08275b.htm.
[62] See Chapter 10.

9

ISLAM, PATRIARCHS AND CHRIST

And who is better in faith than those who 'fully' submit themselves to Allah, do good, and follow the Way of Abraham, the upright? Allah chose Abraham as a close friend. – Surah 4:125

Moslems lay claim to the lineage and covenant of Abraham through Ishmael, Abraham's first son by Hagar, and trace Prophet Muhammad's ancestry to him. *Eid-ul-Adha* – the commemoration of the attempted sacrifice of Isaac by Abraham (Ibrahim) – is one of the two major festivals in Islam. The Quran also recognises Moses as Allah's lawgiver and leader of the Israelites.[1] In fact, it recognises Abraham, Ishmael, Isaac, Jacob, Moses and Jesus as Allah's Prophets preceding Muhammad.[2] However, the Bible tries strenuously to exclude Ishmael and his descendants from the covenant of Abraham,[3] and insists that Yahweh only established the Abrahamic covenant through Isaac, the son of promise.[4]

---

[1] See Surah 10:75-93.
[2] See Surah 2:136; 3:3; 3:84; 4:163.
[3] Genesis 17:19-21.
[4] See Chapter 4

Despite the above links however, Moslems do not claim salvation through the Abrahamic covenant, the Mosaic Law, or Jesus Christ. For them, entry into paradise depends on total submission to Allah, acceptance of Muhammad as Allah's Prophet, observance of the edicts of the Quran, and doing good deeds.[5] The Quran is emphatic that although Jesus (Isa) was a messenger and prophet of Allah, he was not and could not be Allah.[6] In fact, it declares it blasphemous and a bar to paradise for anyone to equate Jesus with Allah:

> *They have certainly disbelieved who say, "Allah is the Messiah, the son of Mary" while the Messiah has said, "O Children of Israel, worship Allah, my Lord and your Lord." Indeed, he who associates others with Allah - Allah has forbidden him Paradise, and his refuge is the Fire. And there are not for the wrongdoers any helpers.*[7]

The Quran also flatly rejects the notion of Holy Trinity and the claim that Allah has a son. According to Surah 9:30:

> *The Jews say, "Ezra is the son of Allah "; and the Christians say, "The Messiah is the son of Allah." That is their statement from their mouths; they imitate the saying of those who disbelieved [before them]. May Allah destroy them; how are they deluded?*

---

[5] See Chapters 1 and 2.
[6] See Surah 2: 87, 253; 3:52; 4:17; 5:45, 75, 110, 116; 43:67; 57:27; 61:6.
[7] Surah 5:72. See also Surah 5:17.

IS JUSTIFICATION BY LAW OR CHRIST?

In Surah 2:116, the Quran declares, 'And yet some people assert, "God has taken unto Himself a son!" Limitless is He in His glory! Nay, but His is all that is in the heavens and on earth; all things devoutly obey His will'. The Quran further rejects the doctrines of Original Sin and justification through the shedding of blood that underpin the salvific mission of Jesus.[8] For Moslems therefore, as for Jews and non-Christians at large, Jesus Christ is not the saviour.

---

[8] See Chapters 1 and 2.

10

PAUL AND THE SALVATION OF CHRIST

As he neared Damascus on his journey, suddenly a light from heaven flashed around him. He fell to the ground and heard a voice say to him, "Saul, Saul, why do you persecute me? – Acts 9:3-4

The Bible's New Testament, as the last chapter shows, indicates that Apostle Paul was largely responsible for the teaching that the Law of Moses, as well as the Abrahamic covenant, has become otiose and irrelevant for salvation, both for Jews and non-Jews. According to him, salvation only comes through acceptance of, and faith in, Jesus Christ as the saviour. Was Apostle Paul entitled to make this claim? Answering this question requires an evaluation of the story of Paul as told in the Bible's New Testament, including the claim that he was commissioned to preach the gospel of Jesus Christ to gentiles.

THE STORY OF PAUL
According to Acts of the Apostles,[1] Paul (then Saul and a Pharisee), one of the chief persecutors of the followers of Jesus, was on his way

---
[1] Acts 9:1-30.

to Damascus to arrest and imprison Christians when he had a supernatural encounter with the ascended Jesus – an encounter that rendered him blind for three days. Following instructions by the voice of Jesus, Paul was taken to the disciples in Damascus, chiefly Ananias, for prayers and instructions as to what he needed to do.[2] While in Damascus, Jesus revealed in a vision to Ananias that, Paul was his 'chosen instrument' to proclaim his name 'to the Gentiles and their kings and to the people of Israel'.[3] After spending several days in Damascus with the believers and preaching the gospel there, Paul left for Jerusalem due to an assassination plot against him. Having overcome their initial scepticism, the Jerusalem disciples accepted Paul in their fold and he went about with them boldly preaching the gospel. However, following another plot to kill him, the Jerusalem believers smuggled Paul away to Tarsus.[4] This conversion story and Paul's alleged commission to preach the gospel is however dubious for many reasons.

DID JESUS CONVERT AND COMMISSION PAUL?

The story of Paul's Damascene conversion contradicts other biblical narratives. The Ananias Paul met in Damascus was described as 'a devout observer of the law' who was 'highly respected by all the Jews living there'.[5] Since at that time, Jewish religious leaders were persecuting the followers of Jesus, it is doubtful that any of these

---

[2] Acts 9:1-; 22:10
[3] Acts 9:15.
[4] See Acts 9:1-30.
[5] Acts 22:12.

followers would be described as highly respected by *all Jews* in Damascus. Conversely, it is doubtful that Jesus would send the converted Paul to a devout observer of the law for briefing on a gospel mission that has supposedly come to supplant it. Further, the claim that the believers smuggled Paul to Tarsus because of a plot to kill him in Jerusalem, is unlikely to be true. This is because according to Acts 22, Paul decided to leave Jerusalem because Jesus had told him in a trance to do so because the people of the city would not accept his testimony about him.[6] Jesus then promised to send him away to the gentiles.[7]

Furthermore, Paul flatly denied any encounter with Ananias or the Christians in Damascus and Jerusalem after his conversion. In Galatians 1:16-20, Paul *swore* that after his conversion, his 'immediate response was not to consult any human being' or the apostles in Jerusalem. Instead, he went to Arabia before returning to Damascus later.[8] Only after three years did he go to Jerusalem to meet Peter and James, but for only fifteen days. He did not meet any of the other disciples or members of the churches in Israel who never knew who he was.[9] Thus, by his own account, Paul's alleged camaraderie with Christians in Damascus and Jerusalem, and his preaching in those places, could not have taken place. However, given that he was blind for three days after the conversion encounter, it is doubtful that Paul

---

[6] Acts 22:17-18.
[7] Acts 22:21.
[8] See Galatians 1:15-17.
[9] See Galatians 1:19, 22-23.

could have gone immediately to Arabia unless the claim in Acts about the blindness is false. The claim that the brethren in Damascus instructed Paul as to his mission appears also to be false since Paul apparently decided by himself what the mission was going to be.

Second, it is unclear whether Paul was supposed to preach the gospel to only gentiles or to Jews as well. In the above narratives, Paul was supposed to preach to both, but this plan subsequently changed for differing reasons.[10] If Jesus had commissioned Paul to preach to Jews as well as gentiles, the question would arise as to why he was needed for the Jewish mission given that he was never a follower of Jesus who had trained disciples and several other followers for this exact purpose. A further question would concern the divinity of Jesus, since he apparently did not foresee that Paul's ministry would not be acceptable to the Jews. On the other hand, if Paul went to the gentiles only after his attempt to preach in Jerusalem had failed, it means that the gentile mission was an afterthought.

Third, Paul preached a different gospel from the one Jesus supposedly left for his disciples. By his own admission, Paul did not follow or learn from Jesus or his disciples. Instead, he received his own gospel 'through a revelation of Jesus Christ'.[11] Paul began to preach immediately after his conversion, even though he was not a member of the early Jerusalem or Damascene church. How, where and when had he learned about Jesus and his teachings? Could his

---

[10] See also Acts 26:16-23.
[11] See Galatians 1:12, 16.

uncorroborated 'revelation' have provided him with all the facts and knowledge of the gospel? This question is very important because Jesus and his disciples, as already noted, remained faithful to the Mosaic Law; and Paul complained that other people, presumably from Jerusalem, preached a gospel of Christ different from the one he preached. This caused Paul to berate, and vehemently caution his listeners against, the 'false' preachers,[12] and insist that there is no other gospel except his.[13]

Indeed, the gospel preached by Paul appears to contradict the one preached by John the Baptist, and by Jesus and his disciples. These all preached a gospel of repentance in the context of the Mosaic Law and imminent arrival of the kingdom of God. It was apparently because of the expected imminent return of Jesus that the early Christians in Israel lived a transient, communal and austere life, selling their belongings and bringing the proceeds to the church for common use (in the manner of the Essenes).[14] On the other hand, Paul went about discrediting the Law and preaching a gospel of grace through faith in Christ. He also created permanent church institutions outside Israel when the disciples of Jesus were awaiting his imminent return. If Jesus' return and the kingdom of God were as imminent as he anticipated – within the lifespan of people of his generation and before his gospel had reached the whole of Israel, the only people he meant

---

[12] See Galatians 1:6-9; 2:4-5; 2 Corinthians 11:1-15, 19-23. See also Myth No. 9 in D Fitzgerald, *Ten Myths that Show Jesus Never Existed at All* (Lulu.com 2010).
[13] See Galatians 1:6-9.
[14] See Acts 4:32-37; 5:1-10; 6:1-6.

it for,[15] – there would be no point in instructing Paul to take the gospel to foreign lands and establish churches.

Finally, the Bible indicates that Paul was not qualified to preach the gospel of Jesus. Jesus had chosen twelve disciples specifically in order for them to closely observe his ministry and preach the gospel after he was gone. The choice of replacement for Judas Iscariot reflected this understanding and reiterated the criteria for preaching the gospel. According to Acts 1:21-22:

> *It is necessary to choose one of the men who have been with us the whole time the Lord Jesus was living among us, beginning from John's baptism to the time when Jesus was taken up from us. For one of these must become a witness with us of his resurrection.*

As Paul did not meet the criteria for discipleship set by Jesus and re-affirmed by Jesus' original disciples – a fact Paul himself appeared to acknowledge[16] – it seems that he lacked the credentials to be a disciple or apostle. Any post-mortem (albeit false) commission to Paul to take the gospel to gentiles would contradict the clearly expressed wishes attributed to Jesus while he was alive and would amount to an afterthought. Since all the statements relating to the alleged commission of Paul came from the man's own unproven, unprovable and contradictory visions and claims, they are not capable of overriding the express instructions apparently given by Jesus.

---

[15] See Chapter 11.
[16] See 1 Corinthians 15:9-10.

11

END TIME AND DAY OF JUDGMENT

Behold I am come quickly, and my reward is with me, to give to each person according to what he has done. - Revelation 22:12

Multitudes who sleep in the dust of the earth will awake: some to everlasting life, others to shame and everlasting contempt. - Daniel 2:2

In Judaism, Christianity and Islam, there is an expectation of a last Day of Judgment. That day is supposed to mark the end of the world or the present system of things and lead to the actualisation of the fruits of salvation. On that apocalyptic day, everyone would come face-to-face with Deity and give account of their life on earth. Closely linked to this idea of a Day of Judgment is the doctrine of resurrection of the body. By this doctrine, all dead people will rise from their graves and, along with the living, face judgment and receive their reward or punishment. The saved would go to heaven, while the unsaved would go to Hell Fire. These beliefs, which existed in the ancient religions of Egypt and in Zoroastrianism, probably influenced Judaism, which in turn influenced contemporary Christianity and Islam. The fervent expectation of the Day of

Judgment by believers has led to the emergence of doomsday cults, failed end-time prophecies, and mass suicides by believers who thought they were going to be with their lord in heaven. So, are these religions right about resurrection of the dead and the Day of Judgment?

DAY OF JUDGMENT IN JUDAISM

The Bible's Old Testament refers in several places to the Day of Judgment or the 'Day of the Lord'. According to Daniel 2:1, 'There will be a time of distress such as has not happened from the beginning of nations until then. But at that time your people—everyone whose name is found written in the book—will be delivered.' Esdras declares that 'after death shall the judgment come, when we shall live again: and then shall the names of the righteous be manifest, and the works of the ungodly shall be declared'.[1] From all indications, the Day of Judgment in Jewish theology would be a terrible one. Describing it as day of complete darkness, Prophet Amos says that, 'It will be as though a man fled from a lion only to meet a bear, as though he entered his house and rested his hand on the wall only to have a snake bite him.'[2] Prophet Joel calls it 'a day of destruction',[3] while Prophet Malachi describes it as a 'dreadful' day.[4] Hebrew Scriptures are however not clear as to when this Day of Judgment would come. In relation to the resurrection of the dead, Daniel 12:2 says that

---

[1] Esdras 14:35.
[2] Amos 5:18-20.
[3] Joel 1:15.
[4] Malachi 4:5-6.

'Multitudes who sleep in the dust of the earth will awake: some to everlasting life, others to shame and everlasting contempt.' 1 Samuel 6:2, states that 'the LORD brings death and makes alive; he brings down to the grave and raises up'. In addition, Ezekiel's vision of a mass of re-animated corpses has been interpreted as indicative of resurrection of the body.[5] Although there is little specific information on who would preside over the judgment, there can be no doubt that, it would be Yahweh, the Jewish God, and the saviour, rewarder and punisher of his people.[6]

DAY OF JUDGMENT IN CHRISTIANITY

The Day of Judgment is ubiquitous in the New Testament. This is because the salvation Jesus supposedly wrought for humanity hinges on his return from heaven at the end of time in order to judge everybody, including the dead and the living.[7] The Bible records Jesus as promising on several occasions that he would certainly return.[8] In a particularly heart-warming message, he told his followers:

> *Let not your heart be troubled; you believe in God, believe also in Me. In My Father's house are many mansions; if it*

---

[5] See Ezekiel 37. See also Esdras 14:34; E Gilad, 'What is the Jewish Afterlife Like,' *Haaretz*, August 15, 2018, https://www.haaretz.com/jewish/.premium-what-is-the-jewish-afterlife-like-1.5362876.

[6] See Deuteronomy 10:18; 32:41.

[7] The idea of end time or apocalypse is a common theme in religion and mythology. For a discussion of these, see T Daniels (ed.) *A Doomsday Reader: Prophets, Predictors and Hucksters of Salvation* (New York and London: New University Press 1999); P Wilkinson and N Phillip, *Mythology* (Doring Kindersley Ltd, London 2007) 30-31. See also *The Encyclopaedia Britannica*, http://www.britannica.com/topic/Last-Judgment-religion.

[8] See e.g., Matthew 23:29; Luke 18:8; John 14:28-29; Revelation 3:11; 22:12, 20.

were not so, I would have told you. I go to prepare a place for you. And if I go and prepare a place for you, I will come again and receive you to Myself; that where I am, there you may be also.[9]

In Acts of the Apostles, angels reportedly told the disciples who were gazing in amazement at the ascension of Jesus that, 'this Jesus, who was taken up from you into heaven, will come in the same way as you saw him go into heaven'.[10] Upon his return, a new heaven and a new earth would emerge and Jesus Christ would rule the world from Jerusalem, ensuring global peace, joy and bliss for a millennium.[11] The promised second coming of Jesus, as well as the judgment day and reward for believers it would bring, is the fundament of the gospel message. According to Apostle Paul 'If only for this life we (i.e. Christians) have hope in Christ, we are, of all people, most to be pitied.'[12]

The purpose of Jesus' second coming will be to gather 'the elect'[13] and pass judgment on the people of the world.[14] Accordingly, Jesus had stated, that it was for the purpose of judgment that he came to the world[15] and that God the Father had committed all the power in this regard to him.[16] When Jesus returns, the Bible says, he would reward

---

[9] John 14:1-3.
[10] Acts 1:9-11.
[11] Revelation 20:1-6.
[12] 1 Corinthians 15:19.
[13] Matthew 24:31.
[14] Matthew 16:27; 25:31-46.
[15] See John 9:39; 1 Corinthians 6:2
[16] John 5:22.

people according to their deeds in life.[17] It sets out the criteria for determining people's fate: the righteous would go to eternal life in heaven, while the unrighteous, would go to eternal punishment in hell.[18] In addition, Jesus would shun anybody ashamed to proclaim him as the Christ.[19] The writer of Revelations apparently received a vision of the court of Jesus, the procedure and criteria of the judgment, and the outcome, as follows:

> *Then I saw a great white throne and him who was seated on it. The earth and the heavens fled from his presence, and there was no place for them. And I saw the dead, great and small, standing before the throne, and books were opened. Another book was opened, which is the book of life. The dead were judged according to what they had done as recorded in the books. The sea gave up the dead that were in it, and death and Hades gave up the dead that were in them, and each person was judged according to what they had done. Then death and Hades were thrown into the lake of fire. The lake of fire is the second death. Anyone whose name was not found written in the book of life was thrown into the lake of fire.*[20]

Great suffering, distress, famines, earthquakes and wars would apparently precede the second coming of Jesus; as well as persecution and killing of believers that would lead many to renounce the faith. There would also be the presence of the 'abomination that causes desolation' in the holy place as 'spoken of by Prophet Daniel'. Moreover, the sun and the moon would go completely dark, while the stars would fall from the sky before Jesus returns in glory and power,

---

[17] Matthew 16:27
[18] Matthew 25:31-46. See also John 5: 28-29.
[19] Mark 8:38.
[20] Revelations 20:11-15.

accompanied by angels and the sound of trumpets.[21] Everybody would witness the event.[22] However, it would be unexpected and sudden and would catch many unawares, as was ostensibly the case in the days of Noah and Lot when people were making merry and going about their mundane businesses, oblivious of the imminent destruction that was to come upon them.[23] Because of the suddenness of the coming, and the absence of warning, Jesus enjoined people to be very watchful, vigilant, prayerful, alert and ready,[24] especially against charlatans who would claim to be the Christ; and prophets who would proclaim false sightings of him or a time or place for his coming.[25] The signs that would precede Jesus' return [26] include the preaching of his gospel to the whole world 'as a testimony to all nations'.[27]

The highlights of the second coming would be mass resurrections of the dead[28] and the 'rapture' of the saints. As Apostle Paul put it:

> *According to the Lord's word, we tell you that we who are still alive, who are left until the coming of the Lord, will certainly not precede those who have fallen asleep. For the Lord himself will come down from heaven, with a loud command, with the voice of the archangel and with the trumpet call of God, and the dead in Christ will rise first.*[29]

---

[21] Matthew 24:9-31; 16:27; 25:31; Mark 8:38; Thessalonians 4:16.
[22] See Matthew 24:27.
[23] Matthew 24:37-39; Luke 17:28-30.
[24] See Luke12:37-38, 40; 21:34-36; Matthew 24:40-44; Matthew 25:1-13. See also 2 Peter 3:10.
[25] See Matthew 24:4-5, 11; 23-27.
[26] See Matthew 24:6-15.
[27] Matthew 24:14.
[28] See John 5:28-29.
[29] 1 Thessalonians 4:15-16.

Paul goes further to say that on that fateful day the dead would be transformed and made fit for heaven:

> *Listen, I tell you a mystery: We will not all sleep, but we will all be changed— in a flash, in the twinkling of an eye, at the last trumpet. For the trumpet will sound, the dead will be raised imperishable, and we will be changed. For the perishable must clothe itself with the imperishable, and the mortal with immortality. When the perishable has been clothed with the imperishable, and the mortal with immortality, then the saying that is written will come true: 'Death has been swallowed up in victory.'*[30]

Paul's declaration appears to align with Jesus' teaching that in the night of his return, 'there will be two in one bed. One will be taken and the other left. There will be two women grinding together. One will be taken and the other left.'[31] Following the destruction of heaven and earth precipitated by the second coming, the headquarters of the newly created earth would be Jerusalem, which would double as the city and habitation of God. The second coming would herald an era of bliss where death, suffering, pain, mourning, crying and sorrow would be no more.[32]

Although he did not state the exact date of the second coming, Jesus was clear that it would be very soon, relative to the time in which he lived and spoke. 'I tell you the truth', he said, 'some who are standing here will not taste death before they see the Son of Man coming in his

---

[30] 1 Corinthians 15:51-54.
[31] Luke 17:34-37.
[32] See also 2 Peter 3:10; Revelation 20:11.

kingdom'.³³ On another occasion, Jesus told his disciples, 'when you are persecuted in one place, flee to another. I tell you the truth, you will not finish going through the cities of Israel before the Son of Man comes'.³⁴ Revelation 1:7 affirms the supposed imminence of the second coming of Jesus by saying that when Jesus returns, everyone would see him, 'even those who pierced him'. In line with Jesus' promise, early Christians expected him to return in their lifetimes and were disappointed and distressed at his failure to do so even though members of their generation, including the disciples, were passing away.³⁵ Their despondency prompted Apostle Paul to assure them that when Jesus returned those of them who had died would rise while those still alive would join them to meet Jesus in the clouds.³⁶ That the Second Coming was supposed to be looming was evident throughout the teachings and ministry of Jesus, the theme of which was the imminent end of the world (or the 'present system of things') and the coming of the kingdom of God.

DAY OF JUDGMENT IN ISLAM

On its part, the Quran speaks of the judgment day in terms of a 'mighty Day' when everyone would stand before the Almighty Allah for a judgment that would determine their fate in eternity:

---

[33] Matthew 16:28; or as reported in Mark 13:30, 'Truly I tell you, this generation will certainly not pass away until all these things have happened.'
[34] Matthew 10:23.
[35] See EP Sanders, *The Historical Figure of Jesus* (London: Penguin Books 1995) 58-59.
[36] See 1 Thessalonians 4:15-17.

> *But when the deafening cry shall be sounded on the Day when each man shall flee from his brother, and his mother and his father; and his consort and his children; on that Day each will be occupied with his own business, making him oblivious of all save himself. Some faces on that Day shall be beaming with happiness, and be cheerful and joyous. Some faces on that Day shall be dust-ridden, enveloped by darkness. These will be the unbelievers, the wicked.*[37]

For the purpose of the judgment, the dead will be raised from their graves in a manner reminiscent of the claim in the Bible. According to Surah 4:87, Allah 'will most certainly gather you together on the resurrection day, there is no doubt in it; and who is more true in word than Allah?' Surah 30:19 states that Allah 'brings forth the living from the dead and brings forth the dead from the living, and gives life to the earth after its death, and thus shall you be brought forth.'[38] The resurrection of the dead, according to the Quran, will be both material and spiritual.[39] The Quran rationalizes the notion of resurrection of the body on the ground that Almighty Allah gives life to the dead and has power over all things,[40] and on the ground that it is easier to create life than to re-animate corpses.[41] It is clear that the Judgment Day, as far as Islam is concerned, would be presided over by Allah. Nevertheless, will that day indeed come? If it does come, who would be the judge? By whose and what standards, would people receive judgment?

---

[37] Surah 80:33-42.
[38] Surah 83:4-6. See also Surah 17: 49; 75: 3-4.
[39] Surah 31:28.
[40] Surah 22:7.
[41] Surah 30:27.

WILL THERE BE A DAY OF JUDGMENT?

For several reasons, it is unlikely that there will ever be a Day of Judgment as anticipated by religion. First, the doctrine of resurrection of the body essential for the event is dubious. It assumes that bodies of innumerable people buried since the world began would somehow come together again and be re-animated. These would include bodies buried so far back in the past that they and their graves are no more; cremated bodies whose ashes could have disappeared into the earth, air or water; and bodies eaten and digested by wild animals. It would also include bodies dissected and dismembered in numerous medical training facilities, and those whose vital parts, including hearts and faces, surgeons have removed and transplanted onto other bodies. Undoubtedly, the notion of the resurrection of the body rests on a limited appreciation of the universe, including its age and size; cultural differences in the handling of the dead, and assumptions on the nature of life after death that are by no means universal. In this connection, and notwithstanding Apostle Paul's claim on transformation, the Christian belief in rapture is also mistaken, assuming as it were, that material bodies would ascend to heaven and inhabit the abode of spirits. It is the same belief that informed the ascension tales of Enoch, Elijah and Jesus. Since material bodies may neither ascend nor belong to the heavens, the idea of rapture would appear to be without merit.

Second, it is unclear who the judge would be on the Day of Judgment – Yahweh, Allah or Jesus. Since each of the religions have earmarked a different judge, will there be one judgment day or several? In respect of a Day of Judgment under Jesus Christ, there is also confusion as to whether he would indeed judge the world. This is because he had taught not only that we should not judge others, but also that he would not judge anybody. In Luke 6:37, he said: 'Do not judge and you will not be judged. Do not condemn, and you will not be condemned. Forgive, and you will be forgiven'. Jesus chastised the Pharisees for judging by human standards and declared that he would 'pass judgment on no one'.[42] More significantly, he declared that he would not judge those who fail to abide by his teaching because he 'did not come to judge the world, but to save it'.[43] However, these teachings on non-judgment directly contradict Jesus' earlier teachings that it was for the purpose of judgment that he came to the world for which cause 'the Father' had given him exclusive prerogative.

Third, the idea of judgment day presupposes that nobody would go to heaven or Hell Fire until that day. However, this flies in the face of many biblical accounts and passages. The Bible reports that Hell Fire is already home to condemned souls to whom Jesus even preached after his death.[44] It also reports that the devil, demons and oppressors, such as the wicked rich man in the Lazarus story, are already burning

---

[42] John 8:15.
[43] John 12:47.
[44] See 1 Peter 3:19; Ephesians 4:8-10.

in hell.[45] In addition, the Bible makes it clear that people who failed to accept Jesus before they died have already been condemned to Hell Fire.[46] The idea of a Day of Judgment also contradicts biblical reports that many people, such as Enoch, Abraham, Moses, Elijah and Lazarus[47] were already in heaven even though they did not face any judgment. Further, it contradicts the Catholic teaching that Mary, the mother of Jesus, is in heaven and answering prayers of the faithful. Allied to this is the fact that the Catholic Church has made many church people saints to whom believers make supplications. This indicates that these people are not awaiting resurrection and judgment but are already in heaven.

Finally, the wait for the Day of Judgment appears interminable. Despite the claims made more than 2000 years ago that the second coming of Jesus was imminent, it has not yet materialised, even though all the supposed signs that would herald it have since come and gone. All the disciples and followers of Jesus and their entire generations are long dead. Numerous earthquakes, terrible wars and conflicts, including two world wars that cost over sixty million lives, have occurred. Indeed, Jews have been victims of wars and conflicts of the types unprecedented in the time of Jesus, including the destruction of Jerusalem and its temple, the cessation of the biblical Israel, and the Nazi holocaust. Moreover, the so-called abomination

---

[45] See Luke 16:19-31.
[46] See Chapters 1 and 2.
[47] See 2 Kings 2:10-11; Genesis 5:34: Hebrews 11:5; Matthew 17:1-3; Luke 9:27-36; Luke 16:19-31.

that causes desolation as referred to by Jesus and Daniel has already occurred. It 'denotes the pagan alter set up in the Jerusalem temple by Antiochus Epiphanes in 167 BCE'.[48] Even the alternative interpretation of the 'prophecy' as a reference to the attempt by the Roman Emperor Caligula to erect his statute in the Jerusalem temple in 40 CE has also long passed.[49]

As observed earlier, the earliest Christians fully expected Jesus to return in their lifetimes and were left disheartened when, after a long time, he had not done so. Consequent upon Jesus' promise, many apocalyptic and millenarian movements have arisen and proclaimed in futility the imminent end of the world and the Judgment Day.[50] Although, the Bible says that a thousand years on earth may be like a day in the sight of God,[51] it is clear that the expectation of the Day of Judgment is reckoned in human terms. In the case of Jesus, he was explicit that the people of his generation on earth would still be alive at the time of his return. Moreover, the fact that he made his return analogous to the legend of Noah and his flood-busting ark[52] renders it incredible. By the words and signs credited to Jesus, it is certain that he would not return, assuming that he had come the first time and did ascend to heaven. The wait for the Day of Judgment has been even

---

[48] The WRF Browning (ed.) *Oxford Dictionary of the Bible* (Oxford University 2009) 84.
[49] Ibid.
[50] See *Encyclopaedia Britannica*, http://www.britannica.com/topic/Apocalyptic-Movements-1891921. See also T Daniels (ed.), supra n 7, 99-223.
[51] See 2 Peter 3:8; Psalm 90:4.
[52] See Matthew 24:36-41.

longer in Judaism, and has exceeded 1400 years in Islam even though in both cases, it was supposed to be imminent. In all three cases, the interminable wait continues.

12

RIGHTEOUSNESS OR GRACE?

That as sin hath reigned unto death, even so might grace reign through righteousness unto eternal life by Jesus Christ our Lord. – Romans 5:21

Assuming the Day of Judgment would come, it is unclear what the main determinant of guilt or innocence would be. Would it be righteousness through the doing of good deeds; or grace through faith? In the gospels and the New Testament in general, there is no clear understanding of the criteria for salvation. In his teachings, Jesus countenanced both, and appeared unwilling to let ordinary people into the secret of his kingdom.[1] According to the gospels, Jesus always taught the people in parables,[2] so that, 'though seeing, they do not see; though hearing, they do not hear or understand'.[3] He only explained the meanings of the parables

---

[1] See Matthew 13:15.
[2] Mark 4:34; Matthew 13:34. Parables are 'teachings by means of comparison; stories of varying length containing a meaning or message over and above the straightforward and literal, with an element of metaphor' – WRF Browning, *Oxford Dictionary* of the Bible (Oxford University 2009).
[3] Matthew 13:11-15, emphasis added. See also Luke 8:9-10; Mark 4:10.

privately to his disciples, who he insisted that they were privileged to receive it.[4] Moreover, although Jesus gave several parables on the kingdom of God involving faith and belief[5] he also gave others on forgiveness, responsibility and the need for good works. In the Hebrew Bible and the Quran, the requirement for salvation seems predominantly to be righteousness.

RIGHTEOUSNESS

In many places, the New Testament insists that righteousness is key for salvation. In Matthew, Jesus stated that he would separate righteous people who would go to heaven from the unrighteous who would go to hell.[6] Jesus also declared, that not everyone who called him 'Lord' would go to heaven but only those who did the will of God;[7] and that those who hunger and thirst after righteousness shall be filled.[8] Further, he declared that he would reward people according to their deeds.[9] In this regard, Jesus told his listeners not to be amazed, 'for a time is coming when all who are in their graves will hear his voice and come out - *those who have done good will rise to live, and those who have done evil will rise to be condemned*'.[10] On a number of occasions, Jesus also advised people to keep the commandments or

---

[4] See Mark 4:10-20; 34. Matthew 13:10-13, 36-43; 15:15; Luke 8:9-15.
[5] These are the parables of the sower, the weeds, the seed growing from the ground, mustard seed, leaven, treasure in the field, and the net. See Matthew 13, Mark 4:26-29
[6] See Matthew 25:31-46.
[7] Matthew 7:21.
[8] Matthew 5:6.
[9] See Matthew 16:27.
[10] John 5:28-29, emphasis added.

to watch their tongue if they were to be saved.[11] Moreover, as discussed earlier,[12] Jesus laid down many specific rules the observance of which could lead to salvation.

Apart from Jesus, some other teachers in the New Testament also insist on the need for righteousness. Citing the righteous works of Abraham and Rahab as examples, James observed that faith in Jesus without works is dead.[13] 1 Peter 1:17 says that God impartially judges people according to their works, while Luke 1:6, observes that Zacharias and Elizabeth were favoured as parents of John the Baptist because of their righteousness. Similarly, Revelation states that everyone would receive a reward according to his or her works as recorded in the 'Book of Life'.[14] Even Apostle Paul wrote that 'everybody should *work* for their own salvation with fear and trembling and in the *doing* of God's good purpose.[15] He enjoined people to strive to please the Lord because, 'we must all appear before the judgment seat of Christ, that each one may receive what is due him *for the things done* while in the body, whether good or bad'.[16] Paul further observed that righteousness inheres not merely in hearing the

---

[11] See Matthew 19:17; Luke 10:26-28; Matthew 12:37.
[12] See Chapter 7.
[13] James 2:14-17; 21-26. Conversely however, Hebrews 11:31 attributed Rahab's salvation to her faith and belief in the god of Israel.
[14] See Revelation 2:23; 20:12-13; 22:14.
[15] Philippians 2:12-14, emphasis added.
[16] 2 Corinthians 5:9-10, emphasis added. See also 2 Corinthians 11:15.

law, but in *obeying* it.[17] He goes on to declare that God cannot be mocked; therefore, everyone will reap whatever they sow.[18]

The New Testament's teachings on the necessity of righteousness agree with those in the Old Testament. Noting that God will judge people according to their ways, Ezekiel states that, 'If a righteous man turns from his righteousness and commits sin, he will die for it [...] But if a wicked man turns away from the wickedness he has committed and does what is just and right, he will save his life.'[19] Ezekiel also states that he that walks in the statutes of God and keeps his commandments and deals truly with others, is a just person and shall live,[20] and that people would live or die depending on whether they have been righteous or wicked.[21] A similar message appears in many other parts of the Old Testament.[22] The fate of a righteous Jew who fails to keep the covenant of circumcision would seem to be a moot point since they invariably do. In Islam, the basis for salvation and entry into paradise, as already discussed, is righteousness or good works.[23]

GRACE

In other places, the New Testament maintains that salvation and entry into heaven would come through Jesus Christ only as a matter of

---

[17] See Romans 2:6, 13, emphasis added.
[18] Galatians 6:7.
[19] Ezekiel 18:26-27, 30.
[20] Ezekiel 18:8-9.
[21] See further, Ezekiel 18:20.
[22] See e.g., Jeremiah 17:10; Psalm 62:12; Proverbs 10:16; 14:34; Ecclesiastes 12:14.
[23] See Chapter 1, 2 and 9.

grace. According to Ephesians 2:8-9, 'it is by grace you have been saved, through faith - and this not from yourselves, it is the gift of God - not by works, so that no one can boast'. If we are saved by grace, Apostle Paul adds, 'then it is no longer by works; if it were, grace would no longer be grace'.[24] Hence, on the question of what people needed to do to please God, Jesus replied that the work of God is 'to believe in the one he has sent'.[25] In the same manner when a jailer asked Paul and Silas what he must do for salvation, they answered: 'Believe in the Lord Jesus, and you will be saved - you and your household.'[26] Insisting that doing good deeds is not the criterion for salvation, Paul using Abraham as an example observes that, 'when a man works, his wages are not credited to him as a gift, but as an obligation. However, to the man who does not work but trusts God who justifies the wicked, his faith is credited as righteousness.'[27] Apostle Paul then states that the minds of unbelievers have been blinded so that they cannot 'see the light of the gospel of the glory of Christ, who is the image of God.'[28] He also states that believers in the gospel of Jesus Christ were the elect while unbelievers have 'a spirit of stupor' and hardened hearts so that they could neither see nor hear and their backs would be 'bent forever.'[29]

---

[24] Romans 11:6.
[25] John 6:28-29.
[26] Acts 16:29-31
[27] See Romans 4:1-5. See also Galatians 3:6.
[28] 2 Corinthians 4:3-4.
[29] Romans 11:7-10.

EXCLUSIVE CRITERIA

The criteria of righteousness and grace are mutually exclusive and irreconcilable. If righteousness saves, there would be no point in accepting Jesus as saviour; but if Christians have already obtained salvation by accepting Jesus as the messiah, they would have no further need for righteousness in order to gain salvation. Their names being already in the Book of Life, they are the elect whom Jesus would take to the many mansions already prepared for them in heaven when he returns. They would rapture - both the living and the dead among them - and meet their Christ in the clouds with no precondition of passing through any judgment. After all Jesus had promised that, he is the resurrection and the life, and whoever believes in him will never die, and if they had died, will live again.[30] He would neither drive away nor lose anybody who has come to him, but would raise them on the last day according to the 'will of his father'.[31] Furthermore, Jesus proclaimed that he only is the true shepherd who would lead his followers to salvation; and that others were hired hands or thieves and robbers who had come to steal, kill and destroy.[32]

Since Judaism and Islam are also insistent on the observance of the tenets of the religions as pre-conditions for admission into paradise, it is reasonable to conclude that unbelievers, even if righteous, would not get into heaven. In fact, since in all of the faiths, unbelief is synonymous with unrighteousness and evil, it is inconceivable that an

---

[30] See John 11:25-26.
[31] John 6:37-40.
[32] John 10:9-12.

unbeliever would enter any heaven conceived by them. However, using belief or religious observances as the criterion for heaven means that just and upright people would be condemned because they professed a different religious faith or no faith. Meanwhile, evil and wicked people who happen to be pious or convert to a given faith shortly before death would obtain salvation. It also appears to be counter-productive in that it provides little disincentive for wrongdoing since the wait for the judgment day is interminable. On the other hand, if righteousness would be the relevant factor on the Day of Judgment, it is unclear what unrighteousness actually means given its designation as sin against God.

SIN AGAINST GOD
The doctrine of salvation relies on the assumption that by 'sinning', human beings offend God so much as to sever the divine-human connection. As the Catholic Encyclopaedia put it, 'the Incarnation of the Word was the most fitting means for the salvation of man, and was even necessary, in case God claimed full satisfaction for the injury done to him by sin.'[33] However, since it is far from clear what objectively amounts to sin against God, the notion of salvation from, or condemnation for, sin also becomes uncertain. In respect of the so-called sins of blasphemy, apostasy and unbelief, for example, it is unlikely that God who has given human beings freedom of conscience would suffer harm when they exercise this one way or another. Concerning things recognised generally as wrongdoings, these would

---

[33] http://www.newadvent.org/cathen/13407a.htm.

primarily be offences against the persons affected and only indirectly against God. If therefore, the offenders ask for and receive forgiveness from the victims, and perform any requisite act of restitution or serve the necessary punishment imposed by the community, it is doubtful that God would still hold the wrongdoings against them. The Bible makes this point when it admonishes us to forgive others their offences[34] and points out that God would only forgive our sins if we forgave others their offences against us.[35] It goes on to indicate that settling our differences with others is a precondition for, and preferable to, offering.[36] Apart from sinning against the victim of one's wrongdoing, the wrongdoer also sins against himself given that the law of cause and effect ensures that he must reap the consequences of his offence against another. This also implies that God suffers no injury from the wrongdoing since a divine mechanism is already in place to deal with the wrongdoer.

Although human beings might feel alienated from God when they do wrong, in reality, there would be no alienation. What might seem to be a severing of the divine relationship would be the feeling of guilt associated with the wrongdoing or the suffering of the natural consequences that the wrongdoing had engendered. The situation could be likened to that of a person who wilfully inserts his hand into a fire and suffers burns as a result. Such a person cannot blame his

---

[34] See Matthew 18: 21-22; 17:3-4; Ephesians 4:31-32; Colossians 3:13.
[35] See Matthew 6:14-15; Luke 6:37.
[36] See Matthew 5:23-24 (NIV).

burns on enmity with the fire or God. As soon as he stops putting his hand in the fire, so soon would the fire stop burning his hand, and the pain consequent upon his initial foolery would be nothing more than a natural outcome. Accordingly, having paid the price for wrongdoing, a wrongdoer discharges himself from his debt and would not need any further atonement or salvation.

The lack of clarity on the requirements of the salvation of Christ reflects in the vast number of Christian sects with serious doctrinaire dichotomies and divergent views on the requirements for, and even the location of the kingdom of God. It also helps to explain the rancour, violence and bloodshed that attended the establishment and consolidation of current Christian orthodoxy.[37] The bloody Inquisition against heretics, the Oriental-Eastern orthodox schism, the rancorous and bloody Roman Catholic-Protestant divisions, and the divisions between Trinitarian and non-Trinitarian sects, etc., are enduring testimonials to the uncertainty of the requirements for salvation.[38] Meanwhile, modern Pentecostals claim to be the ones with the authentic teaching of salvation, which might not avail the more traditional churches. That each sect claims to know The Way, over and above others, demonstrates that Christians, even today, do not understand what it means to gain the salvation of Christ and what is required to enter the kingdom of heaven.

---

[37] See T *Green, Inquisition: The Reign of Fear* (Pan Books 2007).
[38] Ibid.

13

DEVIL AND DEMONS AS REASON FOR SALVATION

He who sins is of the devil, for the devil has sinned from the beginning. For this purpose the Son of God was manifested, that He might destroy the works of the devil. – 1 John 3:8

Inextricably linked to salvation is the existence and machinations of devil and demons: it is from their hold and influences that believers would apparently get deliverance, and it is to their hold and abode that unbelievers would be condemned after the Day of Judgment. Many believe that devils and demons are super-natural beings responsible for the sins of humanity, its apparent fall from the grace of God, and all sorts of misery and disaster. They also believe that these evil beings regularly thwart the good plans of God in their lives. Given the perceived powers of devil and demons, many understandably seek protection and freedom from them. Through the course of history, the fear of these spirits and the desire to be free from their influences have paralysed believers and empowered religious institutions and leaders. Devils and demons must therefore be as real and powerful as claimed by religion in order for any mission or scheme of salvation to be meaningful.

MEANING OF DEVIL, SATAN AND DEMONS

In the Bible, the term 'Satan' denotes somebody who opposes another, whether for good or for ill – an adversary. This opposer may be a good person, a bad person, or an angel.[1] Thus, an angel of Yahweh acted as opposer (Satan) to obstruct Balaam's donkey and change the course of his journey.[2] Satan as a member of the inner council of Yahweh conspired with him to test the faithfulness of Job,[3] indicating that Satan was not and could not be a challenger of Yahweh. As the Jewish Encyclopaedia observes, it is 'evident from the prologue (in Job) that Satan has no power of independent action, but requires the permission of God, which he may not transgress. He cannot be regarded, therefore, as an opponent of the Deity.'[4] Consistent with this position, Jesus told his disciples that, 'Satan *had asked* to sift them like wheat'.[5] It must also have been with this understanding of Satan that Jesus called Peter, his chief disciple, Satan.[6] In a Similar vein, Jesus spoke concerning Judas Iscariot, 'Have I not chosen you, the Twelve? Yet one of you is a devil!'[7] It would also seem that the serpent that

---

[1] See the *Jewish Encyclopaedia*,

http://www.jewishencyclopedia.com/search?utf8=%E2%9C%93&keywords=satan&commit=search.

[2] Numbers 22:34.
[3] See Job 1:6-22; 2:1-10.
[4] See
http://www.jewishencyclopedia.com/search?utf8=%E2%9C%93&keywords=satan&commit=search.
[5] See Matthew 26:31. Emphasis added.
[6] See Mark 8:33. See also 2 Samuel 19:22; 1 Kings 5:4; 1 Kings 11:14, 23-26.
[7] John 6:70.

supposedly talked Eve into eating the 'forbidden fruit' was regarded in this manner in that it acted in apparent opposition to the creation plans of God.[8] The term 'devil' in the New Testament is a translation of the Greek word *'diabolos'* which means slanderer or false accuser – terms having the same connotation as, and thus used in place of, Satan.[9] The personality of the devil exists in Islam as *Shaitan* or *Iblis*,[10] which the Quran describes as the enemy of human beings.[11] He was an angel cast down from heaven for failing to subjugate himself to Adam.[12] In Buddhism, the devil or Satan appears as *Mara*,[13] a demon, tempter and the god of death.[14]

'Demons' popularly denote evil spirits and fallen angels and are synonymous with the devil[15] who is seen as the chief of demons.[16] Demons are supposed to be lieutenants of the devil and inhabitants of its kingdom. They stand accused of inflicting sicknesses and sufferings, causing temptations,[17] opposing or derailing believers,[18]

---

[8] See Genesis 3:1-5.
[9] See e.g., Revelation 20:2.
[10] See https://www.britannica.com/topic/shaitan; http://www.newworldencyclopedia.org/entry/Mara.
[11] See e.g., Surah 2:34, 168-169, 208; 6:142; 7:11; 17:53, 64; 38:74-75.
[12] Surah 7:12.
[13] See https://www.britannica.com/topic/Mara-Buddhist-demon; https://mythology.net/demons/mara/.
[14] Ibid.
[15] *The Catholic Encyclopaedia*, http://www.newadvent.org/cathen/04710a.htm. The fallen angels are those, according to the Bible, who with Lucifer, the archangel, had rebelled against God and were consequently cast down to earth from heaven. See Isaiah 14:12-14; Revelations 12:3-4, 9; 2 Peter 2:4; Jude 1:6.
[16] http://www.newadvent.org/cathen/04710a.htm.
[17] See Matthew 4:1-11.
[18] See Ephesians 6:12; Romans 8:38-39.

instigating and spreading false doctrines,[19] and opposing the work of God,[20] among others. The power of demons is supposed to be so pervasive that Ephesians 6:2 claims that we do not fight against human beings, but against 'principalities, powers, the rulers of the darkness of this world, and spiritual wickedness in high places'. In Zoroastrianism and Islam, demons equate roughly to *Daevas* and *Jinns*[21] respectively, with similar negative attributes and machinations;[22] and in Buddhism as *Mara* as already noted, among other designations.[23]

MISSION AGAINST DEVIL AND DEMONS

The notion that devils and demons cause diseases in and negatively influence human beings is not common in the Hebrew Scriptures. In fact, when lying spirits deceived King Ahab, and the spirit of madness possessed King Saul, they were said to be from God.[24] Similarly, the incidence of devil or demonic possession and influence receives limited attention in the Quran.[25] However, devils and demons are pervasive in the Bible's New Testament and Jesus spoke extensively about them. In one of his many altercations with the Pharisees and teachers of the law, Jesus told them that they were descendants of the devil whose bidding they carried out.[26] In Luke 10:18, he remarked

---

[19] See 1 Timothy 4:1; 1 john 4:1-3; 2 Corinthians 11:14-15; 2 Thessalonians. 2:2.
[20] See Daniel 12:13, 20.
[21] See Surah 2:102-104;
[22] See https://www.britannica.com/topic/shaitan;
[23] See https://www.britannica.com/topic/Mara-Buddhist-demon.
[24] 1 Samuel 16:14, 23; 18:10; 19:9; 1 Kings 22:22; 2 Chronicles 18:21.
[25] See Surah 2:275.
[26] John 8:43-44.

that he 'saw Satan fall like lightning from heaven,' while in Matthew 26:31-32, as noted earlier, he told his disciples that, Satan was keen to sort them out. Jesus also believed that the devil or Satan is the power that controls the world and the people in it. For this reason, the devil reportedly offered Jesus the whole world if he were to bow to him.[27] Jesus reiterated this belief in the devil when he observed that 'now is the time for judgment on this world; now the prince of this world will be driven out. But I, when I am lifted up from the earth, will draw all men to myself.'[28]

Furthermore, Jesus believed that the devil is in a constant power tussle with, and always seeks to undermine the work and purposes of, God. He illustrated this point in the Parable of the Weeds: the 'Son of Man' would plant good seeds, while the devil and his cohorts would plant weeds in their midst.[29] Similarly, in the Parable of the Sower, Jesus explained that, the devil snatches from people the seeds of the good news planted in their hearts'.[30] He also taught that the devil runs the Kingdom of Hell populated by himself and demons – a kingdom parallel to the Kingdom run by God and populated by angels. Jesus affirmed the existence of the devil when he denied casting out demons by the power of Beelzebub, the king of devils.[31] He also claimed that the devil has a retinue of demons who do his bidding, in much the same way, as there are angels who do the bidding of God. In addition,

---

[27] See Matthew 4:1-11.
[28] John 12:31-32.
[29] Matthew 13:37-38.
[30] Matthew 13:19.
[31] Matthew 12:25-28.

Jesus indicated that many diseases and sickness are the manifestations of demonic attack or possession. Consequently, he reportedly performed exorcism on many occasions.[32] It was Jesus' exploits as an exorcist that prompted the Pharisees and Scribes to allege that he worked with the power of Beelzebub.[33]

Indeed, Jesus' primary mission on earth was supposedly to undo the work of the devil.[34] This is, causing human beings to sin, assuming lordship over them and their affairs, and bringing death to the world.[35] The purpose of Jesus' coming was to nullify the hold of the devil by offering up himself as a ransom for the sins of humanity.[36] He also came in order to overcome the stealing, destruction and death wrought by the devil, so that we 'might have life and have it more abundantly'.[37] Jesus' position on the devil and his supposed powers is replicated throughout the New Testament which presents the devil as an adversary of God and humanity.[38] However, Jesus averred that on the Day of Judgment, unrighteous people would be cast into Hell Fire

---

[32] See Mark 1:34, 39; 9:25; 16:9; Luke 4:33-35, 41; 8:28; 9: 37-42; 11:14; 13:32; Matthew 8:16-17, 28-34; 9:33; 12:22.
[33] See Matthew 12:24; Mark 3:22; Luke 11:15.
[34] 1 John 3:8.
[35] See Matthew 4:1-11; John 10:10.
[36] See Mark 10:45; Matthew 20:28; John 15:13-15; Romans 4:25; 5:8-10; Colossians 1:13-14; Hebrews 2:14; 1 Peter 2:24; 3:18.
[37] John 10:10.
[38] See for example, John 13:2; Acts 5:3; 10:38; 26:17-18; James 2:19; Romans 16:20; 1 Corinthians 7:5; 2 Corinthians 2:10-11; 11:14; James 4:7; 1 Peter 5:8-9; Ephesians 6:11; 1 Thessalonians 2:18; 2 Thessalonians 2:9; 3:3; 1 Timothy 5:15; 2 Timothy 2:26; Hebrew 2:14; Revelation 2:13; 3:9; 12:9; 12:12; 20:7, 10.

to join the devil and demons. Do these diabolical beings really exist? Do they lead human beings to sin and separation from God?

CREATIONS OF RELIGION

Despite the powers ascribed to the devil or Satan in religious scriptures as an independent supernatural power contending with God for supremacy, and the fear this inspires in people, he does not in fact exist. In the biblical context, the devil originally appeared to be an agent or manifestation of God. The later biblical (and subsequently Quranic) belief in a supernatural Satan or devil as the architect of all evil and the archenemy of God and humanity is a result of the personification of evil reminiscent of more ancient religions and cultures. Chief among these was Persian Zoroastrianism,[39] and Egyptian, Canaanite and Mesopotamian religions. In Zoroastrianism, there was a marked duality between the cosmic forces of good and evil, with *Ahura Mazda (Spenta Mainyu)* being responsible for all things good, and in eternal battle with *Angra Mainyu* who was responsible for all evil things.[40] In ancient Egyptian religion, there was the good god Osiris and the evil god Seth, while in ancient Mesopotamian mythology, the good god Marduk battled with and

---

[39] See *Encyclopaedia Britannica*, http://www.britannica.com/EBchecked/topic/658081/Zoroastrianism; http://www.worldatlas.com/articles/top-countries-of-the-world-by-zoroastrian-population.html.
[40] See *The Jewish Encyclopaedia*, http://www.jewishencyclopedia.com/articles/13219-satan. See also LRN Ashley, *the Complete Book of Devils and Demons* (Barncade Books 1996) 19; D Heaster, *The Real Devil: A Biblical Exposition* (Carelinks Publishing 2009) 1-28; http://www.worldatlas.com/articles/top-countries-of-the-world-by-zoroastrian-population.html.

eventually prevailed against the chaos-dragon Tiamat. In the land of Canaan, the god Baal contended with Mot, the god of the dead. In short, the concept of a devil as a supernatural power was prevalent in many old religions and cultures around the world.[41]

By virtue of the belief in cosmic duality, people assume that since God is good; evil must come from other powerful supernatural beings. Thus, before the age of science and modern medicine, people attributed almost every serious disease or sickness - epilepsy, schizophrenia and other mental health problems, deafness, dumbness, blindness, etc. – to devils or demons. To this day, despite scientific advances and the widespread realisation that diseases – both physical and mental – have biological, physiological or neurological causes, many still attribute them to devils or evil spirits. Instances of exorcism still occur in many churches and other religious centres,[42] sometimes with fatal consequences,[43] while charges of demon possession or witchcraft led to the 'witch-hunt' and murder of untold number of people in many areas of the world. In addition, many ascribe to devils

---

[41] See generally, *Encyclopaedia Britannica,*
http://www.britannica.com/EBchecked/topic/172631/dualism; D Rosenberg, *World Mythology: an Anthology of the Great Myths and Epics* (McGraw Hill Companies Inc. 1994). A Cotterell (ed.) *The Illustrated Encyclopaedia of Myths and Legends* (Marshall editions Ltd 1989) 10-51; 56, 57, 69, 145, 160.
[42] See https://www.bbc.co.uk/news/uk-20357997;
https://metro.co.uk/2018/02/02/imam-allows-filmed-carrying-muslim-exorcism-7281718/.
[43] See e.g., the UK Daily Mirror, http://www.mirror.co.uk/news/world-news/woman-beaten-death-sticks-religious-5679890;
http://www.mirror.co.uk/news/weird-news/girl-killed-by-family-members-in-suspected-1230197; http://www.mirror.co.uk/news/uk-news/nun-killing-exorcist-is-jailed-14yrs-453374.

or demons the misfortunes that befall them and others in their personal, family, financial and communal affairs.

However, as indicated in Chapter 4, the Supreme Creator or God is the source of all powers in the universe. The existence of devils or demons is inconsistent with the existence of an omnipotent God, as any ascription of power to the devil or demons is tantamount to the diminution of the power of God. If God is all-powerful, there will be no power left for these supposed evil beings. If there were to be a devil that controls the world, holds humans captive and, with his band of demons, frustrates the designs of God, it would follow not only that God is not almighty, but also that the devil is also a god, albeit an evil one, as some religions and cultures indeed teach.[44] This is however contrary to the notion of monotheism apparently professed in Judaism, Christianity, Islam, and many other religions. Indeed, the Bible in many places asserts that all powers – good and evil – come from Yahweh, the biblical God, who does good and evil:

> *Isaiah 45: 5 – 7:*
>
>> *I am the LORD, and there is no other. I form the light and create darkness, I bring prosperity and create disaster; I, the LORD, do all these things.*
>
> *Jeremiah 18:11:*
>
>> *Now therefore say to the people of Judah and those living in Jerusalem, 'this is what the LORD says: Look!*

---

[44] As in Zoroastrianism, ancient Egyptian, Mesopotamian, and Hellenistic religions. The Bible itself describes devil as 'the god of this age' who has blinded the minds of unbelievers in Jesus as God – 2 Corinthians 4:4.

> *I am preparing* a disaster for you and devising a plan against you. So turn from your evil ways, each one of you, and reform your ways and your actions.

Exodus 4:11:

> *The LORD said to him, "Who gave man his mouth? Who makes him deaf or mute? Who gives him sight or makes him blind? Is it not I, the LORD?"*

Amos 3:6:

> *When a trumpet sounds in a city, do not the people tremble? When disaster comes to a city, has not the LORD caused it?*

Genesis tells us that, in the Garden of Eden, God planted the Tree of Knowledge in contrast to the apparent ignorance and blindness in which he had created Adam and Eve. It tells us also that God had planted the Tree of Life in contrast to the mortal existence of the supposed first humans. In these passages, God was the source of blessings, curses and disasters. God was also the source of wisdom and ignorance; as well as the source of mortality and immortality.

In Deuteronomy 28, Yahweh promised the people of Israel numerous blessings if they obeyed him, but terrible curses and disasters if they disobeyed. The Bible indeed claims in many passages that Yahweh was responsible for the evil that befell the people of Israel.[45] In other examples, it was Yahweh that sent the 'evil spirit' to possess and

---

[45] I Kings 14:10; 2 Kings 6:33; 21:12; 2 Chronicles 34:24; Isaiah 31:1-2; Jeremiah 6:19; 11:11; 18:11; 19:3; 23:12; 32:42; 36:3; 42:17; 44:2, 11, 27; 45:5; 49:37; Amos 9:4; Micah 1:12; 2:3.

torment Saul, his anointed King;[46] enabled Satan to destroy Job;[47] and sent 'lying' spirits into the mouths of his prophets so that they prophesied falsely to King Ahab.[48] If God is the source of all things, positive and negative; and if all power belongs to God; it follows that there cannot be a powerful supernatural being who is the devil or Satan, and no demons who do its bidding.

The claim that devil and demons are fallen angels is not credible as there is no scriptural, philosophical or logical basis for it. The passages in the Old Testament, notably, Isaiah 14:12-14 and Ezekiel 28:12-19 often cited in support of this notion are respectively a taunt at the fall of the king of Babylon and a dirge against the king of Tyre, both enmeshed in mythical imagery.[49] They are not references to any devil or any fallen angel. This being the case, the New Testament assumptions in Jude 1:6 and 2 Peter 2:4 that the devil and demons were angels who had 'sinned' and were cast down from heaven;[50] and the statement attributed to Jesus that he saw Satan fall from heaven,[51] are mere myths or allegories. The same is true of the references in Revelations about the dragon, beast, Satan and devil.[52] In fact, although demons are now popularly associated with absolute evil, this was not always the case. The English word 'demon' is a derivative of

---

[46] See 1 Samuel 16:14, 23.
[47] See Job 1, 2.
[48] See 1 Kings 22:19-23; 2 Chronicles 18:18-22
[49] See the annotations to both passages in *The New Oxford Annotated Bible (NRSV)* (Oxford University Press 2001).
[50] See Luke 10:18; 2 Peter 2:4; Jude 1:6.
[51] See Luke 10:18.
[52] See Revelations 12:4, 7-9; 20:1-10

the Greek word *diamon* or *diamonium*, which in classical usage, did not mean evil but rather holy, divine and beneficent spiritual beings in the nature of gods or angels.[53]

Moreover, and ignoring the fact that there were no witnesses to the supposed heavenly event, it is implausible that angels would rebel against God. By their nature, angels are supposed to be devoid of human weaknesses, emotions and vices. Being in a pure and incorruptible spiritual state of existence, they would not be prone to jealousy, envy, ambition, conceit, strife or rebellion.[54] They would know and understand their place and would work in complete unity and harmony with God, the Ultimate Spirit. They would not turn into evil spirits. An acceptance of the narrative on devils and demons as fallen angels would mean that these beings succeeded in thwarting the designs of God. According to the Bible, God's design was for human beings to live in an earthly paradise, while the angels would live in heaven with God.[55] The rebellion of the angels shortly after the creation of the earth, apparently compelled God to send them down here to cause hardship and misery for humans, even though these were

---

[53] See the *Catholic Encyclopaedia*, http://www.newadvent.org/cathen/04710a.htm. See also *Encyclopaedia Britannica*, http://www.britannica.com/EBchecked/topic/149915/demon; WRF Browning (ed.) *Oxford Dictionary of the Bible* (Oxford University 2009) 83.

[54] Contrast with Isaiah 14:12-14; 1 Timothy 3:6.

[55] See Genesis 1:26-30; 2:15-17. The Quran has a similar story as the Bible on creation and the design to reside human beings in paradise – a plan which the devil frustrated. See Surah 7:19-26.

not in God's original blueprint. Implicit in this supposed frustration of the divine plan is a suggestion that God is not omnipotent or omniscient, since God could not anticipate the treachery of the angels, nor forestall it and its ensuing consequences. The absurdity of the claim that devils and demons are fallen angels finds illustration in the popular depiction of angels as graceful, winged and white beings; and the devil and demons as ugly, black, monstrous and horned creatures. This is in spite of the fact that Lucifer, the supposed rebellious chief of the angels was apparently an awesome-looking 'bringer of light' – the title of planet Venus when it rises in the morning.[56]

Furthermore, the attribution of evil things to the activity of devils and demons is largely due to fear of others and the unknown, as well as religious exceptionalism. This is why people perceive the religious beliefs and rituals of other people as devil worship. For example, the Bible, apart from describing the deities of other nations as wood, stone or ornaments,[57] pointedly calls them demons or devils.[58] It condemns the Jews for embracing and worshipping these demons and thereby incurring the anger and jealousy of Yahweh.[59] Apostle Paul expressed

---

[56] See https://www.britannica.com/place/Venus-planet

[57] See e.g. Jeremiah 10:1-25; Deuteronomy 29:17; Psalm 31:6; 115:4-8; Isaiah 44:9-20; 46:6-10; Act 17:22-31; Habakkuk 2:18-20; 2 Chronicles 11:15.

[58] See e.g., See Leviticus 17:7; Deuteronomy 32:17; 1 Corinthians 10:20; Psalm 106:34-37.
[59] Deuteronomy 32:15-18; see also Psalm 106:34-37; Leviticus 17:7; 2 Chronicles 11:15.

this bias when he warned Christians against 'being participants with demons' and eating meat offered by non-Christians in sacrifice since, 'the sacrifices of pagans are offered to demons, not to God'.[60] He went on to declare that, 'You cannot drink the cup of the Lord and the cup of demons too; you cannot have a part in both the Lord's Table and the table of demons'.[61] Because the Bible regards the deities of other people as demons or devils, any wondrous works done by such people were immediately ascribed to the devil or demons, and therefore evil. Because of this, it construed as devilish, the exploits performed by the prophets of Egypt in replication of those performed by Moses, the prophet of Yahweh.[62] Similarly, the Bible generally regards the spiritual exploits of the 'pagan' nations around Israel as demonic even though they were similar to those of the Israelites.

Ironically, Jews who did not believe in the ministry of Jesus expressed the belief that he was the subject of demon possession[63] and performed his miracles by the power of Beelzebub, the so-called Prince of devils.[64] Yet, Beelzebub actually means, 'Lord of Flies'. It is a corruption of Baal-Zebul and synonymous with Beelzebul, which means 'Lord of Heaven' or 'Lord of the House'. Beelzebul was the name of the god of the people of Ekron,[65] an ancient Canaanite and Philistine city. Far from being a devil, the Bible confirms that

---

[60] I Corinthians 10:20.
[61] I Corinthians 10:21.
[62] See Exodus 7:11, 22; 8:7.
[63] See John 8:48-49.
[64] See Matthew 9:34; 12:24; Mark 3:22; Luke 11:15.
[65] See WRF Browning (ed.) supra n 53, 34.

Beelzebub was a god. It recounts that when King Ahazia of Israel suffered a serious injury, he sent messengers to 'Go and consult Baal-Zebub, the god of Ekron' in order to know his fate. Unhappy about this, Prophet Elijah accosted the messengers and demanded why they were going to the god of Ekron instead of inquiring from Yahweh, the god of Israel.[66] The above analysis illustrates the bigoted, hollow and dangerous foundations for the existence of devils and evil spirits. The assumption that the deities of other lands are devils and demons is a strong incentive to people to hate and discriminate against others and commit religiously motivated atrocities.

GOOD AND EVIL

The non-existence of devils and demons does not mean however, that evil or evildoers do not exist. It is therefore important to differentiate between the personality of devils, Satan and demons that do not exist, and the perpetration of evil, although there is no absolute good or absolute evil. Good exists relative to evil, and vice versa: positive and negative; darkness and light; night and day; life and death; sunshine and rainfall; water and fire; black and white etc. None of these phenomena or attributes is inherently good or bad. Sometimes daylight is good, other times darkness is better and preferable to daylight; sometimes we wish for rainfall, and at other times sunshine. Sometimes life is better than death; other times, death may be preferred to life.

---

[66] 2 Kings 1:1-3.

Water is essential for life; yet water, in the form of a storm or flood causes death and destruction. Bodies of water - oceans, river, lake, etc. - have also drowned many people, even though they are essential for sustaining life on earth. The sun is indispensable for life; yet it can cause misery and death through drought and desertification. Knife is a deadly instrument, but without knife, we will struggle to prepare our food. Although gun has been the source of much bloodshed and misery in the world, a person will bless the day of its invention if it saves him from the deathly jaws of a crocodile or the crosshairs of an assassin's rifle. We cannot reasonably say that 'good' water, sun, knife or gun comes from God, while 'bad' ones come from the devil. All these, and other opposite phenomena and attributes come from the same source and complement each other.

Therefore, whether something is 'good' or 'bad' is not so much a question of origin, but a question of circumstances or use. In reality, human beings choose their actions and must take responsibility for them instead of blaming them on devils and demons. We have the capacity and the will to do good or evil; how we deploy this is up to us. We have the freedom to utilise the resources of our being and those of the universe as we choose. In the soul and conscience of everyone is the inclination for good or evil; whichever we allow to prevail at any time manifests in our actions. God will not force our minds or hands one way or another; neither will any Satan, devil or demons.[67]

---

[67] For more information on this subject, see: JB Russell, *The Devil: Perceptions of Evil from Antiquity to Early Christianity* (Cornell University Press 1977); *Satan: the Early Christian Tradition* (Cornel University Press 1987); P Carus, *The History of*

DEVIL AND DEMONS AS REASON FOR SALVATION

The popular but mistaken belief in devils and demons have engendered much fear in people, caused many to feel they are under the spell of evil forces, and rendered others vulnerable to failure, misery and exploitation. By not realising their inextricable connection and oneness with the omnipotent God, and hence their inherent powers, people often feel they need to seek deliverance from the hold of Satan and demons, thereby falling prey to dubious religious leaders and medicine men.

Because human beings have creative spiritual powers and energy, our belief in anything, if strong enough and properly directed, is capable of creating an appearance or reality of it. Our belief is the energy that gives life to things that are otherwise mere illusions. In other words, we can make our own devils and demons. To be free from the so-called attack, works, or possession of devil or demons, we need to free our minds from belief in them and appreciate our connection with God, the source of all energy. Since devils and demons exist only in the abstract and metaphorical sense, any purported mission or scheme to undo their work and save people from their control is meaningless and serves no purpose. What about the mission to save people from Hell Fire, the putative domain of the devil and his demons?

---

the Devil and the Idea of Evil: *from the Earliest Times to the Present Day* (Forgotten Books, Classic Reprints 2012). See also S Mitchell, *the Book of Job* (New York: Harper Collins 1975); E Pagels, *The Origin of Satan* (Hamondsworth: A Lane/The Penguin Press 1996); D Heaster, supra n 40.

14

HELL AS PLACE FOR THE UNSAVED

We have prepared for the wrongdoers a fire whose walls will surround them. And if they call for relief, they will be relieved with water like murky oil, which scalds [their] faces. Wretched is the drink, and evil is the resting place. – Surah 18:19

Directly associated with the supposed existence and power of devils and demons, and the need for salvation, is the belief in the existence of Hell Fire. Assumedly, this is the dominion of devil and demons, and the future home of people who would not make heaven after the Judgment. It is supposed to be a place of excruciating and perpetual anguish. As with devils and demons, the existence of Hell Fire is critical to the dogma of salvation. This is because the purpose of salvation is not only to save people from the hold and power of the devil, but also from eternity in Hell Fire. If there were to be no Hell Fire, the ultimate mission to save people from eternity in it and provide them safe passage to heaven would be useless.

A PLACE OF ETERNAL TORMENT?

The gospels teach that there is a literal Hell Fire where 'sinners' and unbelievers would suffer eternal torment after their death and warn people of the dangers of going there. In his parable of the sower, for example, Jesus promised to send his angels to gather those who cause sin, as well as all evildoers, and throw them into the furnace of fire where they will weep and gnash their teeth.[1] Jesus also advised his listeners to cut off any offending part of their body because it is better to 'enter into life' disabled than to be whole and end up in hell where the worms never die and the fires never quench.[2] On another occasion, Jesus told his listeners not to be afraid of those who could destroy only the body, but to 'be afraid of the One who can destroy both soul and body in hell'.[3] Further, in the well-known story of the rich man and Lazarus, Jesus told of how the poor and deprived Lazarus went to heaven after his death and sat in 'Abraham's bosom' while the mean rich man went to Hell Fire from where he begged Lazarus for a drop of water.[4] Jesus also taught that on the Day of Judgment, those who had lived a bad life would be isolated and sent 'into the eternal fire prepared for the devil and his angels'.[5] Jesus further remarked that the gate to life is small, narrow, and discoverable only by a few, while the gate to destruction is broad and discoverable by many.[6] John the

---

[1] Matthew 13:40-43.
[2] Mark 9:43-48. See also Matthew 18:8-9.
[3] Matthew 10:28.
[4] Luke 16:19-31.
[5] Matthew 25:41.
[6] Matthew 7:13-14. Other teachings or references by Jesus to hell are in Matthew 23:33 and Luke 12:5.

Baptist, the forerunner of Jesus, also spoke about hell and its everlasting fire. According to him, 'the axe is already at the root of the trees, and every tree that does not produce good fruit will be cut down and thrown into the fire.'[7] He stated further that Jesus already has his winnowing fork in his hand with which to 'clear his threshing floor, gathering his wheat into the barn and burning up the chaff with unquenchable fire'.[8]

The Bible book of Revelation insists that hell is an actual place where inmates would roast for eternity[9] in an intense 'Lake of Fire'.[10] Many other passages in the New Testament concur with Jesus on the existence of a hell of fire.[11] Writing about the certainty of Hell Fire, the epistle of Peter states that if God did not spare his rebellious angels but threw them into Hell Fire, dissident human beings should not expect a more favourable treatment.[12] The writer even asserts that, after his death and burial, Jesus went into Hell – assumedly located 'in the heart of the earth'[13] – to preach to the inmates.[14] The Church affirms and propagates the totality of the teachings of Jesus and the Bible on Hell Fire. Asserting that the doctrine 'has never met any opposition worthy of mention,' the Catholic Encyclopaedia, insists

---

[7] Matthew 3:10.
[8] Matthew 3:12.
[9] Revelation 20:10.
[10] See Revelation 20:14-15; 19:20; 21:8.
[11] See e.g., Revelation 14:11; Matthew 25;46; Jude 1:7; 1 Peter 3:19; 2 Peter 2:4-10; Ephesians 4:8-10.
[12] 2 Peter 2:4-10.
[13] Matthew 12:40; Ephesians 4:8-10.
[14] See 1 Peter 3:19. See also Ephesians 4:8-10.

that, 'there is a hell, i.e. all those who die in personal mortal sin, as enemies of God, and unworthy of eternal life, will be severely punished by God after death'. The church also professes the Athanasian Creed, which asserts that, 'they that have done good shall go into life everlasting, and they that have done evil, into everlasting fire.'[15]

The conception of Hell Fire as a literal place of eternal torment also exists in Islam. The Quran describes it as a place of 'chains, shackles and blaze'.[16] It further states that:

> *We have prepared for the wrongdoers a fire whose walls will surround them. And if they call for relief, they will be relieved with water like murky oil, which scalds [their] faces. Wretched is the drink, and evil is the resting place.*[17]

The fire of hell, the Quran says would be severe, unrelenting and all encompassing.[18] The Hebrew Bible is more ambivalent about the issue of Hell Fire. Although it does not generally paint a picture of a literal Hell Fire, it does speak of a Day of Judgment or of The Lord[19] when people would receive eternal blessings or punishment. Jewish tradition however, conceives of Hell Fire in the nature of *Gehenna*

---

[15] See http://www.newadvent.org/cathen/07207a.htm.
[16] Surah 76:4; 14:49-50.
[17] Surah 18:19.
[18] Surah 29:55; 56:41-44; 43:74-77; 77:32-33;
[19] See Psalm 10:5; Isaiah 2:12; 13:6, 9; Ezekiel 13:5, 30:3; Joel 1:15, 2:1,11,31; 3:14; Amos 5:18,20; Obadiah 15; Zephaniah 1:7,14; Zechariah 14:1; Malachi. 4:5.

where unbelievers and oppressors of their nation will receive their just deserts.[20] So, for whom is this Hell of Fire?

WHO GOES TO HELL?

According to Jesus, the list of people destined for Hell Fire includes the devil and his demons;[21] people who blaspheme the Holy Spirit;[22] and those who commit sin[23] or do bad things.[24] The Bible also includes in the list, those who do not believe in Jesus as the Christ or in his gospel;[25] those whose names are not in the 'Book of Life';[26] the sexually immoral, including adulterers, fornicators, and homosexuals; as well as cowards, liars, the vile, idolaters and magicians.[27] Judaism and Islam make non-believers the prime candidates for Hell Fire. In Jewish theology, reading the Shema[28] and the Hallel[29] and eating the three meals prescribed for the Sabbath days protect one from Hell Fire, while Israelites in general are less in danger of going there than heretics and heathens.[30] Meanwhile, the Quran unequivocally declares that Hell Fire is for unbelievers:

---

[20] http://www.jewishencyclopedia.com/articles/6558-gehenna.
[21] Matthew 25:41; 1 Peter 3:19; Revelations 20:10.
[22] Mark 3:29.
[23] Mark 9:43-47; Matthew 18:8-9.
[24] Matthew 13:40-43; 25:41.
[25] Revelation 21; John 3:36; Luke 13:3; 2 Thessalonians 1:8-9.
[26] Revelation 20:15.
[27] Revelation 21. See also Jude 1:7; Galatians 5:19-21.
[28] This is the confession of the Jewish faith in the oneness of Yahweh as stated in Deuteronomy 6:4
[29] This refers to Psalms 115-118 which are a Jewish praise of Yahweh for his goodness to them, especially their deliverance from Egypt. The Psalms are usually sung at the end of the Passover meal.
[30] See *The Jewish Encyclopaedia*, http://www.jewishencyclopedia.com/articles/6558-gehenna.

And for those who disbelieved in their Lord is the punishment of Hell, and wretched is the destination. When they are thrown into it, they hear from it a [dreadful] inhaling while it boils up. It almost bursts with rage. Every time a company is thrown into it, its keepers ask them: 'Did there not come to you a warner?[31]

A number of problems arise from these lists and categories of candidates for Hell Fire. First, since devils and demons do not exist, and these designations encompass gods of other religions or agents of Yahweh,[32] the supposed tenants-in-chief of Hell Fire are likely to be absent from it. Second, the supposedly grave sins of idolatry, apostasy or blasphemy against God punishable with damnation in Hell Fire in Judaism, Christianity and Islam, is not likely to send anyone to the place because it inheres merely in the profession or rejection of a particular religion or its doctrines. As for blasphemers of the Holy Spirit, no one can be sure who these would be since the interpretation of Holy Spirit and blasphemy differs from person to person and from one religion to another. Because one man's Holy Spirit might be another man's devil or demon, this category could potentially include everybody.

---

[31] Surah 67:6-8. See also, Surah 4:5; 17:97; 18:29, 53; 25:26-27; 3 5:36-37; 76:4.
[32] See Chapter 13.

Third, sentencing 'unbelievers' to Hell Fire implies that just people, who follow other religions or belief systems, or indeed none, would receive unjust and unfair punishment. Accordingly, believers in Jesus Christ (who therefore are unbelievers in the eyes of Jews, Moslems and other religious people) would be sure candidates for Hell Fire. In like manner, all adherents of other religions would be unbelievers in Christianity and potential inhabitants of the Hell Fire of its conception. Concerning persons whose names are not in the 'Book of Life', if this book refers to the record of souls' activities in their lifetimes on earth,[33] the name of everybody would be there.[34] However, if it would contain only the names of believers in Christ, it would follow that these peoples' names would not be in the book of life of other religions and would therefore go to Hell.

Fourth, it is unclear who would fall into the general category of 'sinners' since the word is nebulous and has many subjective connotations. Christian theology, defines 'sin' as a moral evil or depravity, or the contravention of the laws or will of God usually due to human disobedience, selfishness or pride,[35] and may arise by acts, omissions or thoughts. It could be actual, in the sense of perpetration by the particular person, or original, in the sense of perpetration by an original ancestor and inherited by his offspring. Sins are also categorised as mortal or venial. Mortal sins are deliberate sins that are

---

[33] See Revelation 20:12-13.
[34] See L Howe, *How to Read the Akashic Records: Accessing the Archives of the Soul and its Journey* (Sounds True Inc. Boulder CO 2010).
[35] See the *Catholic Encyclopaedia*, http://www.newadvent.org/cathen/11312a.htm.

so grave that they would cut off the sinner from the sanctifying grace of God. Venial sins are usually less serious and deliberate, and do not have the same effect as mortal sins, although they could impair a person's relationship with God.[36] While a person could repent from venial sins, the effects of mortal sin are irremovable except with the grace and at the instance of God.[37] Disobedience or rebellion against God, idolatry, and apostasy are examples of Mortal sin.[38] Judaism and Islam have a similar definition and characterisation of sin.

However, many of the things deemed sinful are so-called because a particular religion, culture or belief system has categorised them as sin even though they might be perfectly acceptable in others. For example, the sins of blasphemy, apostasy, idolatry, the worship of 'other gods', or un-belief, vary in their meaning depending on the religion of the judge. Sexual immorality, including adultery and fornication are sins only because religion has defined it as such; and the so-called sin of adultery is a religious contraption that generally favours men at the expense of women.[39] The inclusion of fornicators as candidates for Hell, to the extent that it damns adult human beings for willingly engaging in lovemaking, is unnatural and unreasonable.

---

[36] See generally, *The Catholic Encyclopaedia*, http://www.newadvent.org/cathen/14004b.htm; the Encyclopaedia Britannica, http://www.britannica.com/EBchecked/topic/545534/sin; WRF Browning, *Oxford Dictionary of the Bible* (Oxford University 2009) 333.
[37] See e.g., Romans 7; John 3:3.
[38] See the *Catholic Encyclopaedia*, http://www.newadvent.org/cathen/11312a.htm. See also, e.g., Genesis 3; Exodus 20:3-6; 1 Samuel 15:23; Romans 5:19; Hebrews 10:26; 1 Corinthians 10:14.
[39] Ibid.

What is better, consenting adults having sex without marriage, or subjecting minors to it within forced or arranged marriages, as obtains in certain cultures and religions?[40] On the issue of homosexuality, the edict on it is mean and unsympathetic as it condemns people for their inherent sexual disposition;[41] while in the case of magicians, one person's magician may be another person's miracle worker.[42]

As for lying, it is clearly not the case that every lie would amount to a sin, since a lie could be for a good cause, or otherwise perfectly harmless. Who has not lied to a child who has asked an awkward question, the answer to which the child is not entitled? Who would reasonably be expected to tell the truth when a lie could save another's life, or protect them from imminent harm or danger? The Bible even records in a number of places that Yahweh had lied. In Genesis, the alleged promise to Adam and Eve that they would die if they ate from the 'Tree of knowledge' proved not to be true.[43] Elsewhere, Yahweh's angels acting as lying spirits in the mouth of his prophets deceived King Ahab into war and his death.[44] Jesus also appeared to have lied (or misled people) on occasions, such as when he promised to grant

---

[40] For minimum marriage age around the world, see https://www.independent.co.uk/news-19/the-lowest-age-you-can-legally-get-married-around-the-world-10415517.html.
[41] See Chapter 5.
[42] Ibid.
[43] Ironically, it was the serpent that proved to be truthful. See Genesis 2:17; 3:4, 7, 22.
[44] See 1 Kings 22:18-38; 2 Chronicles 18:18-34. See also Jeremiah 4:10; 20:7; Ezekiel 14:9 for other instances where the Bible God was accused of being deceitful.

any request made in his name,[45] and with regard to the time of his Second Coming.[46] Are Yahweh and Jesus also bound for Hell Fire?

GOING TO HELL IN ANGER

According to Jesus, 'anyone who is angry with his brother will be subject to judgment' and presumably Hell Fire.[47] Accordingly, Apostle Paul lists anger as one of the works of the flesh, the practitioners of which would not enter heaven,[48] and the Catholic Church includes it among the seven capital sins that would deprive a person of a place in heaven.[49] Yet, Jesus himself got angry on occasions. He angrily cursed a fig tree with unproductivity because it yielded no fruit to him out of season.[50] He got angry with people trading in the temple, overturned their tables and chased them away.[51] He also got angry and distressed at the Pharisees who opposed his healing of a sick man on the Sabbath.[52]

In addition, the Bible states that Yahweh expresses his wrath every day,[53] and that he became extremely angry on many occasions – sometimes for no reasonable cause. For example, Yahweh's anger 'burned' against Moses when he doubted his own suitability to lead

---

[45] See John 14:13-14.
[46] See Matthew 16:28 and pp. 153-154.
[47] Matthew 5:22.
[48] See Galatians 5:19-21.
[49] See *The Catholic Encyclopaedia*, http://www.newadvent.org/cathen/14004b.htm.
[50] See Mark 11: 12-14; Matthew 21: 18-19.
[51] Mark 11:15-17.
[52] See Mark 3: 1-6.
[53] See Psalm 7:11.

the Israelites out of Egypt.⁵⁴ Yahweh was also very angry when Moses struck a rock for water instead of merely speaking to it⁵⁵ notwithstanding that Yahweh had previously asked him to strike it,⁵⁶ and Moses was in distress over his people's rebellion.⁵⁷ Yahweh was so angry at the complaints of the Israelites about the hardships they had to endure in that he burned down parts of their camp;⁵⁸ and was 'exceedingly angry' when the people cried and complained of hunger in the wilderness.⁵⁹ Similarly, the anger of Yahweh 'burned' so much against Miriam and Aaron for questioning Moses' marriage to an Ethiopian wife that he inflicted the former with leprosy.⁶⁰

Furthermore, Yahweh became so angry with a certain Uzzah that he struck him instantly dead merely for touching the 'Ark of Covenant' in order to steady it.⁶¹ Yahweh was also angry at the Israelites such that he commanded King David to carry out a census⁶² and became angry with Solomon for worshipping foreign gods.⁶³ Ultimately, Yahweh became so angry at the Israelites for their idolatry, worship of other gods, and rejection of his commandments that he gave them and their land up to the Assyrians.⁶⁴ The New Testament also says

---

[54] Exodus 4:14.
[55] Numbers 20:8-12
[56] Exodus 17:6
[57] Numbers 20:1-7.
[58] Numbers 11:1.
[59] See Numbers 11:10.
[60] See Numbers 12:9-10.
[61] See 2 Samuel 6:6-7.
[62] See 2 Samuel 24:1.
[63] See I Kings 11:9-10.
[64] See 1 Chronicles 5:26; 2 Kings 17:5-6; 2 Chronicles 32:22; Deuteronomy 28:62-65; 2 Kings 17.

that, 'the wrath of God is revealed from heaven against all ungodliness and unrighteousness of men, who by their unrighteousness suppress the truth.'[65] If the Bible records Yahweh as regularly getting seriously angry,[66] why should mere mortals be condemned to Hell Fire for having a similar emotion?

In addition, the Bible reports that many acknowledged and venerable servants of Yahweh got angry. King Saul 'burned with anger from the Lord' when the Ammonites insulted Israelites by offering them a peace treaty on the condition that they would gauge out the eyes of every Israelite.[67] He became very angry when the people praised David more than him,[68] and against his son Jonathan for befriending David and helping to save his life.[69] King David was angry when Yahweh killed Uzzah for touching the 'Ark of Covenant'.[70] Prophet Elisha was angry with King Jehoash for striking an arrow on the ground three times, instead of five or six times;[71] and was so angry with forty-two youths who called him baldhead that he caused wild bears to devour them.[72] Prophet Jonah was angry with Yahweh for not destroying Nineveh and its people.[73] For his part, Apostle Paul was

---

[65] See Romans 1:18.
[66] See 2 Kings 17. For some other instances when God was reported to be very angry against the people of Israel, see Exodus 32:10-11; 15:7; Deuteronomy 9:8; 31:17; Judges 2:14; 20; Judges 10:7; 2; Psalm 78:59; 106:40; Job 4:9; 2 Kings 13:3; 23:25-27; Ezekiel 7:8; Habakkuk 3:12; Isaiah 13:9; Jeremiah 30:24.
[67] See 1 Samuel 11:1-11.
[68] See 1 Samuel 18:6-8.
[69] See 1 Samuel 20:30-31.
[70] See 2 Samuel 6:8.
[71] See 2 Kings 13: 18-19.
[72] 2 Kings 2:23-24.
[73] See Jonah 3, 4.

angry with Peter and other Jerusalem Christians who had refused to interact with Galatian Christians.[74] Were all these eminent people of Yahweh subject to Hell fire?

It is difficult to comprehend how merely being angry, irrespective of cause, could subject somebody to judgment and everlasting punishment in Hell Fire. Despite the suggestion in Ecclesiastes 7:9 that only fools get angry, the emotion is natural and cannot be a wrongdoing in itself. Although prolonged and uncontrolled anger could damage a person psychologically and physiologically, and a rash action in anger could occasion unpleasant and regrettable consequences, this would be indicative of a human weakness for which they would need help. The unreasonableness of the position on anger is further illustrated by the fact that, a person might get angry but prudently control and restrain himself from speaking out or reacting rashly in that state.[75] What sense would it make to condemn the person for showing restraint in the face of provocation?

Jesus also said in Matthew 5:22, that, 'anyone who says to his brother, *'Raca*,' is answerable to the Sanhedrin. But anyone who says, 'You fool!' will be in danger of the fire of hell.' However, it is hard to rationalise that a person could go to hell simply for calling a person a fool or indeed for giving him or her any other insult, even if the insult was totally justified by the person's acts or utterances. As if to illustrate the fallacy of his own teaching, Jesus called the Pharisees

---

[74] See Galatians 2:11-21.
[75] See Proverbs 29:11; 15:18; Ephesians 4:26-27.

'blind fools' for teaching that swearing by the temple gold was worse than swearing by the temple itself.[76] He went on to suggest that God called people fools when they had deserved that label, as demonstrated by his parable of the 'Rich Fool'.[77] In addition, following his 'resurrection', Jesus described two disciples on the Emmaus road, as foolish for their failure to understand the prophecies about him.[78] Apostle Paul also called people fools. In Galatians 3:1, he described the people of Galatia as foolish for subscribing to Mosaic Law instead of remaining steadfast in his teaching that salvation was by faith in Jesus Christ. This is notwithstanding the Bible's claim that the Law of Moses came directly from God.

The Old Testament refers to many people as fools or foolish. These include those who denied the existence of God[79] and those who are quick to anger.[80] It describes King Saul as foolish for daring to offer sacrifice to Yahweh instead of waiting for Prophet Samuel.[81] Clearly then, referring to somebody who has behaved or spoken foolishly as a fool cannot be a wrongdoing. It certainly cannot be something so wrong as to put a person at risk of Hell Fire - were such a place to be in existence. Of course, unnecessarily and unjustifiably insulting somebody in the presence of others could be hurtful and should therefore be refrained from both for spiritual and legal reasons. This

---

[76] Matthew 23:16- 17.
[77] Luke 12: 13-21.
[78] See Luke 24:25.
[79] See Psalm 14:1.
[80] See Ecclesiastes 7:9; Proverbs 29:11.
[81] See 1 Samuel 13:1-15.

is why libel and slander are actionable wrongs in law as defamation. However, an evidently foolish person is not entitled to complain if he or she is called a fool, as the statement would be a true description of their conduct.

Indeed, the Bible records in a number of places that sometimes foolishness would be a virtue and preferable to apparent wisdom. In the words of Apostle Paul, if anyone thinks, 'he is wise by the standards of this age he should become a 'fool' so that he may become wise'.[82] Paul also states that, 'we are fools for Christ'.[83] This seems to accord with Jesus' teaching that whoever does not change and become like a little child will not enter into the kingdom of God.[84] In any case, the teaching of Jesus on this matter is irreconcilable with the punishment he envisaged for saying *raca* to another person. According to him, such a person would face the Sanhedrin for some kind of censure. Now, *raca* is a derogatory Hebrew word meaning empty or worthless – an abuse seemingly more serious than being called a fool. Yet the punishment for saying *raca* to someone is much less than calling him or her a fool. Nevertheless, is Hell Fire really a literal place or something else?

MEANING OF HELL
The word hell is used in the English Bible in place of the Hebrew word *Sheol* and the Greek word *Hades,* both of which refer to the 'dwelling

---

[82] 1 Corinthians 3:18.
[83] 1 Corinthians 4:10, See also 1 Corinthians 1:21.
[84] See Matthew 18:3; Mark 10:15; Matthew 19:4; Luke 18:17; 1 Peter 2:2.

place of the departed who continue a shadowy existence'.[85] According to the Catholic Encyclopaedia, hell 'is cognate to 'hole' (cavern) and 'hollow' and a substantive formed from the Anglo-Saxon *helan* or *behelian*, 'to hide' [...] Thus by derivation hell denotes a dark and hidden place'.[86] Similarly, the Encyclopaedia Britannica states that, 'In its archaic sense, the term *hell* refers to the underworld, a deep pit or distant land of shadows where the dead are gathered' and derives from the old English word *hel*, which means to conceal or cover'.[87]

By these definitions, hell is not an extra-terrestrial place of torment but simply an underground place of burial – the home of dead bodies.[88] Accordingly, the Bible records that Jacob believing Joseph his son to be dead, refused to be comforted and insisted on going down with him into *Sheol*.[89] In like manner, Jesus observed that just as Jonah spent three days and three nights in the belly of a huge fish, so would he spend three days and three nights in the heart of the earth.[90] Accordingly, after his death and entombment, Jesus allegedly descended into hell, from which he emerged after three days.[91] Several other passages in the Bible make it clear that *Sheol*, hades, or hell

---

[85] WRF Browning (ed.) *Oxford Dictionary of the Bible* (Oxford University 2009) 139, 336. See also Isaiah 14:9-10; Job 10:19-22.
[86] http://www.newadvent.org/cathen/07207a.htm.
[87] http://www.britannica.com/EBchecked/topic/260218/hell.

[88] Ibid. See also Revelations 20:13.
[89] Genesis 37:35.
[90] Matthew 12:40.
[91] In the words of the Christian church's 'Apostles' Creed'.

simply means grave.[92] Being an underground, airless, lightless, and condensed place, and a place where the body rots and from which it never returns, the grave is obviously and understandably an unattractive place.[93] Thus, in a metaphorical sense, going to hell would be a very unwelcome idea. So, why has hell become widely designated as a literal place of eternal torment burning with unquenchable fire and brimming with devils and demons?

The designation of hell as a place of eternal torment has a lot to do with *Gehenna*, a term denoting the Valley of Hinnom (*ge-hinnom*) in Jerusalem where people burned large numbers of children with sulphur as sacrifice to the god Molech.[94] This practice was so huge and pervasive that Prophet Jeremiah renamed the place 'the Valley of Slaughter'.[95] The word ge-hinnom seems to have evolved later into *geena* or *gehenna*, the English translation of the Greek word for hell. Because the Valley of Hinnom unceasingly burned with fire, from either human sacrifice or latterly rubbish, and became a place for the burial of criminals, it provides an abiding image of fire, suffering and badness. Thus, the metaphor of ge-hinnom became a literal Hell-

---

[92] See Job 7:9; Psalm 30:3; 31:17; 49:15; Isaiah 14:11, 15; Numbers 16:31-33; Proverb 1:12; 1 Samuel 2:6; Hosea 13:14;1 Corinthians 15:55; Revelation 20:13. See also D Heaster, *The Real Devil: A Biblical Exposition* (Carelinks Publishing 2009) 142-146.
[93] See, e.g., Job 10:19-22, Psalm 9:17; 16:9-11; Proverbs 15:24; Ezekiel 26:20. Apparently, persons whose bodies were cremated would not have the feeling of being in this hellhole or hades.
[94] See 2 Kings 23:10; Jeremiah 2:23; 7:30-33; 19:1-6, 13-14.
[95] See Jeremiah 7:32; 19:6.

Fire,[96] a designation that found accommodation in the sister religions of Christianity and Islam.[97]

DIVINE PUNISHMENT FOR EVIL

The conception of hell as an extra-terrestrial and eschatological place of torment appears to have much to do with the misconception, by religion and the masses, of death and sin, and the manner of punishing evil doers. The Catholic Church, for example, rationalises Hell Fire as being necessary to ensure divine justice for evil doers even in the afterlife since they might evade justice in their lifetime:

> *In His sanctity and justice as well as in His wisdom, God must avenge the violation of the moral order in such wise as to preserve, at least in general, some proportion between the gravity of sin and the severity of punishment. But it is evident from experience that God does not always do this on earth; therefore He will inflict punishment after death. Moreover, if all men were fully convinced that the sinner need fear no kind of punishment after death, moral and social order would be seriously menaced. This, however, Divine wisdom cannot permit. Again, if there were no retribution beyond that which takes place before our eyes here on earth, we should have to consider God extremely indifferent to good and evil and we could in no way account for His justice and holiness.*[98]

---

[96] See notes on Matthew 18:8-9 in *The New Oxford Annotated Bible* (*NRSV*) (Oxford University Press 2001). See also the *Jewish Encyclopaedia*, http://www.jewishencyclopedia.com/articles/6558-gehenna; *Encyclopaedia Britannica*, http://www.britannica.com/EBchecked/topic/227782/Gehenna.

[97] This popular understanding of hell has been aided by such works of fiction as J Milton, *Paradise Lost* (Oxford World Classics, 2004); D Alighieri and DH Higgins, *The Divine Comedy* (Oxford World Classics Paperback 1988).

[98] See the *Catholic Encyclopaedia*, http://www.newadvent.org/cathen/07207a.htm.

HELL AS PLACE FOR THE UNSAVED

While the justice of inflicting some form of repercussion on evil doers is correct, the belief that this would happen post-mortem through eternal roasting in hell is not. In Biblical reckoning, once a person dies, his life and everything about him entirely end. According to Ecclesiastes, 'the living know that they will die, but the dead know nothing, and they have no more reward, for the memory of them is forgotten',[99] while Psalm 11:17 asserts that, 'the dead do not praise the Lord, nor do any who go down into silence'. What would happen at some point after death, Christians believe, is the resurrection of the dead and a final judgment. Depending on the verdict, the person would proceed to the eternal bliss of heaven or the everlasting torment of Hell Fire.[100] Therefore, Hebrews 9:27, declares that, 'it is appointed unto men once to die, but after this the judgment'. In Matthew 25, Jesus taught that on the Judgment day, those who failed to make the required grade would receive a marching order 'into the eternal fire prepared for the devil and his angels'.[101] This point is emphasised graphically in Revelation with a description of the court and judgment process.[102] The belief in a day of final Judgment and reckoning, as already discussed, also exists in Judaism and Islam.[103]

---

[99] Ecclesiastes 9:5.
[100] The Catholic Church teaches that there are grades of condemnation and sentencing. These range from limbo (for infants who died without baptism and for the just who died before the advent of Christ) to purgatory (where those who committed only venial sins are cleansed in preparation for heaven) and ultimately hell fire for those who had committed mortal sin).
See http://www.newadvent.org/cathen/07207a.htm.
[101] Matthew 25:41.
[102] Revelation 20:11-15.
[103] See Chapter 11.

Hell is also rationalised as the antithesis of heaven: If there is heaven, where God, the angels and the souls of good people reside and rejoice, then there must also be Hell Fire where devil, demons and the souls of bad people would stay and be tortured. As has clearly been seen in the preceding chapter, devils and demons as powerful evil beings working in opposition to God and human beings do not exist. This being the case, there is no need for a hell of fire where they, along with people they lead astray, would face perpetual punishment in eternity. In any event, people do not have to die before they experience the consequences of their wrongdoings. They do so here on earth under the law of cause and effect.

THE LAW OF CAUSE AND EFFECT

In the law of nature, for every act a consequence would follow and invariably come upon the perpetrator in due course on earth – a state of affairs confirmed by the Bible. In Matthew, Jesus stated that, 'all who draw the sword will die by the sword'.[104] Revelation reiterates this by stating that, 'He that leadeth into captivity shall go into captivity: he that killeth with the sword must be killed with the sword […].'[105] The Bible's Old Testament also teaches that, 'whoever sows calamity will reap injustice, and the rod of his fury will fail',[106] and

---

[104] Matthew 26:52.

[105] Revelation 13:10 (KJV). The alternative (NIV) translation, 'If anyone is to go into captivity, into captivity he will go. If anyone is to be killed with the sword, with the sword they will be killed. This calls for patient endurance and faithfulness on the part of the saints', also suggests pre-destination, itself an indication of re-incarnation and karma.

[106] Proverbs 22:8.

that, 'those who plow evil and those who sow trouble reap it'.[107] The book of Galatians decisively affirms this principle as follows:

> *God cannot be mocked. A man reaps what he sows. The one who sows to please his sinful nature, from that nature will reap destruction; the one who sows to please the Spirit, from the Spirit will reap eternal life. Let us not become weary in doing good, for at the proper time we will reap a harvest if we do not give up.*[108]

The above biblical statements do not suggest or imply that the consequences of misdeeds are post-mortem or eschatological. The Quran also appears to affirm the law of cause and effect.[109]

Moreover, Hell Fire as a place of punishment for evildoers is of doubtful effect. First, it is unclear how the souls or spirits of the dead would suffer in Hell, as they are not likely to feel pain or discomfort from any fire or torture. Second, the doctrine of eternal punishment in Hell Fire has largely not deterred people from doing evil. Given that no one, including Jesus,[110] knows when the judgment day would come; given that thousands of years have passed since Jesus was allegedly on earth; and given that human beings have lived and died since the world began, people are likely to regard the supposed punishment in Hell Fire as something very remote, if not fanciful or illusory. The amount of evil and wickedness in our world, despite thousands of years of the propagation of this doctrine by major

---

[107] Job 4:8.
[108] Galatians 6:7-9.
[109] See e.g., Surah 13:11; 22:45.
[110] See Mark 13:32; Matthew 24:36; Acts 1:7.

religions, is testimony that any fear of Hell Fire has not been much of a deterrence to evildoing. Third, the Bible records many instances when dead people were brought back to life, including three by Jesus.[111] Although these people had died once, they did not face any judgment or the possibility of Hell Fire for any sins they might have committed.

Finally, and to make matters worse, the religions espousing the existence of Hell Fire, as already noted, make their own followers virtually immune from it and reserve the place primarily for unbelievers. Thus, the New Testament claims that the acknowledgment that one is a sinner and the confession of Jesus as Lord and saviour furnishes the confessor with salvation, making them free from Hell Fire.[112] It was perhaps pursuant to this teaching that the 'repentant' robber who purportedly accepted Jesus while being crucified received the promise that he would get into paradise immediately,[113] without facing any judgment or consequences for his sins. Moreover, on occasions, Jesus had forgiven people all their sins;

---

[111] Prophet Elijah raised from the dead the son of the 'Widow of Zarephat' (1 Kings 17:17-24). Prophet Elisha raised to life the dead son of the Shunamite woman (2 Kings 40:20-37). Another dead body was restored to life after it was thrown into Elisha's tomb (2 Kings 13:21). Jesus returned to life Lazarus (John 11:1-44). Jairus' daughter (Mark 5:35-43)) and the son of the widow of Nain (Luke 7:11-15). Apostle Peter reportedly raised Tabitha from the dead (Acts 9:36-41) while Apostle Paul reportedly restored Eutychus to life after the former fell down to his death from a third floor window during Paul's preaching (Acts 20:7-12). The Bible also recounts that at the point of Jesus' death, there was an earthquake which opened graves and many dead people came back to life (Matthew 27:51-53).
[112] See John 1:2; 3:36; 10:9; Romans 6:23; 8:1; 10:3; Acts 2:38; 16:31; 2 Corinthians 5:17; 1 John 4:14. See also Chapters 1 and 2 for a discussion of the doctrine of salvation.
[113] Luke 23:43.

and confessional priests still do the same in the Catholic Church. What then would stop a person from doing as much evil as he could in the knowledge that he would someday become a believer, be saved, and avoid Hell Fire?[114] How would this person receive punishment for his wickedness? It seems clear therefore, that the notion of Hell Fire as a place of eternal punishment for wrongdoers reflects erroneous popular culture and theology and has no basis in reality.

Nevertheless, although an eschatological and physical hell might not exist, hell in a metaphorical sense had been, and remains, real for many people on earth. This is because human beings create conditions of torment for others by acts of discrimination, injustice, oppression wickedness and brutality. It is from this type of hell that people need salvation. Although unhelpful to the ordinary person and the society, the concept of Hell Fire and the prospect of eternal punishment in it has proved a useful instrument of fear and control that enables religious authorities to keep believers pliant and in the faith. More damagingly, the doctrine of eternal punishment in Hell Fire has shifted the focus of many a religious person from the alleviation of human suffering and the improvement of the human condition on earth to the escapist race for heaven.

---

[114] See Romans 5, 6:1-3.

15

HEAVEN AS HOME OF THE SAVED

In my Father's house are many mansions: if it were not so, I would have told you. I go to prepare a place for you. And if I go and prepare a place for you, I will come again, and receive you unto myself; that where I am, there ye may be also. - John 14:2-3

The ultimate goal of salvation is the entry of the saved into heaven, the assumed kingdom of God. The notion of heaven as the home of gods, angels or spirits or as the ultimate place of reward for humans after death, existed and exist in many ancient and modern religions. Many religious people believe that after their death or the end of the earthly system of things, they would go to their real home in this heavenly kingdom. The notions of End Time and the Day of Judgment stem from this belief and the desire of people to escape from the troubles of this world. However, the nature of heaven and the people entitled to enter it differ among the religions. So, what and where is heaven? Would departed believers or righteous people go to heaven? This chapter addresses these questions in the context of the foremost modern religions that teach apocalyptic eschatology – Judaism, Christianity and Islam.

HEAVEN IN JUDAISM

The Hebrew Bible seems ambivalent on the subject of life after death and heaven as a home for the departed, depicting heaven as the abode of God and earth as the abode of living human beings. According to Psalm 115:16, 'the heaven, *even* the heavens, *are* the LORD's; But the earth He has given to the children of men'. The Old Testament then indicates that the home of the dead is the grave or *sheol*,[1] with Ecclesiastes being the most emphatic about the absence of life after death:

> *I also said to myself, "As for humans, God tests them so that they may see that they are like the animals. Surely, the fate of human beings is like that of the animals; the same fate awaits them both: As one dies, so dies the other. All have the same breath; humans have no advantage over animals. Everything is meaningless. All go to the same place; all come from dust, and to dust all return. Who knows if the human spirit rises upward and if the spirit of the animal goes down into the earth?" So I saw that there is nothing better for a person than to enjoy their work, because that is their lot. For who can bring them to see what will happen after them?*[2]

Ecclesiastes also insists that 'the living know that they will die, but the dead know nothing; they have no further reward, and even their name is forgotten' and would have no further part in anything.[3] In

---

[1] The notion and nature of *sheol* has already been discussed in Chapter 14 in the context of Hell Fire.
[2] Ecclesiastes 3:18-22.
[3] Ecclesiastes 9:5. See also Ecclesiastes 9:10.

support of this position, 2 Samuel 14:14 says that death is as irrecoverable as water spilled on the ground.

Yet, in other places, the Old Testament seems to envision life after death in heaven. Prophet Daniel states that after a period of unprecedented distress, those whose names are in 'the book' would be delivered; and multitudes who had died would rise from the grave, 'some to everlasting life, others to everlasting contempt'.[4] In Psalm 49:14-15, the psalmist declares that the body of people who trust in themselves will decay in the grave, but that God will redeem him from the realm of the dead and unto himself.[5] Similarly, he rejoices that God would not abandon his body in the grave or allow it to decay; instead, God would fill him with joy in his presence and right hand.[6]

Judaism perceives heavens (*Shamayim*) as the third part of the cosmos – the others being earth (*eret*) and the underworld (*sheol*). It conceives of heaven in the plural to encompass the space above the earth, from the sky and beyond.[7] It recognises seven layers of heavens, which correspond with the Sun, Moon, and the observable planets of Mercury, Venus, Mars, Saturn and Jupiter.[8] Therefore, the Old

---

[4] Daniel 12:1-2.
[5] See also Psalm 73:23-24.
[6] Psalm 16:10-11. See also Job 14.
[7] See Genesis 14:22; 27:39; Exodus 16:4; 17:14; 20:4; Deuteronomy 2:25; 4:19; Isaiah 65:17; Judges 20:40; Joshua 2:11.

[8] See Psalm 8:3. The Hebrew terms for the seven heavens are Vilon or Araphel, Raqia, Shehaqim, Zebul, Maon, Makon and Araboth.

Testament has used the term 'heavens' in respect of the sky and the Outer Space,[9] as well as the dwelling of God,[10] which is supposed to be beyond the seventh heaven. The Second Book of Enoch however identifies ten heavens and locates paradise (containing the Tree of Life) on the third, and God, on the last.[11] Presumably, the third heaven is the paradise where the faithful departed would live in a new Eden-like existence, with freedom to enjoy the fruits of immortality from the Tree of Life.

However, residents of the Jewish heaven are unlikely to live with God, whose home (in the seventh or tenth heaven) appears unwelcoming to humans. Prophet Daniel reports a vision in which 'the ancient of Days' in the form of a man sat on a wheeled throne of fire in sparkling white garments and woollen hair,[12] in the midst of fierce and monstrous-looking animals. In his own vision of heaven and God, Prophet Ezekiel also painted a picture of a man on a flaming wheeled throne surrounded by fire. Around him were flaming man-like creatures each with four faces – of man, lion, ox and eagle – and four wings.[13] Similarly, in the Second Book of Enoch, Enoch, who had

---

[9] Genesis 1:6-8; 22:17.
[10] Genesis 21:17; 22:11; 28:12; Exodus 20:22; Joshua 10:11; Psalm 11:4; Psalm 14:2; 102:19; Job 1:6-8; Isaiah 66:1; Nehemiah 1:4.
[11] JB Lumpkin, *The Second Book of Enoch (also called the Secrets of Enoch and the Slavonic Book of Enoch)* (Fifth Estate 2009); https://archive.org/stream/pdfy-R9zRtlssi4sDgDNt/The%20Second%20Book%20Of%20Enoch%20%5BThe%20Book%20Of%20The%20Secrets%20Of%20Enoch%5D_djvu.txt.

[12] Daniel 7:9.
[13] Ezekiel 1:

assumedly gone to heaven to intercede for the fallen angels, depicts the abode of God as a formidable place of fire, ice, snow and hailstones. God himself sat on a wheeled throne of fire and ice, surrounded by fire and ten thousand times ten thousand attendants.[14]

In any case, given that the above description of heaven are dreams or visions and that the accounts attributed to Enoch are legendary,[15] it is uncertain what weight could be given to them. In fact, the Bible's Old Testament also depicts God (Yahweh) as living on the Mountain of God,[16] in the Jerusalem temple,[17] and in the Ark of Covenant.[18] Moreover, it is uncertain whether the Jewish heaven is really the ultimate home for departed souls. This is because, although the Book of Enoch speaks of a paradise in the third heaven, Prophet Daniel explained his vision of heaven as meaning that the people of Israel, led by their messiah, would dominate and rule the world forever.[19]

---

[14] I.e., One hundred million. See also Daniel 7:9
[15] See http://www.jewishencyclopedia.com/articles/5773-enoch-books-of-ethiopic-and-slavonic.
[16] See Numbers 10:33; Isaiah 2:1-2; 25:6-9, 56:7; Ezekiel 28:16; Micah 4:1-2.
[17] 1 Kings 8:10-11;
[18] See Exodus 25:22; Numbers 10:35; 1 Samuel 4:3-9; Psalm 11:4.
[19] Daniel 7:15-28.

HEAVEN IN CHRISTIANITY

As in Judaism, the notions of layers of heaven, and heaven as the abode of God, exist in Christianity. In 2 Corinthians 12:2-4, Paul spoke about a man who was caught up to the third heaven and paradise. The third heaven would correspond to the abode of God, while the other two heavens would correspond to the sky and outer space.[20] During his teachings, Jesus expressly suggested the existence of heaven as the home of God where the faithful would eventually enter: In Matthew 12:50, he stated that his father was in heaven;[21] and in Matthew 5:19, declared that:

> *Anyone who sets aside one of the least of these commands and teaches others accordingly will be called least in the kingdom of heaven, but whoever practices and teaches these commands will be called great in the kingdom of heaven'. For I tell you that unless your righteousness surpasses that of the Pharisees and the teachers of the law, you will certainly not enter the kingdom of heaven.*

Jesus promised to take the 'repentant' criminal crucified with him to his paradise kingdom,[22] having earlier comforted his disciples with the following promise:

> *Do not let your hearts be troubled. You believe in God; believe also in me. My Father's house has many rooms; if that were not so, would I have told you that I am going there to prepare a place for you? And if I go and prepare a place for you, I will*

---

[20] See Acts 10:11.
[21] As are angels – Matthew 22:30.
[22] Luke 23:42-43.

> *come back and take you to be with me that you also may be where I am.*[23]

In line with this promise, the New Testament claims that Jesus ascended to heaven and would return from there to take his followers with him.[24] Revelation 2:7 promises 'victorious' ones the right to eat from the Tree of Life in Paradise, while Apostle Paul promises that the citizenship of believers is in heaven from where they would await Christ who would transform their lowly bodies like his own.[25] In heaven, the saved would be in Mount Zion, the presence of God and an innumerable company of angels:[26]

> *They shall neither hunger anymore nor thirst anymore; the sun shall not strike them, nor any heat; for the Lamb who is in the midst of the throne will shepherd them and lead them to living fountains of waters. And God will wipe away every tear from their eyes.*[27]

The Christian heaven would be a restored Garden of Eden where there will be no nights but only bright days powered, not by the sun, but light from God.[28] However, there would be neither marriage nor given in marriage in the place where the residents would be like angels rather than material beings.[29] Ironically, the Christian heaven, like the heaven of Judaism, is also essentially and exclusively Jewish – a

---

[23] John 14:1-3.
[24] See Acts 1:11; Luke 24:50-53.
[25] Philippians 3:20-21. Other biblical passages on heaven as a place of reward for believers include Luke 15:7, Matthew 7:21-23, Revelation 21:23.
[26] Hebrews 12:22-23.
[27] Revelation 7:15-17.
[28] Revelation 22:1-5.
[29] Matthew 22:30.

restoration of the Garden of Eden. The New Testament describes it as Jerusalem, the city of God[30] surrounded by twelve gates representing the twelve tribes of Israel,[31] and Mount Zion.[32] One hundred and forty-four thousand Israelites, twelve each from the twelve tribes, would receive the seal for heaven.[33] Even the 'Tree of Life' would bear twelve kinds of fruits.[34] The heaven also contains Yahweh's Jerusalem temple and the Ark of covenant.[35] Finally, after the Day of Judgment, Jesus would supposedly rule the world for a millennium from Jerusalem and the throne of David, while his disciples would be the new judges of Israel.[36]

HEAVEN IN ISLAM

Islam also recognises seven layers of heaven[37] as levels of paradise to which believers would go depending on their level of piety. Prophet Mohammed apparently went through the heavens where he met Old Testament prophets, including Jesus in a trip reminiscent of the one allegedly undertaken by Enoch and the Zoroastrian priest, Arda Viraf.[38] The Quran envisions heaven (*Jannah*) as a beautiful and bountiful garden (paradise) where people would eventually live in eternity in the presence of Allah after the Day of Judgment.[39] The

---

[30] Revelation 21:9-11; 19-20.
[31] Revelation 21:21.
[32] Hebrews 12:22-23.
[33] Revelation 7:1-8.
[34] Revelation 22:22.
[35] Revelation 11:19.
[36] Matthew 19:28; Revelation 20.
[37] Surah 2.29; 65:12, 22; 71:12.
[38] For an account of this, see http://www.avesta.org/mp/viraf.html.
[39] Surah 2:28; 3:15.

Islamic paradise is a place of fun and merry-making. According to the Quran, there would be in paradise:

> *Rivers of water unaltered, rivers of milk the taste of which never changes, rivers of wine delicious to those who drink, and rivers of purified honey, in which they will have all kinds of fruits and forgiveness from their Lord.*[40]

Apparently, in the Islamic heaven, married people will re-unite blissfully with their spouses,[41] beautiful and perpetual virgins would become spouses to unmarried men,[42] and beautiful young boys of eternal youth will attend to unmarried women.[43] Who however, are the candidates for heaven?

WHO GOES TO HEAVEN?

For a number of reasons, it is doubtful that the expectations of believers to go to heaven would be realised. First, the expectation of salvation and heaven are religion-oriented and have no universal formula or criteria. The heaven of Jewish imagination would be the home of faithful departed Jews. This is because all the key Jewish descriptions and accounts of heaven are Jewish-centric with little reference to other peoples or nations of the world. Circumcision, observance of the Mosaic Law and the prayers and rituals of Judaism are pre-conditions for entry into paradise and constitute an antidote to Hell Fire.[44] Conversely, the New Testament insists that those who

---

[40] Surah 47:15.
[41] Surah 36:56.
[42] Surah 56:35-38.
[43] Surah 76:19.
[44] See Chapter 3.

believe in Jesus would receive salvation and enter heaven, while those who do not are condemned.[45] Even descendants of Abraham and followers of the Mosaic Law, would not enter heaven unless they accept and follow Jesus Christ.[46]

In Islamic conception, those who would enter paradise are believers,[47] people who obeyed Allah and His messenger, the steadfast affirmers of truth, the martyrs, and the righteous.[48] Of course, those who obey Allah and the Prophet and steadfastly affirm the truth would be people who observe the pillars of Islam[49] and follow its teachings, while the martyrs would be those who give their lives for the cause of Islam, including during Jihad. Therefore, unbelievers and people who failed to follow the teachings of the Quran are unlikely to make heaven.[50] As Surah 3:91 makes clear, 'those who disbelieved and died as unbelievers, not even an earth full of gold will be accepted from them as ransom. For such people there is painful chastisement; and none shall come to their help'. Since the criteria for heaven among the religions are mutually exclusive, the implication is that all believers are likely to miss out.

---

[45] See Mark 16:16; John 3:18; 36. See also Romans 1:16-17; 5:1; Galatians 2:16; Titus 3:5.
[46] See Luke 18:18-23.
[47] Surah 2:82; 18:107; 80:38-39.
[48] Surah 4:69.
[49] The five pillars of the faith are (1) declaration and belief that Allah is the One and only God and that Mohammed was His prophet. (2) Praying five times a day (3) Fasting during specified festivals, especially Ramadan (4) Giving alms (5) Making the pilgrimage to Mecca, unless one is crippled, or too poor to afford it.
[50] Surah 3:85; 51:56; 78:40; 80:40-42.

Second, the idea of heaven as a place of reward for the righteous at the end of time is doubtful. Given the untold number of years that have elapsed since the world began, the number of people that have died within that time, and the non-arrival of the Day of Judgment, it would seem that the reward of a heavenly home remains relevant only in the realms of fantasy. Moreover, the nature of life expected in heaven differs across the religions. While Judaism and Islam depict a wonderful Garden or paradise of bliss and merry-making, Christianity envisions heaven as a place in which human beings would only reside in the form of angels. Moreover, while Islam promises marital re-unions and new spouses in heaven, Christianity discountenances such a possibility.

Third, the notion of heaven as a place of eternal reward and Hell Fire as a place of eternal torment might make some sense if human beings live only one physical life on earth. However, if souls re-incarnate and experience many lifetimes in different bodies, there would be no need for a final judgment, heaven or hell after death. Although departed souls would recognise the errors they made while on earth and the need to make amends for them in their subsequent lives, these would be for the purpose of growth and perfection and not as punishment. However, before souls re-incarnate in new bodies, and at the end of the re-incarnation cycle, they would apparently stay in the heavens or spiritual realms.[51] They would not stay in the grave or in hell.[52] Although, the Bible appears in places to oppose the notion of re-incarnation,[53] the belief in it was virtually universal among ancient peoples and religions all over the world, including Jews.[54] Even Jesus, whose messiahship depended on the re-incarnation of Elijah as John the Baptist,[55] appeared to believe in it. Similarly, although the idea of re-incarnation is a matter of theological contest and debate in Islam, and the Quran appears in places to reject it,[56] its recognition seems implicit in some passages.[57] In any case, even though one may not be in a position accurately to explain what transpires after death, the billions of dead people still awaiting the Day of Judgment and bodily resurrection would make re-incarnation a much more sensible and

---

[51] For evidence and discussions of re-incarnation, see T Shrodder, *Old Souls: Compelling Evidence from Children Who Remember Past Lives* (Simon & Schuster Paperbacks 1999); M Newton, *Journey of Souls: Case Studies of Life Between Lives* (Minnesota: Llewellyn Publications 1994); *Destiny of Souls: New Case Studies of Lives between Lives* (Minnesota: Llewellyn Publications 2000). See also B Weiss, *Many Lives, Many Masters: The True Story of a Prominent Psychiatrist, His Young Patient and the Past-Life Therapy that Changed Both Their Lives* (Piatkus 1994); I Stevenson, *Children Who Remember Previous Lives: A Question of Re-incarnation* (McFarland & Co; Revised edition 2001). See further E Cayce, *Reincarnation and Karma* (ARE Press 2006); S Lonnerstrand (Translated by Leslie Kippen), *I have Lived Before: the True Story of the Reincarnation of Shanti Devi* (Ozark Mountain Publishers 1998); D Chopra, *Life after Death: the Book of Answers* (Crown Publishing Group 2006). Finally, see A Moorjani, *Dying to be Me: My Journey from Cancer, to Near Death, to True Healing* (London: Hay House UK Ltd 2012).
[52] Ibid.
[53] See e.g., Psalm 78:39; John 5:25-29; Hebrews 9:27.
[54] See e.g., Ecclesiasticus/Sirach 48:4-10; Malachi 4:5-6.
[55] See Matthew 11:13-14; 16:14; 17:10-13, 22; Mark 6:14-16; Luke 1:16-17; 9:7-9; John 9:1-3.
[56] See Mark 12:18-27; Matthew 22:23-32; Luke 20:27-38; Acts 23:8;
[57] See Surah 23:99-100; 40:11.

realistic prospect. Otherwise, where would the souls of all those people supposedly awaiting judgment be?

Finally, the Bible indicates that the faithful (both Jewish and Christian) will receive their reward on earth. As already indicated, Daniel interpreted in his own vision of heaven as such, and went further to state that, 'One like the Son of Man' approached the throne and received glory and power to rule all the peoples of the world forever.[58] Similarly, Revelation states that there will be two resurrections: in the first one, only those martyred for Christ would rise and rule for a thousand years with Jesus who would bind Satan and throw him into the abyss for this period.[59] The second resurrection would happen after this millennial rule following the temporary release of Satan from his bondage, his final consignment to Hell fire,[60] and the arrival of the Day of Judgment.[61] At this period, there would be a new heaven, a new earth, and a New Jerusalem, while God's dwelling place would be among the people here on earth.[62] In this new earth, God would wipe away every tear and banish death, mourning, crying and pain; and give water to the thirsty.[63] Then, 'the cowardly, the unbelieving, the vile, the murderers, the sexually immoral, those who practice magic arts, the idolaters and all liars', would be

---

[58] Daniel 7:13-14.
[59] Revelation 20:1-6.
[60] Revelation 20:7-10.
[61] Revelation 20:11-15.
[62] Revelation 21:1-7.
[63] Ibid.

consigned to Hell fire.[64] It is in a new earth that believers in Jesus who happen to be alive when and if he returns would enjoy their reward. As explained by the Seventh Day Adventist Church:

> *On the new earth, in which righteousness dwells, God will provide an eternal home for the redeemed and a perfect environment for everlasting life, love, joy, and learning in His presence. For here God Himself will dwell with His people, and suffering and death will have passed away. The great controversy will be ended, and sin will be no more. All things, animate and inanimate, will declare that God is love; and He shall reign forever.*[65]

This outcome seems to tally with biblical teachings in both the Old and New Testament that the poor, the meek and the righteous would inherit the earth.[66] It is also probably for the same reason that the Jewish sect of Sadducees reject the idea of resurrection of the body, insisting that the journey of life begins and ends on earth.[67]

---

[64] Revelation 21:8.
[65] Fundamental Belief, Number 28, The General Conference of Seventh-day Adventists, Adventist Fundamental Beliefs, 2006. This is also the position of the Jehovah's Witnesses, who assert that only 144,000 Jewish people would go to heaven in accordance with Revelation 7:1-8; 14:1-5.
[66] See e.g., Psalm 37:9, 11; Matthew 5:5; 2 Peter 3:13; Revelation 5:9-10.
[67] See Matthew 22:22-33; https://www.britannica.com/topic/Sadducee.

A POPULAR MISAPPREHENSION

It would seem that the doctrine of heaven as a place of eternal reward arose because of a misunderstanding of the universe and the purpose of human beings on earth. The idea of seven heavens was the way ancients tried to explain the Solar System. Since it is now clear that the Sun and Moon are not planets, and that other planets apart from Mercury, Venus, Mars, Saturn and Jupiter exist, the notion of the heavens, as the abode of God would seem misguided. Being Omnipresent, the Spirit or energy of God pervades every part of the universe unconfinable to a particular location.

Similarly, the conception of heaven as a place of eternal reward and residency for the faithful departed is a way certain religions, notably Zoroastrianism, Judaism, Christianity and Islam, attempt to explain the destiny of faithful people after their death. Since unbelievers would go to Hell Fire (which does not exist), it would follow in their reckoning that believers would go to heaven. This theology though is fallacious as evident from foregoing analyses. It also ignores the fact that the earth is God's kingdom, as Jesus reportedly alluded to when he observed that the kingdom of God is within and in the midst of us.[68] Equipped with all kinds of resources and facilities to make it a wonderful and joyous place, the fact that the world has not felt like God's kingdom to most of its inhabitants is a testament to how human beings have mismanaged it.

If human beings spend many lifetimes on earth before they achieve the perfection that would enable them to stay in the spirit realm forever, it means that the only home we have in this physical existence is the earth. The expectation of an end to the world and the hope for heaven has been responsible for the many apocalyptic prophecies, missions and movements in religious and world history[69] and the tragedies of mass deception, killings, and suicides in anticipation of the end of the world.[70] Instead of fantasising about heaven, we should strive in love to make the earth a reflection of the glory and love of God for the benefit of present and future generations.[71]

---

[68] See Luke 17:21; Matthew 12:28.
[69] See *Encyclopaedia Britannica*, for an account of apocalyptic movements in world history, at http://www.britannica.com/topic/Apocalyptic-Movements-1891921. In the Bible, the foremost examples of this are the books of Daniel and Revelation.
[70] See *Encyclopaedia Britannica*, http://www.britannica.com/topic/Apocalyptic-Movements-1891921. See also T Daniels (ed.) (ed.) *A Doomsday Reader: Prophets, Predictors and Hucksters of Salvation* (New York and London: New University Press 1999) 99-223.
[71] See Matthew 6:10 for The Lord's Prayer that God's kingdom should come on earth.

16

LOVE AND PEACE

If a man says, "I love God," and hates his brother, he is a liar; for he who does not love his brother whom he has seen, how can he love God whom he has not seen' – 1 John 4:20

Love is advocated by many religions and philosophies,[1] including the Abrahamic faiths on which this book focuses. However, it has proved elusive, as the world continues to have deep disunity and little peace. The history of the world is replete with religious intolerance and religiously motivated conflicts and bloodshed that have consumed countless human lives. Even sects of the same religion fight one another. Nations have enslaved, colonised and exploited other peoples while their missionaries purport to give messages of salvation to the victims. Terrorists claiming to fight for God destroy with impunity human lives and properties across the world. Incidences of racism, discrimination, and hate-induced

---

[1] See https://www.britannica.com/topic/Golden-Rule;
http://www.jewishencyclopedia.com/articles/3744-brotherly-love;
http://www.jewishencyclopedia.com/articles/10112-lord-s-prayer-the.

violence continue to rise, while political leaders fill their coffers at the expense of suffering and impoverished masses. In the corporate world, greed and exploitation have no limit, as a tiny percentage of the world's population control most of its wealth. Yet, the world is full of religious people most of whom hope for salvation and afterlife in paradise. Love and peace have been very difficult to find despite exhortations to both effect in philosophies and religious scriptures. Is it realistic for human beings to seek an escape to heaven while failing to do what is required to make the world a better place for its inhabitants?

LOVE

The Bible's New Testament captures well the essence and meaning of love. It states that, all kinds of spiritual endowments and prowess, such as prophecy, speaking in tongues, wisdom, faith, charitable giving and martyrdom, are meaningless without love.[2] On the nature of love, it posits that:

> *Love is patient, love is kind. It does not envy, it does not boast, it is not proud. It is not rude, it is not self-seeking, it is not easily angered, it keeps no record of wrongs. Love does not delight in evil but rejoices with the truth. It always protects, always trusts, always hopes, always perseveres. Love never fails.*[3]

True love therefore is non-discriminatory and synonymous with godliness. As the Bible avers, 'love comes from God', and 'everyone

---

[2] 1 Corinthians 13:1-3.
[3] 1 Corinthians 13:4-7.

who loves has been born of God and knows God'.[4] Conversely, 'whoever does not love does not know God, because God is love.'[5] Accordingly, Galatians 5:22 observes that the fruit of the spirit is love, joy, peace, forbearance, kindness, goodness and faithfulness. Love is the antithesis of fear, which is at the root of most things wrong with human beings: jealousy, hatred, conflict, destruction, and all manners of wrongdoing, among others. As rightly pointed out in 1 John 4:18, 'There is no fear in love. But perfect love drives out fear, because fear has to do with punishment. The one who fears is not made perfect in love'. Not only does love overlook wrongdoings from others,[6] it does not also countenance doing wrong to others.[7] The Bible also rightly says that a person cannot hate his brother while claiming to love God.[8]

In some of the teachings attributed to him, Jesus reportedly emphasised the need for love. In a re-statement of the Golden Rule, he stated that the love of neighbours, second only to the love of God, is one of the two greatest commandments on earth.[9] He enjoined his disciples to love one another, just as he had loved them.[10] Further, in one of the most memorable teachings credited to him, Jesus taught that, in order to be perfect, we should extend love not just to neighbours or friends, but also to strangers and enemies[11] - a point he

---

[4] 1 John 4:7.
[5] 1 John 4:8.
[6] 1 Peter 4:8; Proverbs 10:12; 17:9.
[7] See Romans 13:8-10.
[8] See I John 4:20.
[9] See Mark 12:30-31; Matthew 22:37-40; 19:19.
[10] See John 13:34.
[11] Matthew 5:43-48.

illustrated with the parable of the Good Samaritan.[12] He also taught that we should forgive those who sin against us up to seventy times seven, i.e., four hundred and ninety times.[13]

Exhortations on love are not wanting in other religious scriptures and philosophies. The Hebrew Scriptures, for example, command Jews not to 'seek revenge or bear a grudge against one of your people, but love your neighbour as yourself.'[14] Similarly, the Quran enjoins Moslems to be kind, generous, loving and compassionate to others, especially those who are in need or less privileged.[15] It also calls on believers to respond to evil with good.[16] All these are expressions of the so-called Golden Rule found in traditional spirituality and the words of philosophers across the ages. According to Encyclopaedia Britannica, the rule, for example:

> *is to be found in Tob. 4:15, in the writings of the two great Jewish scholars Hillel (1st century BC) and Philo of Alexandria (1st centuries BC and AD), and in the* Analects *of Confucius (6th and 5th centuries BC). It also appears in one form or another in the writings of Plato, Aristotle, Isocrates, and Seneca.*[17]

---

[12] See Luke 10:30-37.
[13] See Matthew 18:22.
[14] See Leviticus 19:18.
[15] See e.g., Surah 2:178; 16:91, 128; 29:70; 55:61.
[16] See Surah 41:34.
[17] https://www.britannica.com/topic/Golden-Rule.

PEACE

Flowing from and connected to love is peace. Not only does love enthrone tranquillity in one's spirit, it eliminates the propensity towards enmity and conflict in one's utterances and dealings with others. Peace cannot exist without love because only a loving person or situation enjoys peace and can project it to others. As pointed out in James 3:17, 'the wisdom that comes from heaven is first of all pure; then peace-loving, considerate, submissive, full of mercy and good fruit, impartial and sincere.' Moreover, as noted in Galatians 5:22-23, 'the fruit of the Spirit is love, joy, peace, patience, kindness, goodness, faithfulness, gentleness and self-control.'[18] In short, a loving person is a peaceful person who abhors injustice, discrimination, jealousy and violence against others.

The scriptures are replete with exhortations to maintain peace. According to Proverbs 12:20, 'deceit is in the hearts of those who plot evil, but those who promote peace have joy'. Psalm 34:14 enjoins people to turn from evil, do good, seek and pursue peace, while Psalm 37:37 says that a future awaits those who seek peace. The New Testament credits Jesus with the teaching of pacifism towards people who do evil or invite us to conflict[19] by attacking us, taking our possessions or otherwise causing us pain.[20] He reportedly told his disciples that in him they would have peace even though they would

---

[18] See also Romans 14:17; Isaiah 32:17.
[19] See Matthew 5:38-41; Luke 6:29. See also Proverbs 20:22; 24:29.
[20] See Luke 6:30.

have trouble in the world, because he has conquered the world.[21] He declared that, he has bestowed his peace on his followers, who should therefore not be troubled or afraid.[22] Indeed, the New Testament projects the birth of Jesus as the dawn of peace for humanity. Angels from heaven heralded his birth to shepherds with the words: 'Glory to God in the highest, and on earth peace to men on whom his favour rests.'[23] It claims that God had sent, 'the good news of peace through Jesus Christ who is Lord of all'.[24] The New Testament further describes Jesus as the 'Prince of Peace',[25] 'our peace' and the preacher and bringer of peace to the world.[26] Several other passages in the New Testament also emphasise the need for peace.[27]

Admonitions on peace also abound in the Quran. It says for example, 'O You who believe! Enter absolutely into peace. Do not follow in the footsteps of Satan. He is an outright enemy to you.'[28] It also says that, 'You may fight in the cause of GOD against those who attack you but do not aggress. GOD does not love the aggressors';[29] that religion

---

[21] See John 16:33. See also Matthew 26:51-53.
[22] John 14:27.
[23] Luke 2:14.
[24] Acts 10:36.
[25] Isaiah 9:6 is appropriated to Jesus.
[26] See Ephesians 2:14-18.
[27] See e.g., 1 Peter 3:11; James 3:18; Romans 12:18; 14:17-19; Hebrews 12:14; Galatians 5:22.
[28] Surah 2:208.
[29] Surah 2:190. See also Surah 2:193; Surah 8:61.

does not allow compulsion;[30] and that believers should do good and avoid destruction.[31]

The Quran goes on to condemn violence by stating that:

> *Whoever killed a human being, except as punishment for murder or other villainy in the land, shall be regarded as having killed all mankind; and that whoever saved a human life shall be regarded as having saved all mankind.*[32]

Given the above admonitions on love and peace in their scriptures, why are love and peace lacking so much within and among these religions?

RELIGIOUS LOVE AND PEACE
It would seem that the beneficiaries of the love and peace in the scriptures discussed above are believers only. The treatment and prescriptions for the treatment of non-believers in the religions' scriptures bear out this observation.

JESUS AND NON-BELIEVERS
From the very beginning of his ministry, the gospels depict Jesus as irritable and intolerant towards people who were not well disposed to his teaching. In the first evangelistic mission to which he sent his disciples, Jesus instructed them that in every home or town that failed to welcome or listen to them, they should shake off the dust of the place from their feet when they left. The punishment for members of that home or town would be worse than that of Sodom and Gomorrah

---

[30] Surah 2:256. See also Surah 109:1-6.
[31] Surah 2:195.
[32] Surah 5:32.

(which were reportedly destroyed by fire and brimstone) on the Judgment Day.[33] Similarly, Jesus pronounced curses and woes on the people of towns that did not immediately accept his message.[34] Might this hostile attitude not inspire preachers and zealots to commit acts of discrimination and violence against unbelievers, seeing that Jesus had already condemned them to destruction?

On another occasion, Jesus declared unforgivable and subject to Hell Fire Pharisees who 'blasphemed' the Holy Spirit by questioning the source of his power of exorcism.[35] This attitude is not indicative of love given that it is common for doubters to suggest that somebody was using unholy means to perform miracles. In the Bible for example, the Israelites believed that their own diviners and magicians worked with the power of God while those of other nations used the power of the devil. Yet, John the Baptist and Jesus labelled these same Israelites, especially their scribes, 'brood of vipers' and 'sons of the devil'.[36] If Jesus were a loving teacher, would he not have understood this inherent human prejudice especially given that his own family and crowd of listeners on occasions appeared to share the view that he had demons.[37] Jesus' attitude and injunctions above correspond with the message all through the New Testament that unbelievers would be

---

[33] Matthew 10:11-15. Jesus repeated this injunction when he sent out seventy-two disciples on a similar mission, see Luke 10:1-10.

[34] Luke 10:13-15; Matthew 11:21-23; Luke 10:13-15.
[35] Mark 3: 28-29. See also Luke 12:10; Matthew 12:31-32.

[36] See Matthew 3:7; 23:33; John 8:42-44.
[37] See Mark 3: 20-22; John 7:20; 8:48, 52; 10:20.

condemned to Hell Fire,[38] and contradict his teachings on love. They also contradict his admonition that we should repay evil with good, and turn the other cheek when we receive a slap on one.[39]

Furthermore, Jesus did not appear to respect his own teachings on loving one's enemies. According to him, those who abide in him and his words would receive whatever they ask from him,[40] but those who do not do so would wither, be cast into the fire and consumed.[41] Jesus made it clear that, those who are not with him are against him and those who do not gather with him scatter.[42] He also appeared to show little compassion for followers who were bereaved or wishing to bid farewell to their families,[43] or for his family members worried about his well-being.[44] Furthermore, Jesus exhibited a racist tendency;[45] supported slavery, and other discriminatory and cruel prescriptions of the Mosaic Law;[46] and was apparently only concerned about the well-being of Israelites. Jesus' brand of love appears therefore to be selective and self-serving, and 'neighbours' appear to be only those who subscribe to the same philosophy or religion as he did.

Therefore, Christians are to love one another; encourage the disheartened; help the weak; be patient and kind; and refrain from

---

[38] See Chapter 14.
[39] Matthew 5:39-41.
[40] John 15:7.
[41] John 15:6.
[42] Matthew 12:30-31.
[43] See Matthew 8:22; Luke 9:59-62.
[44] See Matthew 12:46-50; Luke 2:45-50.
[45] See Matthew 15:22-26.
[46] See Chapter 8.

repaying wrong with wrong.[47] However, there is no requirement for them to extend the same sentiment or treatment to unbelievers. In the words of Paul, Christians are not to be 'yoked' with unbelievers. This he says is because righteousness and light have nothing in common with darkness, idolatry and wickedness, which unbelievers represent.[48] Apostle Paul also insists that everybody who does not follow the gospel of Jesus 'will be punished with everlasting destruction and shut out from the presence of the Lord and from the majesty of his power'.[49]

Similarly, notwithstanding admonitions to placidity and pacifism, Jesus did not embody or purport to bring peace; and his attitude and utterances towards dissenters and unbelievers contradict his characterisation as 'Prince of Peace'. In fact, Jesus made it clear that he came to the world to bring a sword rather than peace, and division instead of unity:

> *Do you think I came to bring peace on earth? No, I tell you, but division. From now on there will be five in one family divided against each other, three against two and two against three. They will be divided, father against son and son against father, mother against daughter and daughter against mother, mother-in-law against daughter-in-law and daughter-in-law against mother-in-law.*[50]

In Luke 22:36, Jesus advised those who had no swords to sell their clothes and buy swords in readiness for conflicts that would be

---

[47] See 1 Thessalonians 5:14-15.
[48] 2 Corinthians 6:14-16.
[49] 1 Thessalonians 1:8-9.
[50] Luke 12:51-53. See also Matthew 10:34.

incidental to the gospel message. He also encouraged his followers to hate and abandon their spouses, children, parents and siblings in order to follow him or have everlasting life.[51] These are recipes for domestic and societal upheavals and conflicts, instead of peace and unity.

It is no wonder then that the love and peace of Christ did not prevent Christian European elites from eliminating or enslaving Native Americans, Africans, and the indigenous peoples of Australia and New Zealand. It did not prevent them from colonising and expropriating Africa, Asia, the Americas and other parts of the world even while taking the gospel of Christ to them;[52] neither did it prevent the churches from participating in and profiting handsomely from these atrocious acts.[53] Similarly, the love and peace of Christ did not stop the Christian Hitler and his Christian lieutenants from slaughtering and despoiling millions of Jews in the holocaust.[54]

JUDAISM, ISLAM, AND NON-BELIEVERS
The attitude of Judaism and Islam to love and peace in relation to non-believers is similar to the position of Jesus and the New Testament. The Hebrew Bible insists that Yahweh is the only true God while the Gods of other nations are not just false, but also devils.[55] As in Christianity, professions of love in Judaism stand parallel to prescriptions of harsh treatment and damnation for unbelievers. Accordingly, while Jews must love their own people, it seems okay

---

[51] See Luke 14:26-27; Matthew 19:29. See also pp. 110-112.
[52] Ibid.
[53] Ibid; https://www.theguardian.com/uk/2006/feb/09/religion.world.
[54] D MacCulloch, *A History of Christianity* (Penguin Books 2012) 915-958.
[55] See e.g., Deuteronomy 32:17; 1 Corinthians 10:20.

for them to destroy or annihilate others and take their land, possession and virgin girls.[56] It also seems okay for them to kill anybody who 'would not seek the LORD God of Israel, or who entices others to worship other gods.[57] In fact, the Bible designates Yahweh as 'a man of war' who brings destruction and doom to his enemies, while showing love and kindness to his chosen people.[58] Today, the love of Yahweh has not prevented Israeli authorities from ill-treating Palestinians in Israel and the occupied Palestinian territories.

Similarly, while the Quran enjoins Moslems to treat their fellows with love, kindness and compassion, they need not extend similar treatments to non-Moslems who are destined for Hell Fire.[59] Thus, the love and peace proclaimed in the Quran did not prevent Islamic elites and merchants from enslaving others and profiting from their misery.[60] Today, Islamic fundamentalists commit gruesome acts of terror and brigandage against non-Muslims, and Muslims of different sects, whom they consider infidels. Renunciation of Islam is also punishable by death,[61] or condemnation to Hell Fire.[62]

---

[56] See Chapter 5.
[57] Ibid. See also 2 Chronicles 15:13; Deuteronomy 13:6-10.
[58] See Exodus 15:3-21.
[59] See e.g., Surah 2:6-7; 3:32, 56, 85; 4:91, 101; 5:51; 8:38-39; 9:5, 29, 68, 73, 123; 28:86; 30:45; 58:22; 60:1, 13; 66:9.
[60] See http://www.bbc.co.uk/religion/religions/islam/history/slavery_1.shtml
[61] See e.g., Sura 4:65, 89, 90-91; 5:54; 9:11-12. Different Islamic traditions also support the death penalty for apostates.
[62] See e.g., Sura 2:217; 9:73-74.

RELIGIOUS EXCLUSIVISM

The selective and parochial character of religious love and peace is attributable to religious exclusivism. Since organised religions believe themselves to be the exclusive mouthpieces of God and the guardians of the gate of heaven, it is not surprising that conflict is prevalent among them given their divergent, and often contradictory, doctrines and messages, and the perception of others as heathens or infidels. For example, the backing of Christianity and suppression of alternative religions and philosophies by Roman emperors propelled it to the dominant religion it eventually became.[63] The desire to show the superiority of Christianity over Islam and reclaim the 'Holy Land' for Christ was the catalyst for the brutal and bloody crusades by Christian warriors against Muslims and Jews.[64] Similarly, the motivation to spread and enforce the rules of Islam is a major reason behind 'holy wars' and efforts by fundamentalists forcefully to establish an Islamic Caliphate.[65] The conflicts between religious sects, and the atrocities of numerous terrorist religious groups around the world, further demonstrate the damaging effects of religious intolerance.

---

[63] See D MacCulloch, supra n 54, 189-222; S Lunn-Rockliffe, 'Christianity and the Roman Empire', http://www.bbc.co.uk/history/ancient/romans/christianityromanempire_article_01.shtml

[64] For an account of these, see T Asbridge, *The Crusades: The War for the Holy Land* (Simon & Schuster 2012).

[65] See MA Khan, *Islamic Jihad: A Legacy of Forced Conversion, Imperialism, and Slavery* (New York Bloomington: iUniverse, Inc. 2009).

AG Bostom, *The Legacy of Jihad: Islamic Holy War and the Fate of Non-Muslims* (Prometheus Books 2008)

Even among adherents of the same broad faith, there is much hatred, violence and bloodshed in the struggle for doctrinaire control and supremacy. In Christianity for example, the papacy instituted the Inquisition to hound, torture and eliminate an untold number of dissenters and critics whom the church branded as heretics.[66] Likewise, several millions of people lost their lives in Europe in the century-old wars of reformation and counter-reformation involving Catholics and Protestants.[67] In Islam, battles of supremacy and control have historically raged between the Sunni and Shia branches of the faith. Presently, the dichotomy manifests in wanton acts of terrorist savagery against rival worshippers by sectarian fundamentalists in different parts of the world.

In short, organised religion, despite platitudes of love and peace, have not enabled these virtues in human beings. Although some religious men and women have done and still do commendable acts of charity and love, institutionalised religious hatred, divisions, exploitation and violence have unfortunately blighted and still blight humanity, even within and among religions that traditionally seem to advocate love and non-violence. Clearly, the messages of love and peace in the typical religious scripture is of insufficient service to humanity. If religions, which are supposed to be the guardians of morality,

---

[66] For an account of the Inquisition, see T Green, *Inquisition: The Reign of Fear* (Pan Books, 2007); https://www.britannica.com/topic/inquisition; http://www.newadvent.org/cathen/08026a.htm.
[67] See D MacCulloch, supra n 54, 551-703; https://www.history.com/topics/reformation.

goodness, and love, have proved unable to do it, how then can we achieve genuine love and peace among all the peoples of the world?

17

UNITY

Replace fear-based thinking with love-based thinking. Every time you are making a choice, ask yourself if it is going to cultivate the experience of unity and love or the experience of separation and stress. – Deepak Chopra

Religious bigotry, and the wickedness and injustice prevalent among human beings, are due largely to separation consciousness arising from a deficit of spiritual awareness. This mind-set makes us to see people as different from us and focus on our perceived differences. It is this consciousness that generates fear, jealousy, wickedness and violence. It is also this consciousness that makes us insensitive to the travails of people we consider not one of us, or ignore injustice emanating from those we see as our own. Religions typically thrive on, and inculcate in believers, the consciousness of separation and group righteousness and exclusivism. There is not likely to be universal love and enduring peace and unity in the world unless we abandon this mind-set in favour of a consciousness of unity.

UNITY

Unity consciousness is the awareness and understanding that all are one, and there are no 'others'. Unity consciousness does not perceive racial, national, ethnic, sexual, religious, sectional, class and other differences. It enables us to see apparent human differences as positive expressions of different aspects of one humanity. It enables us to see God and ourselves in our fellow humans. It promotes universal love and peace. One may draw a loose analogy here with the children of the same parents. Although these children might appear different in looks, size, orientation, talents and characteristics, they have similar genetic make-up and remain aspects of the same parents and part of one family. In like manner, although our colour, tongue, nationality, religion and ethnicity differ, we remain the products of one creator and possess the Divine imprint. After all, if the creator had desired all human beings to be the same or alike, that would have been the outcome of creation. Seeing all as one will eliminate fear, jealousy, hatred and discrimination among human beings. This in turn will remove the propensity to do people harm or injustice.

In addition to understanding our oneness with one another, unity consciousness enables us to understand our oneness with God. It makes us understand that the Divine energy or essence is never away from us, that it is not elsewhere but everywhere, and that it is not just without but also within us. Unity consciousness is therefore much higher than the consciousness of unity among siblings since the latter is merely biological, physical, and limited to family connections. Spiritually, unity of all human beings implies oneness at the soul level.

This means that whatever we do to others, whether good or evil, we do to ourselves. It also implies that whatever we do for or against others, we do for or against God, since God inheres in all human beings, and indeed in all God's creations. 1 Corinthians 3:16-17 appears somewhat to capture this philosophy with the observation that God's spirit dwells in us; and that whoever destroys another human being brings Divine destruction upon himself or herself. Inevitably, therefore, unity consciousness will make us desist from evil.

If we understand our unity with God, we would of course understand that we do not need religion or dogma to get to God, and that we do not need any mediator or intermediary between God and us. Then, it would become clear to us that religion merely represents ways in which different peoples attempt to relate to God in line with their own history, circumstances, world-view and understanding, and that God did not found any religion. Then, we will realise that many religious doctrines, including the belief in and the expectation of a saviour, hinder our spirituality, block our direct line to God and curtail our experience of the Divine.

Rather than dwelling on religion and religious dogma, we need to spend more time, thought, energy and resources on looking after the welfare of fellow human beings. The real worship we may give to God is the love and care we give to the creations of God. This is not merely the love only of one's family, nor the love only of one's religious brothers and sisters, nor the love only of people of one's race and nation. It is the love of all. It is universal love arising from unity consciousness that will enthrone peace and unity in our individual, communal, national and global relationships and eliminate injustice, oppression, exploitation and war.

Instead of waiting in endless hope for heaven or a saviour, we should strive in love to create the conditions of peace, justice, unity and prosperity on earth with the abilities and resources God has placed at our disposal. We need to allow the Divine Spirit to guide our lives and deeds in order to project outward, the Kingdom of God, which is already within us. By so doing, we would be manifesting the love of God and on the way to realising the Kingdom of God on earth. Although it might sound idealist and overly optimistic to hope that humanity would achieve this outcome anytime soon, it has little option than to try as hard as it can to do so. Otherwise, human disunity and suffering, as well as the forlorn and unending wait for salvation and paradise in the skies, will continue.

CONCLUSION

This book has outlined, analysed and critically evaluated the doctrine of salvation, especially from the Christian, Jewish and Islamic perspectives, relying largely on Scriptures and objective sources. The aim has been to enlighten readers – believers and unbelievers alike – on an important subject, which has long closed people's minds and divided the human family. The book has shown that the purport of salvation and the means earmarked for achieving it are different and contradictory and depict the beliefs and biases of the religions that espouse it. Accordingly, salvation under one religion would mean damnation under another. It has also shown that the expectation of an apocalypse, the hope for heaven, and the fear of Hell Fire are misplaced. These reflect flawed human attempts to explain Divine reward for good and punishment for evil, as well as the desire of religious institutions to keep the faithful loyal.

It is clear that the gospel of Christ aims to supplant Judaism and promote Christianity as the new paradigm for Divine-human relationship. However, this attempt failed as the Bible makes it clear that Jesus Christ, the beacon of the putative new order, had declared and made himself fully compliant with the old order as underpinned by the Abrahamic covenant and Mosaic Law. Nevertheless, the nationalist and traditionalist Jewish scheme of salvation as embodied in the Hebrew Scriptures is dubious, has no universal application, and is inconsistent with salvation through Christ or under Islam.

In any case, the idea of salvation through an incarnate God relies on the unethical and incorrect supposition that all human beings are disconnected from God because of inherited sin that needed to be atoned by the shedding of divine blood. This claim rests squarely on religious dogma, mythology and rituals of the type seen in some more ancient religions whose own saviours are now derelict or defunct. Since individual human beings are fully responsible for their own wrongdoings; since the blood of another person - human or divine - cannot obliterate the consequences of evildoing; and since God does not incarnate in anybody, the supposed saving mission of Jesus Christ and other putative saviours appears baseless and useless. In addition, the belief in incarnation for the salvation of humanity undermines the essence of God and the divine-human connection. It is also detrimental to the spiritual enlightenment and empowerment of the individual, and the unity of humanity.

The culmination of the scheme of salvation is the expectation of an end of the world. A final Day of Judgment, mass resurrections of the dead, and the entry of believers into heaven, and unbelievers into Hell Fire, would assumedly mark this supposed apocalypse. However, the promise of heaven and the expectations of life in it appear to be the products of religious imagination and faith. So is the claim that unbelievers would go to Hell Fire. Thus, while believers of different religions may obtain salvation according to the tenets of their faith, they would be unbelievers in other faiths, according to which rules they would go to Hell Fire. This religion-oriented salvation is a fantasy and the hope in it nugatory. We do not need this salvation, which, with its contradictions and dichotomies across faiths, has caused enormous conflicts, bloodshed and misery within, and to, humanity. It has also stifled spiritual development in, and the empowerment of, individuals.

What we do need is universal love and a realisation that humanity is one and connected to the source of all creation – God. Accordingly, there is no need for an intermediary, and people would understand that they hurt themselves when they hurt other people. This spiritual re-orientation would eliminate fear, empower individuals to realise their potentials and mission on earth, and lead to the enthronement of justice and equity in the affairs of human beings. This state of being would in turn promote enduring peace and unity among all peoples and nations of the world, and enable us to bequeath on future generations a better world. This is the real salvation. This is what we need.

BIBLIOGRAPHY

Acharya S, *The Christ Conspiracy: The Greatest Story Ever Sold* (Adventures Unlimited Press 2012).

Alighieri D and DH Higgins, *The Divine Comedy* (Oxford World Classics Paperback 1988).

Ancient History Encyclopaedia, http://www.ancient.eu.

Asbridge T, *The Crusades: The War for the Holy Land* (Simon & Schuster 2012).

Ashley LRN, *The Complete Book of Devils and Demons* (Barncade Books 1996).

Bartlett R, *Trial by Fire and Water: The Medieval Judicial Ordeal* (Vermont: Echo Point Books and Media 2014).

Belinerblau J, *The Secular Bible: Why Nonbelievers must Take Religion Seriously*, Cambridge University Press 2005).

Bible, New King James Version (Collins, Box Lea edition 2011).

Bible, New Revised Standard Version (with Apocrypha) (Oxford University Press 2001).

Bible, New International Version (Hodder & Stoughton 2015).

Bible, New Jerusalem Version (Pocket Edition) (New York: Double Day 1990).

Bible, The New Oxford Annotated (NRSV) (Oxford University Press 2001).

Bostom AG, *The Legacy of Jihad: Islamic Holy War and the Fate of Non-Muslims* (Prometheus Books 2008).

Bremmer JN (ed), *The Strange World of Human Sacrifice* (Peeters Publishers 2007).

Browning WRF, *Oxford Dictionary of the Bible* (Oxford University 2009).

Carpenter E, *Pagan and Christian Creeds: Their Origins and Meanings* (Scriptura Press 2015).

Carus P, *The History of the Devil and the Idea of Evil: from the Earliest Times to the Present Day* (Forgotten books, Classic Reprints 2012).

Catholic Encyclopaedia, http://www.newadvent.org/cathen/.

Cayce Edgar, *Reincarnation and Karma* (ARE Press 2006).

Chesnut GF, *Images of Christ: An Introduction to Christology* (Seabury Press 1984).

Chopra D, *Life After Death: The Book of Answers* (Crown Publishing Group 2006).

Cotterell A, *The Illustrated Encyclopaedia of Myths and Legends* (Marshall editions Ltd 1989).

Cross FM, *Canaanite Myth and Hebrew Epic: Essays in the History of the Religion of Israel* (Harvard University Press 1973).

Daniels T (ed) *A Doomsday Reader: Prophets, Predictors and Hucksters of Salvation* (New York and London: New University Press 1999).

Dever W, *Did God Have a Wife? Archaeology and Folk Religion in Ancient Israel* (Eerdmans 2008).

BIBLIOGRAPHY

DiMattei Steven, *Are Yahweh and El the Same God or Different Gods?* http://contradictionsinthebible.com/are-yahweh-and-el-the-same-god/.

Ehrman BD, *Whose word Is It? The Story behind who changed the New Testament and Why* (The Continuum International Publishing Group 2006).

Encyclopaedia Britannica, http://www.britannica.com/topic/creation-myth.

Fitzgerald D, *Nailed: Ten Myths that Show Jesus Never Existed at All* (Lulu.com 2010).

Fox RL, *The Unauthorised Version* (Penguin Books 1991).

Friedman RE, *Who Wrote the Bible?* (Harper Collins 1997).

Girard R, *Violence and the* Sacred (Baltimore: the John Hopkins University Press 1993).

Goring R, *Larouse Dictionary of Beliefs and Religions* (Kingfisher Publications PLC, New ed. 1994).

Green MA, *Dying for the Gods: Human Sacrifice in Iron Age & Roman Europe* (Stroud, Gloucestershire; Charleston, SC: Tempus, 2001).

Green M, *Animals in Celtic Life and Myth* (London and New York: Routledge 2002).

Green T, *Inquisition: The Reign of Fear* (Pan Books 2007).

Heaster D, *The Real Devil: A Biblical Exposition* (Carelinks Publishing 2009).

Hoffman M, *A Twist in the Tale: Animal Stories from around the World* (Frances Lincoln Ltd 1998).

Howe L, *How to Read the Akashic Records: Accessing the Archives of the Soul and its Journey* (Sounds True Inc., Boulder Co 2010).

Johnston SI (ed) *Ancient Religions*, (The Belknap Press of Harvard University 2007).

Josephus F, *Antiquities of the Jews* (Acheron Press 2012)

Josephus F, *The Wars of the Jews* (Palatine Press 2015)

Khan MA, Islamic Jihad: *A Legacy of Forced Conversion, Imperialism, and Slavery* (New York Bloomington: iUniverse, Inc 2009).

Lonnerstrand S, *I have Lived Before: the True Story of the Reincarnation of Shanti Devi* (Translated by Leslie Kippen) (Ozark Mountain Publishers 1998).

Lumpkin JB, *The Second Book of Enoch (also called the Secrets of Enoch and the Slavonic Book of Enoch)* (Fifth Estate 2009).

Lumpkin JB, *The Life of Saint Issa, Best of the Sons of Man: The Missing Years of Jesus and His Travels in the East* (Fifth Estate 2012).

Lunn-Rockliffe S, *Christianity and the Roman Empire*, http://www.bbc.co.uk/history/ancient/romans/christianityromanempire_article_01.shtml.

MacCulloch D, *A History of Christianity* (Penguin Books 2012).

Mbiti JS, *African Religions and Philosophy* (Heinemann Educational Books Ltd 1969).

Milton J, *Paradise Lost* (Oxford World Classics, 2004)

Mitchell S, *The Book of Job* (New York: Harper Collins 1975).

Moorjani A, *Dying to be Me: My Journey from Cancer, to Near Death, to True Healing* (London: Hay House UK Ltd 2012).

Newton M, *Journey of Souls: Case Studies of Life between Lives* (Minnesota: Llewellyn Publications 1994).

Newton M, *Destiny of Souls: New Case Studies of Lives Between Lives (*Minnesota: Llewellyn Publications 2000).

Pagels E, *The Origin of Satan* (Hamondsworth: Allen Lane/The Penguin Press 1996).

Ranke-Heinemann U, *Eunuchs for the Kingdom of Heaven: Women, Sexuality and the Catholic Church* (Penguin Books Limited 1991).

Ranke-Heinemann U, *Putting Away Childish Things: The Virgin Birth, the Empty Tomb, Hell and Other Fairy Tales You Don't Need to Believe to Have a Living Faith* (Harper San Francisco 1994).

Russell JB, *The Devil: Perceptions of Evil from Antiquity to Early Christianity* (Cornell University Press 1977).

Sanders EP, *The Historical Figure of Jesus* (London: Penguin Books 1995).

Shrodder T, *Old Souls: Compelling Evidence from Children who Remember Past Lives* (Simon & Schuster Paperbacks 1999).

Smith M, *The Early History of God: Yahweh and the Other Deities in Ancient Israel* (Eerdmans 1990).

Spence L, *An Encyclopaedia of Occultism* (New York: Cosimo Inc. 2006).

Spinoza B, *Tractatus theologico-politicus* (1670), cited in Richard Elliot Friedman, *Who Wrote the Bible?* (Harper Collins 1997).

Stanton G, *The Gospels and Jesus* (Second ed.) (Oxford University Press 2002).

Stevenson I, *Children Who Remember Previous Lives: A Question of Re-incarnation* (McFarland & Co; Revised edition 2001).

The Catholic Encyclopaedia, http://www.newadvent.org/cathen/11312a.htm.

The Illustrated Encyclopaedia of Myths and Legends (Marshall Editions Ltd 1989) 85.

The Jewish Encyclopaedia, http://www.jewishencyclopedia.com/articles/13236-savior.

Trumbull HC, *The Blood Covenant* (Literary Licensing, LLC 2014).

Ward H, *Unwitting Wisdom: an Anthology of Aesop's Fables* (Chronicle Books 2004).

Weiss B, *Many Lives, Many Masters: The True Story of a Prominent Psychiatrist, His Young Patient and the Past-Life Therapy that Changed Both Their Lives* (Piatkus 1994).

Wilkinson P and N Phillip, *Mythology* (Doring Kindersley Ltd, London 2007).

Zeitlin IM, *Jesus and the Judaism of His Time* (Policy Press 1988).

INDEX

a man of war' 244
Aaron................. 63, 90, 201
Abimelech 48
abomination that causes desolation' 152
Abraham... 45, 46, 47, 48, 49, 50, 51, 52, 54, 55, 59, 66, 72, 73, 75, 97, 99, 103, 109, 117, 123, 124, 125, 126, 139, 159, 165, 167, 192, 224
Abrahamic covenant......... 91, 139
Abram...45, 46, 48, See Abraham
absolute evil 183, 187
absolute good 187
Achan 88
Adam .. 33, 52, 94, 95, 96, 97, 98, 100, 101, 104, 116, 175, 182, 199
Admah 48
adultery 71, 72, 73, 114, 115, 198
Africans 243
Ahab 176, 183, 199
Ahura Mazda........................ 179
Allah. 20, 40, 139, 140, 155, 156, 158, 222, 224
Amalek 69, 81, 88
Ammon............................. 52, 55
Ammonites 68, 202
Amorites.......................... 46, 88
Amram 63
Analects of Confucius............ 236
Ananias................... 119, 143, 144
Angel Gabriel 124
Angra Mainyu 179
Antiochus Epiphanes............. 160
apocalypse 150, 252

apocalyptic 22, 39, 112, 148, 160, 215, 230
apostasy 79, 80, 169, 196, 198
Apostle Paul ...30, 59, 78, 81, 87, 91, 107, 112, 118, 131, 135, 151, 153, 155, 157, 165, 167, 185, 200, 202, 204, 205, 212, 221, 242
Apostles' Creed 31, 42, 206
Arabia.............................. 46, 144
Arda Viraf 222
   Zoroastrian priest .... See
Aristotle 236
Ark of Covenant 84, 201, 202, 219
arrest.............................. 105, 143
ascension 121, 151, 157
Asherah.............................. 60, 80
Asia............................... 136, 243
Assyria
   Assyrians............................ 201
Astarte .... 60, See Ashtoreth
Athanasian Creed 194
atone 19, 25, 31, 32, 68, 106
atonement . 26, 27, 28, 30, 31, 32, 33, 70, 99, 102, 106, 171
atoning sacrifice 25, 93
Baal 30, 60, 80, 180, 186
Baal-Zebub . 187, See Beelzebub, Beelzebul
Babylon 89, 183
Balaam................................. 174
baptism 147, 209
beast 84, 183
Beelzebub 177, 186
Beelzebul 60, 186, See Beelzebub

i

believers *15, 21, 22, 110, 111, 115, 119, 122, 125, 143, 144, 149, 151, 152, 159, 167, 173, 175, 195, 197, 213, 215, 221, 222, 223, 224, 228, 229, 236, 239, 248, 252, 253*
Benedictus *124*
Benjamin *53, 77*
Beth Peor' *63*
Bethlehem *83*
betrothed *71, 74, 76*
Bilhah *53, 54, 73, 117*
Bill of Divorce' .... *75, See* Get
blasphemy *169, 196, 198*
Book of Enoch *218, 219, 258*
Book of Life .. *165, 168, 195, 197*
bronze snake *84*
Buddhism *20, 61, 175, 176*
Caligula *160*
Canaan *45, 48, 55, 82, 88, 180*
Canaanites *45, 46, 81, 88*
Cannon *132*
career 110
castration .... *113, See* Eunuchs
Catholic .... *30, 33, 39, 43, 50, 66, 103, 112, 113, 137, 159, 169, 171, 175, 184, 193, 197, 198, 200, 206, 208, 209, 213, 256, 259, 260, See* Catholic Church
Catholic Church ... *113, 159, 200, 208, 209, 213, 259*
Catholics *246*
celibacy *112, 118, 119*
celibate ... *112, 114, See* Celibacy
charitable giving *234*
Cherubim *84*
Christ *146*
Christian .... *See* Christianity
Christianity. *19, 41, 42, 130, 135, 136, 137, 148, 181, 188, 196, 197, 208, 215, 220, 225, 229, 243, 245, 258, 259*

Christology *106, 136, 256*
Christos *41*
circumcision *46, 54, 55, 126, 131*
clairvoyance *83*
conception *39, 51, 114, 124, 127, 194, 197, 208, 224, 229*
concubines *73, 86, 89, 117*
conflict *60, 75, 123, 235, 237*
consciousness of separation .. *248*
Constantine *137*
Counter-Reformation *246*
covenant ... *31, 45, 46, 47, 51, 52, 53, 54, 55, 91, 99, 102, 123, 124, 125, 126, 130, 131, 133, 135, 139, 140, 222, 252*
cowrie shells *84*
The use of *84*
cross *93, 111*
crucifixion *104, 108*
crusades *245*
Cyrus the Great *39*
Daevas .... *176, See* Demons
Damascus *143, 144*
Daniel *83, 89*
David .. *38, 39, 40, 41, 51, 68, 72, 73, 117, 124, 201, 202, 208, 222*
Day of Atonement *29, 70*
Day of Judgment .. *148, 149, 150, 157, 158, 159, 160, 163, 173, 178, 192, 194, 215, 222, 225, 226, 227, 253*
Day of the Lord' *149, See* Day of Judgment
demons ... *84, 158, 173, 175, 176, 177, 179, 180, 181, 183, 184, 185, 187, 188, 189, 191, 195, 196, 207, 210, 240*
devil .. *42, 82, 106, 120, 121, 126, 158, 173, 174, 175, 176, 177, 178, 179, 181, 183, 184, 185,*

186, 188, 189, 191, 192, 195, 196, 209, 210, 240
devils *58, 60, 173, 176, 177, 180, 181, 184, 185, 186, 187, 188, 189, 191, 196, 207, 210, 243*, See Devil
diabolos .... *175*, See Stan, Devil
diamon or *diamonium* ... 184, See Demon
Dinah *54*
disciples .. *41, 102, 103, 107, 110, 119, 121, 129, 130, 134, 136, 137, 143, 144, 145, 146, 147, 151, 155, 159, 164, 174, 177, 204, 220, 222, 235, 237, 239, 240*
discipleship *111, 147*
discrimination *213, 233, 237, 240, 249*
divination *83, 84*
Divine energy or essence *249*
Divine imprint *249*
Divine Spirit *251*
diviners *81, 84, 240*
divinity *145*
divorce *75, 76, 114, 115, 116, 118*
divorcees .. *114, 119*, See Divorce
doctrinaire control and supremacy *246*
doomsday cults *149*
dragon *180, 183*
dynasty *38, 39, 88*
earthquake *212*
Edom *55*
Egypt *46, 48, 54, 55, 66, 82, 108, 148, 186, 195, 201*
Ekron 186
El *58, 59, 60, 103, 257*
El Elyon .... *58*, See El
El Shaddai .... *58, 59*, See El
Elijah *80, 157, 159, 187, 212, 226*

Elisha *202, 212*
Emmaus *204*
end of the world .... *122, 148, 155, 160, 230, 253*, See Apocalypse
Enoch *157, 159, 218, 219, 222, 258*
Esau *47, 53*
eschatological ... *16, 39, 208, 211, 213*
Essene *136*
Essenes *130, 146*
Esther *89*
eternal life *43, 102, 128, 152*
eternal reward *225, 229*
eternal torment *192, 194, 207, 225*
Eucharist *102, 103*
eunuchs *112*
Eutychus 212
Eve *33, 52, 94, 95, 96, 97, 100, 101, 116, 175, 182, 199*
exclusivism *80, 248*
exorcism 178, 180, 240
expiation *27, 28, 29, 32, 102*
Ezra *140*
faith *15, 16, 21, 66, 120, 123, 125, 128, 131, 133, 135, 146, 152, 165, 167, 169, 195, 204, 213, 224, 234, 246, 253*
faithfulness *47, 174, 210, 235, 237*
fallen angel 183
fallen angels ... 175, 183, 184, 219
family . *13, 14, 15, 34, 46, 48, 52, 68, 76, 98, 110, 111, 180, 181, 240, 241, 242, 249, 250, 252*
fantasy *225, 254*
fear *22, 87, 101, 103, 108, 165, 173, 179, 185, 189, 208, 212, 213, 235, 248, 249, 252*
Feast of Tabernacles *29, 70*
Feast of Trumpets *70*

Feast of Weeks 70
first bishop of Rome 136
First Fruits 70
forbearance 235
forbidden fruit' .... 175, See Eve, Garden of Eden
forgiveness of sins 30, 31
fornication 113, 198
fortune telling 83
fruit of the spirit 235
fundamentalists 21, 244, 245
Gad 50, 53
Galatia 204
Garden of Eden . 94, 95, 182, 221
Gehenna 194, 207, 208
Gentiles 143
Get .... 75, See Bill of Divorce
Gibeonites 68
Gideon 72, 73, 117
Gilead 50
Gilgal 69
God the Father 151
God's creations 250
godliness 234
Golden Rule . 235, 236, See Love your neighbour as yourself
Gomorrah 48, 239
goodness 195, 235, 237, 247
grace due to faith 163
greatest commandment 128
guardians of morality 246
Hades 152, 205
Hagar 46, 47, 73, 75, 117, 139
Ham 99
Haran 45, 48, 49
hate-induced violence 234
hatred 17, 235, 246, 249
heaven 14, 19, 20, 22, 31, 39, 40, 41, 42, 81, 84, 93, 104, 112, 115, 119, 124, 127, 148, 150, 151, 152, 153, 154, 157, 158, 160, 164, 166, 168, 175, 177, 183, 184, 191, 192, 200, 202, 209, 210, 213, 215, 216, 217, 218, 219, 220, 221, 222, 223, 224, 225, 227, 228, 229, 230, 237, 238, 245, 251, 252, 253
heavenly realms .... See Heaven
heavens. 101, 141, 152, 157, 216, 217, 220, 222, 225, 229
hel .... 206, See Hell, Hell Fire
helan or *behelian* 206
Hell Fire 13, 14, 81, 113, 148, 158, 178, 189, 191, 192, 193, 194, 195, 196, 197, 200, 202, 203, 204, 205, 208, 209, 210, 211, 212, 213, 216, 223, 225, 229, 240, 244, 252, 253
hell of fire .... 193, 210, See Hell Fire, Hell
heretics .... 171, 195, 246, See Heresy
heterosexuality 77
High Priest 38, 41
Hillel 236
Hindu 14, 62, 103
Hinduism 20, 61
Hitler 243
Hittites 46, 88
Hivites 88
holiness 208, 242
holocaust 159, 243
Holy Land' 245
Holy Spirit. 43, 51, 195, 196, 240
Holy Trinity 140
holy wars 245
homosexuality 77, 78, 199
Huitzilopochtli 103
Iblis .... 175, See Shaitan, Devil, Satan
Ibrahim 139
idolatry 196, 198, 201, 242
illegitimate children 90
incarnate 31, 225, 253

incarnation............. *226, 253, 260*
incestuous........................ *52, 116*
India *79*
indigenous peoples of Australia and New Zealand *243*
Inquisition *171, 246, 257*
intermediary *61, 250*
Isa *140*
Isaac ... *46, 47, 48, 51, 52, 58, 59, 66, 75, 97, 139*
Ishmael *46, 47, 139*
Isis *60*
Islamic Caliphate.................... *245*
Isocrates *236*
Issachar............................. *50, 53*
Jacob... *47, 49, 50, 51, 52, 53, 58, 59, 72, 73, 75, 97, 117, 139, 206*
Jainism *20, 61*
Jairus' daughter *212*
James..... *120, 137, 144, 165, 178, 237, 238, 255*
Jannah .... *222,* See Heaven
Japheth *99*
jealousy .. *81, 184, 185, 235, 237, 248, 249*
Jebusites *46, 88*
Jehovah's Witnesses............... *228*
Jephthah *67, 79*
Jericho *79*
Jeroboam *68*
Jerusalem *29, 39, 59, 60, 84, 103, 128, 143, 144, 145, 151, 154, 159, 181, 203, 207, 219, 222, 227, 255*
Jesus Christ *13, 15, 16, 19, 30, 32, 41, 42, 59, 87, 102, 108, 123, 124, 125, 127, 131, 134, 140, 141, 145, 151, 158, 166, 167, 197, 204, 238, 253*
Jewish Christians............ *134, 135*
Jihad *224, 245, 256, 258*

Jinns .... *176,* See Demons
Job .. *79, 174, 183, 189, 202, 206, 207, 211, 217, 218, 258*
Jochebed.................................. *63*
John the Baptist *51, 124, 146, 165, 193, 226, 240*
Jonah............................. *202, 206*
Joseph *40, 53, 83, 206*
Josephus *40, 130, 131, 258*
Joshua *46, 49, 55, 79, 80, 88, 133, 217, 218*
joy.......... *151, 217, 228, 235, 237*
Judah... *50, 53, 54, 68, 73, 79, 80, 181*
Judaism........ *19, 29, 39, 129, 130, 131, 135, 136, 148, 161, 168, 181, 195, 196, 198, 209, 215, 217, 220, 221, 223, 225, 229, 243, 252, 260*
Judas Iscariot *147, 174*
judgment... *39, 79, 134, 148, 149, 151, 155, 156, 158, 165, 168, 169, 177, 200, 203, 209, 211, 212, 225*
Judgment Day *156, 160, 240,* See Day of Judgment
Jupiter............................. *217, 229*
justification *43, 95, 130, 131, 141*
Kaffarah *28*
Keturah..................... *51, 73, 117*
kindness.................. *235, 237, 244*
King Agag *69*
King Ahazia........................... *187*
King Cyrus *38*
King Jehoash *202*
king of Tyre........................... *183*
Kingdom of Christ.................. *112*
kingdom of God *78, 120, 122, 146, 155, 163, 171, 205, 215, 229*
Kingdom of God..................... *251*

Kingdom of Hell 177
Krishna *79*
Lake of Fire... 193, *See* Hell Fire, Hell
Lamb of God *32*
Last Supper *102*
Lazarus *124, 158, 192, 212*
Leah *53*
Levi *40, 50, 53, 54*
levirate law *72, 73, 76*
Levites 66
life 11, 13, 27, 31, 32, 33, 37, 42, 71, 74, 85, 88, 96, 97, 101, 102, 103, 104, 105, 106, 108, 110, 111, 114, 115, 118, 119, 120, 127, 128, 130, 133, 136, 146, 148, 150, 151, 152, 156, 157, 166, 168, 178, 187, 188, 189, 192, 194, 197, 199, 202, 209, 211, 212, 216, 217, 225, 228, 239, 243, 253
Lord's Prayer *230*
Lot *45, 46, 47, 48, 49, 52, 153*
love. *11, 15, 16, 31, 43, 101, 111, 117, 118, 120, 121, 128, 132, 228, 230, 233, 234, 235, 236, 237, 238, 239, 240, 241, 246, 248, 249, 250, 251, 254*
love your neighbour as yourself *129, 236*
lovemaking *74, 114, 198*
Lucifer 175, 185
lust *114*
Machir *50*
magicians .. *81, 83, 195, 199, 240*
mammon *120*
Manasseh *50, 80*
Manna *62*
Mara. *175, 176, See* Devil, Satan, Shaitan, Iblis
Marcion *132*

Marcionite 91, 132, *See* Marcion, *See* Marcion
Marduk 179
marriage *54, 71, 74, 77, 112, 113, 116, 117, 119, 199, 201, 221*
Mars 217, 229
martyrdom *20, 136, 234*
Mary *51, 124, 140, 159*
Media *89*
Medianite *59*
mediator *250*
medicine men *189*
mediums *81, 82, 83*
Melchizedeck *59, 103*
Melchizedek *59*
Mercury 217, 229
Meroz *50*
Messiah *37, 39, 41, 140*
messiahship *226*
messianic *130*
Methuselah *96*
Midrash and *Talmud* 57
millenarian movements *160*
millennial rule *227*
miracles *51, 186, 240*
Miriam 201
missionaries *136*
Moab *52, 55, 63*
Molech *30, 60, 69, 80, 207*
Moon 62, 217, 229
Mordecai *89*
Mortal sins 197
Mosaic Law *31, 66, 91, 114, 115, 123, 127, 130, 132, 133, 135, 136, 140, 146, 204, 223, 241, 252*
Moses . 33, 50, 55, 59, 61, 62, 63, 82, 83, 109, 117, 124, 126, 129, 133, 139, 159, 186, 200, 204
Mot 180
Mount Carmel *80*

Mount Everest *61*
Mount Kailash *61*
Mount Nebo *62, 63*
Mount Olympus *61*
Mount Sinai *61*
Mount Zion *221, 222*
Mountain of God *61, 219*
Naboth *79*
Nahor *49*
Native Americans *243*
Nazarenes *134*
new earth *151, 227, 228*
new heaven *151, 227*
New Testament .. *16, 41, 81, 113, 123, 124, 125, 129, 136, 150, 164, 165, 175, 176, 178, 183, 193, 201, 212, 221, 222, 223, 228, 234, 237, 240, 257*
Nineveh .. 202, See Prophet Jonah
Noah *49, 98, 153, 160*
non-Trinitarian *171*
offering. *29, 32, 47, 69, 120, 170, 178, 202*
offerings *26, 28, 29, 67, 68, 90*
Oholah *79*
Oholibah *79*
Old Testament *28, 37, 50, 91, 99, 107, 111, 127, 130, 132, 136, 149, 166, 183, 204, 210, 216, 217, 218, 219, 222*
Old Testament prophecies *127*
Onesimus *87*
only begotten son *106*
opposer .... *174,* See Satan
Original Sin' *33, 98, 100*
Osiris *179*
our peace' *238*
pacifism .... *237, 242,* See Peace
palmistry *84*
papacy *246*
parable of the 'Rich Fool 204

parable of the Good Samaritan *236*
Parable of the Sower 177
Parable of the Weeds 177
parables 163
paradise... *15, 140, 168, 184, 212, 218, 219, 220, 222, 223, 224, 225, 251*
parents *14, 85, 99, 110, 111, 114, 115, 165, 243, 249*
Passover *29, 66, 70, 128, 195*
Paul *11, 81, 87, 113, 130, 131, 132, 134, 135, 137, 142, 143, 144, 145, 146, 147, 154, 165, 167, 205, 212, 220, 242*
peace... *16, 38, 87, 151, 202, 235, 237, 238, 239, 242, 243, 246, 248, 249, 251, 254*
Pentateuch *61, 62, 63*
Pentecostals *171,* See Pentecostal
Perizzites *46, 88*
Persia *39, 83, 89*
Peter *11, 30, 32, 41, 106, 126, 130, 136, 144, 153, 154, 158, 160, 165, 174, 175, 178, 183, 193, 195, 203, 205, 212, 228, 235, 238*
Pharaoh *48, 82, 83*
Pharisees *129, 158, 176, 178, 200, 203, 220, 240*
Philemon *87*
Philistine *186*
Philo of Alexandria *236*
pillars of Islam *224*
plagues *82, 83*
Plato *236*
polygamous marriages *117*
Pontius Pilate *41*
preacher and bringer of peace to the world ...... *238, See* Prince of Peace, Our Peace
pre-marital sex *74, 113*

Prince of Peace' *238, 242*
principalities, powers, the rulers of the darkness of this world *176*
Promised Land *62, 87*
prophecy................... *68, 160, 234*
Prophet Jonah......................... *202*
Prophet Mohammed............... *222*
Prophet Muhammad............... *139*
Prophet Samuel *51, 68, 81, 82, 204*
Protestant.............................. *171*
Protestants *246*
psychics................................... *81*
purification............................. *31*
Queen of Heaven...................... *60*
Quran.... *139, 140, 141, 155, 156, 175, 176, 184, 194, 195, 211, 222, 224, 226, 236, 238, 239, 244*
Quranic...... See Quran, See Quran
rabbi *128*
raca *205*
Raca *203*
Rachel *53*
Racism................................... *233*
Rahab *80, 165*
ransom.. *29, 37, 42, 67, 105, 178, 224*
rapture *153, 157, 168*
Re *226, 260*
Rebecca *48*
redeemer................................ *108*
redemption *31, 34, 37, 42, 66, 67, 86, 108*
Reformation *246*
Rehoboam *72, 73, 117*
re-incarnation .. *20, 210, 225, 226*
religious doctrines............ *22, 250*
religious exceptionalism *185*

resurrection...... *34, 107, 127, 147, 148, 149, 156, 157, 159, 168, 204, 209, 226, 227, 228*
Reuben *50, 53, 54*
righteousness *30, 38, 100, 163, 164, 165, 166, 168, 220, 228, 242, 248*
righteousness,........................... *30*
rituals.......... *25, 27, 185, 223, 253*
Roman Emperor *160*
Roman Empire *137, 245, 258*
Sabbath.. *28, 29, 62, 70, 195, 200*
sacrifice *25, 26, 29, 30, 31, 32, 34, 47, 60, 65, 66, 67, 68, 69, 93, 95, 102, 103, 104, 106, 139, 186, 204, 207*
Sadducees.............................. *228*
salvation ... *13, 14, 15, 16, 20, 28, 31, 34, 37, 40, 42, 69, 91, 93, 95, 102, 103, 107, 108, 110, 112, 115, 122, 123, 124, 125, 127, 136, 140, 148, 150, 164, 165, 166, 168, 169, 171, 173, 191, 204, 212, 213, 215, 223, 233, 251, 252, 253*
Samson............................. *51, 79*
Sarah... *46, 47, 48, 51, 66, 75,* See Sarai
Sarai *45, 46, 48, 49, 52*
Satan *84, 174, 177, 179, 183, 187, 188, 227, 238, 259*
Saturn *217, 229*
Saul..... *38, 49, 51, 68, 69, 81, 82, 88, 142, 176, 183, 202, 204*
saviour *13, 14, 16, 19, 21, 37, 41, 42, 107, 108, 122, 136, 141, 150, 168, 212, 250, 251*
Seal of Solomon *84*
second coming of Jesus *151, 152, 155, 159*
Seneca *236*
Seth... *179*

seven capital sins 200
seventh heaven 218
sex 52, 71, 74, 75, 76, 80, 86, 110, 112, 113, 118, 199
sexual immorality *113, 115*
Sexual immorality .... 198, *See* Adultery, pre-marital sex
Shabbath Sabbathon *29*
Shaitan ...... *175*, *See* Devil, Satan
Shamayim .... 217, *See* Heaven
Shechem 54
Shem *49, 99*
Sheol 205, 206
shepherds *238*
Shiva *62*
Shunamite woman 212
signs *78, 153, 159, 160*
Simeon *50, 53, 54*
Simon 226, 245, 255, 259
sin. 19, 27, 28, 29, 30, 33, 34, 42, 67, 77, 93, 94, 95, 96, 97, 99, 100, 101, 104, 106, 113, 114, 166, 169, 178, 192, 194, 195, 197, 198, 199, 208, 209, 228, 236, 253
Sin 33, *62*, 98, *100*, *102*, *141*
slaves 46, 75, 86, 87
Sodom 46, 48, 239
Solar System *229*
Solomon ... 38, 60, 72, 73, 79, 84, 117, 201
son of Allah *140*
Son of God 42, 173
Son of Man *102, 154, 177, 227*
Song of Deborah 50
sorcerers *81*
sorcery *81, 83*
speaking in tongues *15, 234*
Spenta Mainyu .... 179, *See* Ahuza Mazda
spirit of divination *81*
Spiritism *81*

spiritual wickedness in high places' *176*
spouses ... *78, 110, 111, 112, 113, 117, 118, 223, 225, 243*
Stephen *79*
substitutionary doctrine *106*
Sun 217, 229
Sunni and Shia branches *246*
Syria *46*
Tamar *80*
Tammuz *60*
Tarot cards *84*
Tarsus *143, 144*
temptations *175*
Ten Commandments *85, 115, 128*
Terah *48, 49*
the Americas *243*
the book' ... 217, *See* The Book of Life
the elect 151, 167, 168
the fruit of the Spirit *237*
the Sanhedrin *203, 205*
the seed of Abraham' *125*
the Shema and the Hallel 195
Theodosius *137*
third heaven 218, 219, 220
Tiamat 180
Tibet *62*
Torah *57*
transubstantiation *103, 104*
treaty of peace *88*
Tree of knowledge *94, 199*
Tree of Knowledge *97, 182*
Tree of Life *94, 97, 182, 218, 221, 222*
Tree of Life' *94, 222*
trial *41, 74, 163*
Trinitarian *171*
true shepherd *168*
twelve disciples *147*
twelve tribes *50, 222*
Ultimate Spirit 184

unbelievers *21, 86, 156, 168, 173, 181, 192, 195, 197, 212, 224, 229, 240, 242, 243, 252, 253*
unfaithfulness ... *73, 115, 119*, See Sexual immorality
Unity consciousness *249*
universal love *16, 250*
Unleavened Bread *70*
Ur *45, 48*
Urim and *Thummim* *84*
Uzzah 201, 202
Valley of Hinnom ....207, See Gehenna
Valley of Slaughter' 207
Venial sins............................. 198
Venus *185, 217, 229*
vicarious liability *19, 34, 99*
virgin *71, 74, 75, 86, 89, 244*
virgins .. *26, 74, 75, 88, 114, 117, 223*

wealth 48, 110, 119, 120, 121, 122, 131
wickedness and injustice *248*
widow of Nain....................... *212*
Widow of Zarephat 212
wilderness......................... *62, 201*
wisdom .. *182, 205, 208, 234, 237*
Witch of Endor........................ *83*
witchcraft .... *81, 83, 180*, See Witches, wizards
witches *81*
wizards *81*
wonders *78, 113, 115*
Zacharias and Elizabeth *165*
zealots...................................*240*
Zeboiim and Bela *48*
Zechariah............................. *124*
Zilpah *53, 73, 117*
Zoroastrian priests.................... *83*
Zoroastrianism...... *148, 176, 179, 181, 229*

www.ingramcontent.com/pod-product-compliance
Lightning Source LLC
Chambersburg PA
CBHW031947080426
42735CB00007B/296